BEYOND THE
TRAUMA VORTEX
INTO THE
HEALING VORTEX

A GUIDE FOR THE MILITARY

SPONSORED BY

*THE INTERNATIONAL
TRAUMA-HEALING INSTITUTE*

GINA ROSS AND PETER LEVINE

INTERNATIONAL TRAUMA-HEALING INSTITUTE
A NON-PROFIT ORGANIZATION DEDICATED TO GLOBAL TRAUMA HEALING

Published by International Trauma-Healing Institute
In cooperation with SP Turner Group
Copyright © 2009 by Gina Ross

www.traumainstitute.org
www.beyondthetraumavortex.com

International Trauma-Healing Institute is a registered 501c3
California corporation.

For information address:
International Trauma-Healing Institute
269 South Lorraine Boulevard
Los Angeles, California 90004
www.traumainstitute.org

Library of Congress Control Number: 2009939646

ISBN: 978-0-9815283-4-2

1.   2. Gina Ross   3. Title

Printed in the United States of America

Cover design and book design
by Ryan Scheife, Mayfly Design (www.mayflydesign.net)

I dedicate this book to the members of all militaries, who have served their countries with courage and honor while following the Rules of Engagement in the Laws of Armed Conflict

TABLE OF CONTENTS

FOREWORD

Retired now from United States military service, I served in the Middle-East, Southeast Asia, South America, Africa, Europe and was assigned to domestic service. I was both an officer and a military dependent. My academic studies were in military history at one of our service academies.

I want to share my own firsthand knowledge and personal experiences with two veterans of World War II. One veteran was my own father who served as a gunner on B-17s in the air campaign over Europe and who passed away when I was 18 years old; the second was my stepfather, a Navy Pearl Harbor survivor who has also passed away. My mother was married to both, each for 25 years in turn.

I was raised by both men. In recalling them, each had in common a reluctance to talk about their wartime experiences. Although they were physically close to me, they never expressed any personal thoughts beyond the weather or similar mundane matters. They were very withdrawn from any social interaction, even among family members, and rarely participated in social events outside the home.

I learned about their service experiences from their rows of awarded ribbons and their official records. But there was never anything forthcoming as to their personal experiences or feelings. I knew the cumulative records of these men from others, but never from their own lips. Both of these men experienced intense combat scenarios.

Had they still been in shock? Is this why they excluded others from entering their private hells? Could they have shared their traumas and gotten better? After reading this book and becoming familiar with the concept of the trauma vortex and personally experiencing Gina Ross' Somatic Experiencing® work, I formed a new view of trauma and, by extension, re-evaluated my own encounters with trauma, its causes and healing.

The more I looked at the traumas experienced by others, the more I saw a mirror reflection of my own experiences. I have experienced, heard, and read about many traumatic events. Prior to my experience with this book, I had not found viable release from the physical, mental, and emotional stress caused by these traumas. For example, upon learning of the death of close fellow service members I went through the expected public rituals, such as attending memorial services or participating in small group gatherings of intimates, followed by a few obligatory words of remembrance. But there was no counseling offered, no show of official concern from our leadership. Then came the years, even decades, of living with the traumatic experiences with no healthy release, marked by isolation, drinking, depression, feelings of guilt and shame—and still no help.

I have more questions now than when I began my own journey, about the process of healing and looking for answers. How many waypoints did I pass without pausing to reflect upon what had happened? What could I have done to recognize trauma and its symptoms? Could emotional first aid have been given to me and to others then? I certainly cannot undo the traumatic events themselves, but the lessons from this book have at least provided much comfort in recognizing the origins and signs of trauma, and in learning about the methods available to deal with the traumas, whether immediately or years later.

The big question in my mind is why has so little been done for our service personnel before, during, and after any traumatic military service? After reviewing the *Guide for the Military*, I saw that the need for a book like this is long overdue. Now I feel that the path is open for a useful healing approach to the military experience and also for others likely to be placed in harm's way.

I have personally experienced and witnessed in others the tremendous need for understanding the forces at work in trauma and the healing process described in this book. The ever-changing world of armed conflict and the trauma it generates makes the use of this book imperative. N*ot* recognizing, *not* treating and not *healing* are often worse than the original injury in the long term. For ourselves, our fellow military members, and those close to us, we must do a better job of understanding the trauma and healing vortices.

I sincerely trust that all those who have gone in harm's way or who face the prospect, whether members of the armed forces, their families and/or their care providers, may read this book with the goal of understanding and ultimately healing trauma.

—**Chris Rubacha,** Major (USAF Ret.)

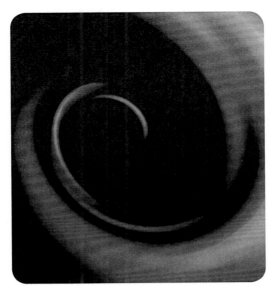

ACKNOWLEDGMENTS

I want to thank the people who helped with the writing and editing of this book, without whom my grasp of the military culture would have been less comprehensive.

Vivian Gold, Ph.D. and Major Tuly Flint were instrumental in the development of the book, in providing the vivid real-life stories, and in their accurate depiction of military culture.

Major Flint, a reserve regiment commander in the Israeli Defense Forces (IDF), a narrative therapist and a Somatic Experiencing® (SE®) practitioner, depicted the Israeli military experience helping me understand Israeli military culture. He shared Israeli soldiers' stories of courage and pain. He used SE®, the healing tool presented in this book, with his unit before, during and after the latest Lebanon War. He used it with active military personnel during war, implementing it on the battlefield. He also introduced SE® to veterans. Vivian Gold, a psychologist and SE® practitioner in Los Angeles, has worked with the United States Veterans Administration

Hospitals for 20 years. She generously shared her knowledge of the poignant suffering of traumatized veterans and the special issues that face the American military. She contributed the American stories in the book that discuss an often-agonizing recovery process.

Additionally, Ralf Zimmerman, Lt. Col., USAF (Ret.), a combat veteran and expert strategist of both U.S. and German military forces, supported the writing of the book. Cassandra Wang, a disable U.S. Navy veteran turned SE® practitioner, helped me better understand the military sensibility regarding trauma. Navy Seal J.T. Pietrzak provided valuable help in editing some of the chapters.

Primarily, I want to thank the brave young soldiers and veterans who fight for their countries and who had the courage to tell their stories. This book was written against the backdrop of the Afghanistan and Iraq War theatres, the Intifada that started in 2000, the Hezbollah/ Israel War of 2006 and Operation Cast Lead in Gaza in 2008-2009. These conflicts brought new levels of awareness to the devastating traumas modern warfare wreaks on its combatants.

Most of all, I am deeply thankful to my friend and teacher Dr. Peter Levine, the creator of Somatic Experiencing® theory and method, author of *Waking the Tiger: Healing Trauma* and co-author of *Trauma Through A Child's Eyes*. Peter provided the tools that make healing trauma at mass levels possible and collaborated in the writing of this book. His theory and method facilitated my vision of healing global trauma and brought it from theory to a very possible future reality. His magnificent treatment work with veterans showed the extent to which SE® can help these worthy young people.

I also want to thank my family in Brazil; my children and my granddaughters in the US, for their love and patience with me during the writing of the book. Finally, I want to thank my dear husband Reg Wilson for his unconditional support. He was an endless source of material about the trauma of returning soldiers, trusting that this book could bring relief to all the young people participating in events so much bigger than they.

—**Gina Ross**, Founder and President
International Trauma-Healing Institute

INTRODUCTION

In the last two decades, modern warfare tactics have included carpet-bombings on one side and, on the other, guerilla tactics such as suicide bombings, IED attacks and shooting from within civilian populations on the other. Military personnel face situations where it is difficult to distinguish enemies from allies, and militants from civilians; where the threat of ambush is relentless, and the civilian toll enormous. These realities make war more lethal and military trauma more serious and costlier than ever. Furthermore, the concept of the soldier as hero/warrior has undergone a radical transformation with modern warfare, making it more difficult to give a positive context to the horrors of warfare.

War trauma is undeniable and the military is now turning its attention to resolving this problem. Currently, the U.S. offers screening and treatment for military trauma to all returning personnel from Iraq and Afghanistan. Some are even receiving treatment for traumatic shock on the battlefield, as mental health providers accompany soldiers on missions, despite commanders fear this will slow their operations, or open up excuses for unwilling soldiers. Substantial healing information is offered on websites and weblogs, and other multimedia sites are giving access to an unlimited number of soldiers' wartime stories. As we go to print, the US Army has just announced plans to give intensive training in emotional resiliency, the exact subject of this book. The Army's Chief of Staff expressed worries that the military culture is not ready to accept a program that seems too touchy-feely. Some agreed with him but others have said the program was desperately needed, not only for the soldiers but for their families and community as well. We hope this book will contribute the crucial missing piece of the nervous system in the healing of trauma and resiliency training being considered.

For the last 20 years, the Israeli military has been studying the long-term effects of war on personnel and implementing helpful coping interventions. With the help of Israeli professor and researcher Zahava Solomon, Ph.D. from Tel Aviv University and other professionals, the Israeli military is monitoring Post-Traumatic Stress Disorder (PTSD) and pioneering new trauma research on the battlefield. Other countries, such as Sri Lanka, routinely rehabilitate returning military personnel.

Nevertheless, too many veterans still do not receive the help they need. Too many people continue to stigmatize trauma and too little is done to prevent trauma. Some of the most cutting-edge methods to heal it still are not widely known. Research is needed for these innovative theories about the nature of trauma and for vanguard tools which have been clearly successful at treating it.

These tools have the ability to transform the issue of war trauma: *they not only heal but also help prevent trauma*, a potentially crucial innovation for the military field. Taught during basic military training, these tools can make trauma have a much less negative impact on personnel's performance during military duty and on their lives keep after service, resulting in fewer costs to society.

Because we now have a better understanding of the brain, we have developed powerful new techniques to heal trauma. For the first time in 130 years of trauma studies, we may be able to permanently and effectively deal with the issue of trauma and institutionalize its healing. We finally have the possibility to end a perpetual cycle characterized by a forced recognition of trauma during times of crisis, followed by its denial because the tools to heal it were not yet available.

New brain technology provides more precise maps to the devastating effects of unresolved trauma. It shows that trauma generates a chronic biological cycle of arousal and dissociation that leads to painful physical, emotional, cognitive, and behavioral symptoms. We also know that symptoms can be triggered years after the traumatic event, a previously misunderstood fact which complicated recovery. For decades, it made trauma a daunting and seemingly unsolvable problem with severe personal and social outcomes for soldiers, veterans, their families and for society.

The burgeoning field of trauma studies has established enough information, so that, for the first time, what we know about the neurobiology of trauma enables us to organize it's healing in a systematic way. Recent findings in the fields of neuroscience have validated some of the powerful groundbreaking healing techniques that have emerged. With them we can institutionalize trauma healing and resiliency development fully and permanently.

Currently, a remarkably innovative paradigm offers us a significant breakthrough in the treatment of trauma. This paradigm proposes that at the same time as traumatic arousal is triggered (the trauma vortex) an innate healing ability (called the healing vortex) is generated in the nervous system. This healing ability is the seed of our human resiliency against trauma. In the traumatized, it just needs to be strengthened.

We also present the concept of the *collective trauma vortex*, the trauma of whole groups or whole nations, as a strategic tool for the military.

We explore its impact on war decisions and military interventions. We propose that the understanding and awareness of this vortex can be beneficial in the design and execution of military operations. It potentially can achieve quicker and better military success.

The paradigmatic theory and method presented in Part I and Part II of the book, breaks through trauma's stigma: the theory adds original information on the impact of repeated extreme events on troops and commanders; and provides tools of *Emotional First Aid* for military personnel to reset the nervous system and for prevention, which military personnel can use on their own. It can prevent the impact of traumatic stress on the military, their families and their communities. It offers a better understanding of the bigger picture. We hope this information will further contribute to the military's efforts to help impacted personnel and impacted populations better.

The book provides:

- Emotional first aid tools for active personnel to release, within the context of military training, their own stress and the stress of their comrades. This is beneficial on the battlefield, providing better performance and group morale, which is also beneficial after discharge from service.

- Tools to 'practice resiliency' against traumatic events, lowering the rate of traumatization.

- Tools to lessen the physical impact of military training (chronic tension and aches).

- Additional knowledge about war trauma, identifying wide-ranging and often hidden symptoms of psycho-biological and emotional trauma beyond the conventional definition of PTSD.

- Self-diagnostic tools to help active military personnel learn to track traumatic activation better, identify the symptoms developed when war has affected them and to seek healing without stigma during service. Veterans can use the information to process their traumatic war experiences and seek professional help when necessary.

- A body-based oriented therapy for trauma treatment, which speeds up healing and lessens the costs of rehabilitation programs for veterans.
- Tools for commanders to enhance group morale.
- Guidelines to recognize a collective vortex.
- Guidelines to apply the concepts of collective trauma vortex and collective healing vortex for military planning, in order to lessen trauma-driven violence and the resulting drive for revenge.
- Examples of addressing a collective trauma vortex from a military point of view.

Reading this book during military training will widely disseminate a fuller understanding of trauma within the military. It provides a common language for soldiers and their commanders to identify and handle traumatic experiences during armed conflict preventing individual trauma. Immediate detection, treatment and prevention of trauma enhances military personnel performance and well being, lessening the costs of war trauma.

In addition, the book contains guidelines to identify and diminish collective trauma, with the potential of reducing levels of collective violence. Recognition and prevention of collective trauma will enhance military strategies and lessen collateral damage.

Raising trauma awareness and trauma prevention in the military further contributes to placing trauma prevention on the global agenda.

THE BOOK'S STRUCTURE

In addition to theoretical frameworks and tools for healing, this book presents stories of war-generated traumatic stress and of stress release in the military theatre. It also includes examples of coping with potential war situations. As a practical matter, it may be helpful to read the text first, while noticing the emotional and physical changes which occur—we call it tracking the body/mind—and just read the exercises within the text. Later, when the reader is ready to practice them, re-read them at the end of the book where we have gathered them as a convenience.

The book is divided into four PARTS in order to accomplish its goals:

- PART I covers the information about the theory of trauma and healing. It offers information on the basics of trauma, the characteristics of war-related traumatic stress, their impact on the brain, on individual body/mind and nervous systems, and their symptomatic manifestation at the bio-physiological, emotional, psychological, cognitive, behavioral and spiritual levels.

- PART II discusses the tool for healing called Somatic Experiencing®. It outlines tools for diagnosing traumatic stress and discharging traumatic activation; resourcing, emotional first aid tools for self-regulation, tools for developing resilience to stressful events and for better mental/physical precision and endurance during combat and obstacles that might be encountered. It also contains examples of using this tool on the battlefield and immediately after traumatic events.

- PART III covers the issues of the impact of second-hand trauma (both media and event generated) and the role of the media in healing it. It introduces the concept of collective trauma and its impact on the intensity, recurrence, perpetuation, and intractability of a conflict. It covers the new role of modern militaries, their dilemmas with Rules of Engagement (ROE) and awareness, tools and guidelines to engage the collective healing vortex, which can lessen war's impact and facilitate peace. Finally, Chapter 16 covers several military voices that have contributed to our understanding and Chapter 17 covers the role of the International Trauma-Healing Institute (ITI).

- PART IV contains appendices, resources, and examples of using the metaphors of the vortices on real conflicts, in addition to other helpful healing methods, healing resources on line and the list of references used.

- PART V includes all the exercises grouped together for your convenience.

THE THEORY AND TOOLS OF SOMATIC EXPERIENCING

The information from the *decade of the brain* and the interface of the fields of trauma studies, neuroscience, psychology and physiology have yielded a better understanding of how exposure to traumatic events influences the functions of all these systems that cause a physical and mental damage. However, while war trauma may be inevitable, the good news we need to grasp and integrate is that not only can trauma can be healed but also can be prevented.

Military personnel are already being screened for emotional strength, taught about combat stress and given suicide-prevention briefings every two months. But it is possible to do more and train personnel to become physiologically better prepared against the traumatic events they inevitably encounter on the battlefield by learning to discharge traumatic arousal on a regular basis.

Developed by Dr. Peter Levine, Somatic Experiencing® (SE®) is a science-based method that gathers the information from the disciplines mentioned above and forms the theoretical background of our approach. Initially developed as an organic and innovative tool to heal multiple shock trauma and deep developmental trauma, SE® was later used to cope with highly stressful situations, and with chronic traumatic stress. Recent research in neuroscience in the U.S. has confirmed its effectiveness as Emotional First Aid in the treatment of post-disaster trauma symptoms helping to minimize the impact of cumulative trauma and as a prevention tool.

A gentle and compassionate technique, SE® allows people to connect with their deepest healing resources while addressing the difficulties of trauma. It is based upon the observation that animals in the wild, though routinely threatened, are rarely traumatized.

They utilize innate mechanisms to regulate and discharge the high levels of arousal associated with defensive survival behaviors. These mechanisms provide animals with a built-in *immunity* to trauma that enables them to return to normal in the aftermath of highly charged, life-threatening experiences. SE® teaches us to do the same.

SE®-trained commanders better understand how unresolved trauma affects involuntary survival responses, and thus military objectives. They become more effective at enhancing their personnel's performance, group morale and military goals, and subsequently better supporting their troops' emotional health and moral bearings.

Training military personnel in self-regulation tools lessens the incidence of combat shock and the potential for spreading traumatic reactions among the troops. SE® trainings normalize the impact of extreme events, overcoming the stigma of trauma. They teach how to maintain balance through self-testing for symptoms of activation and learning to release hyper-arousal.

The ability of each individual to release traumatic stress and remain in control of his emotions and actions benefits military maneuvers and personnel at all levels. These same tools can be used after leaving military service to spare veterans, their families and communities from unnecessary suffering, thus saving scarce financial resources and helping society better support its veterans.

INDIVIDUAL AND COLLECTIVE BENEFITS OF
TRAUMA-AWARENESS AND CULTURAL SENSITIVITY

Military personnel, who despite the difficulties of war return with a healthy sense of self, are able to establish the positive aspects of their difficult experiences improve their survival skills and develop a deeper appreciation for life. They learn to identify resources and utilize them for their benefit. They can return to their communities with new leadership skills and renewed strength.

A recently defined term in the military field perfectly illustrates this phenomenon: *Post-Trauma Growth (PTG)*, or *Post Traumatic Strength*—it is an opportunity for military personnel to review their values and goals and accomplish personal transformation, informed by what they saw of the difficulties of war.

The gift of transformation, which results from healing traumatic experiences, can be witnessed in the lives of military personnel at the collective level, too. For example, in Israel the military has produced many political leaders that are inspired to fight for peace to create a safer country because their previous military service has make them first-hand witnesses to the suffering of war. It is not unusual for commanders to caution their political leaders against taking the decision to engage in war too lightly.

Yitzhak Rabin was a PTG leader. In one of his famous speeches, he gave his personal Army identification number and told the public how he had fought all his life and was now excited to be there as a soldier to create peace:

I am Itzhak Rabin, Reserve IDF Chief of Staff Number 30476. I am a soldier in the Israeli Defense Forces and now a soldier in the Army of Peace. I who sent soldiers and troops to the fire and death, say today we are embarking on a war with no wounded, no blood, and no suffering. We are participating in a war that is a joy—the War for Peace.

THE ROSS MODEL: HEALING THE COLLECTIVE NERVOUS SYSTEM

Learning to heal trauma at collective levels is an important step in diminishing violence worldwide. Understanding what triggers or amplifies the collective trauma of one's adversary may make the difference between shorter or protracted conflicts and less or more damage for both sides. The detailed understanding of how psychological war trauma affects soldiers and civilians on both sides of a conflict can inform military decisions and the assessment of tactical considerations in constructive ways. Such initiatives lessen trauma-driven violence and its resulting resentment and revenge.

In addition to a trauma-sensitive military, the Ross Model for collective trauma identifies twelve relevant social sectors which can help lessen the adverse effects of collective trauma. The common understanding we propose helps these sectors build on a universal language to deal with trauma, provide care for the traumatized, help societies increase resiliency and stop violence. The International Trauma-Healing Institute (ITI) has developed trainings and written material for professionals in the medical, mental health, and educational fields, as well as the justice system, for non-governmental organizations (NGOs), diplomats and peace workers, politicians and first responders, the military, clergy, media and the public. Trained in SE® tools, these sectors have the ability to influence the cycles of trauma and violence, both by identifying and avoiding actions that amplify trauma and by designing interventions that promote healing.

MILITARY VOICES

A series of military trauma and healing stories, which can provide a more personal account of the difficulties and possibilities of traumatic experiences, is included in Part IV, Chapter 16, entitled Military Voices. Some stories are lengthy in order to assure their integrity as they were related to us. You may want to take the time to read some of the stories now as they lay the groundwork for both the theory and method of SE®.

We have chosen to keep two of the stories here. An account by a soldier referred to as "AK" is the only story of a war trauma therapy described at length in this book. It shows the possibility for healing, as well as the difficulty of letting go, when the world does not change, when things are not different from the times of the traumatic events.

AK's Recovery

AK was unaware that his 33-year-long suffering was due to a deep war trauma. He had spent the last three decades feeling as if life were meaningless and empty. He could not find anything good about life. He was very easy to anger and sprinkled his conversations with negative and pessimistic comments, to the frustration and chagrin of his wife and children.

AFTER TWO SE® SESSIONS
After two sessions and after reading the book for the military, AK believed that all soldiers should have this information available to them as soon as they entered the military. He believes he would not have done the destructive things he did in his life if he'd had access to this information about trauma:

> "I realize now that just recognizing and accepting 'the situation' as a problem would have helped me. Instead, I totally disconnected myself from 'the situation.' I left the country, cut contact from all, and did not see or speak to any Israeli for seven years. I would not even speak Hebrew. Nobody knew where I was. Seven years later, I met my sister again in Europe and could hardly speak my native language. It felt awkward.

"I have always been easy to anger, and I react aggressively to any frustration, large or small. I thought of it as my temper reacting to my day-to-day life difficulties. When I reconnected with my country, my troubled reactions became stronger, and the memories started coming back more vividly. My wife thoughts my outbursts were related to 'the situation.'

"The haunting thought was, 'Why me? Why was I spared? Why did I not die like my companions in my unit?' What bothers me the most is how much I feel out-of-control. The images of the war come up and in a second, my tears pour like a fountain, uncontrollably, no matter where I am or with whom. I am overwhelmed by emotion and feel tension in my lower back.

"Now I understand how this technique works. We are speaking with ourselves, to ourselves. The Felt Sense is new, and yet it is something I know."

AFTER SIX SESSIONS

AK's spontaneous and uncontrollable crying decreased by 40 percent and he was much nicer with his wife and son. His amazed wife could not really believe it would last. For the first time in their marriage, he was paying her compliments and was not reacting to all the little things that had upset him before.

When I asked him what he found most helpful in the therapy, AK replied,

"The paragraph about 'Why me?' I understood that this is a normal response, that what I went through will always be there and I cannot erase what took place. Now I can put a lid on it. It was my personal agony and I do not need to hurt others with it.

"I now know that 'Why me?' and 'Why did I survive?' are normal questions to ask when we survive terrible situations in which many others have died. I realize also that I associated the war vortex material to my relationship with my wife. I cannot change many things that happened. They will always haunt me. But I can live with them and change how I think about them. I cannot change the past with her either, but I now accept what I cannot change in her and take things in a calmer, more relaxed way. I am not as triggered and frustrated by everything as I used to be. I am able to take a moment before I object to something and do it calmly. She is really surprised."

The reaction of AK's wife was "Can I really trust his change? Is it going to last, or am I going to be disappointed?" She needed support to accept her husband's change, and handle her fears of future disappointment, and to learn how to deal with these disappointments.

AFTER 12 SESSIONS
"I did what you suggested: I stopped listening to the radio and reading the papers for a while. You were right. I needed a change in diet until I could re-establish my balance. Now I do not get the tightness I used to get when I had conversations with people. Everything felt so uptight, so intense, so matter of life and death. Now I am calmer. I used to live in the past only. Today I concentrate more on the now. The string of bad things and terrible images that came up all the time stopped. I am trying to open a new chapter and make it easier to communicate with my wife, my older son, and my employees. I almost do not cry anymore.

"However, my internal struggle is ongoing. I do not believe it will ever go away. I cannot, I do not want to see the world, the situation from a different angle, because it would disconnect me from my experience and from my understanding of the world. I usually listen to a radio program and I realize nothing has changed in the world. I see the same problems, situations, dangers, human weaknesses and the same waste of lives. I would have to stop listening."

AFTER 20 SESSIONS

I will never forget what happened. I owe it to those who died and to myself. I know I should try to allow a bit more joy in my life without feeling I am betraying them; but I must repair some of the damage my trauma exacted from my life and from my loved ones and that will take more time.

> "I am glad you are not asking me to forget. It is impossible to forget. It does not make sense. At most, you try to bury it and mask it, but it does not really work. It also does not make sense to forget. I am always concerned about forgetting the lessons I learned about war and the world that brings the wars. We must never forget the terrible waste, the unnecessary tragedies and the irreparable damage of wars."

For months, AK wrestled with philosophical and emotional issues still gripping him 30 years later. He did not accept the idea of choosing the healing vortex because for him, recuperating hope meant forgetting what men are still doing to each other, and forgetting the knowledge that hatred was still governing the actions of so many people around the world.

> "I think I can reach acceptance of what is, but it is still the acceptance of the despair in you and in others. You continue to live but without full meaning because you know hatred and war are still there, in disregard of the human voices of despair. I do not really want to live in a society that does not change, where people still make others suffer in the name

of God, where there is still violence, war and harm. It is so easy to destroy and much more difficult to rebuild.

"I still do not feel like I want to wake up in the morning; nothing ever changes. Hope is just not realistic. It is a dream world. People want to believe."

AK briefly considered the possibility of confronting hatred and war through philanthropic work:

"Helping people is nice. Having the motivation to help is nice, especially when you find out that so many people are selfish and cruel, and you still help. But I am not there yet."

AK is reflecting on his present private life. His wife stopped therapy abruptly and the changes that were happening between them did not resolve fully. AK is faced with whether he continues in an unhappy marriage or leaves, although his financial situation does not lead to this yet.

Despite his feelings of despondency, when asked what he would recommend to soldiers coming back from war, AK spoke with words full of compassion and heart.

"Yes, I will tell the young people who come back from war today, scarred by its brutality, not to hold onto anything that keeps them in despair, or onto anything that will not help them get out of suffering and pain. Do not let anything stop them from changing the painful states they feel. I know that I am against hatred, against killing out of hate, against the brutality that comes from man against man, driven by trauma and prejudice. Believe in that and move on."

On one of his last sessions, AK came with yet other insights:

"I finally realize that for my own integrity, I have to accept whatever happened to me and let go. I need to accept it is a misfortune that I was in the wrong place, at the wrong time and I need to drop the anger and not pass it onto others.

"When you have someone to blame and to forgive, or someone to ask forgiveness of, you can get closure. But when there is no responsible party, it is difficult to forget. It leaves you with a void, feeling angry, disillusioned, and creating situations for which you have to ask forgiveness. The only thing you can do for yourself in order to bring yourself inner peace is to understand it as a misfortune that happened."

When he was ready to go more fully into the shattering images of his military trauma, AK brought me a video copy of the movie "Waltz with Bashir." While AK went inside the bunker to get a book, his unit was wiped out by an enemy bomb, right after he had told with insistence to his newly arrived commander that they should not be meeting outside the bunker. The commander did not listen; the young soldiers died and AK was the only one to survive from his unit. Later on, he was not successful in his attempts to bring this information to military court.

AK understands that complete healing will come when he can turn his anger about what is still wrong in the world to a focused effort to help change that world.

Daniel and the Stigma of Trauma

"Trauma is not a word used lightly in any part of the world, but I find that sometimes the fear of trauma is more frightening than the trauma itself. I see so many of my friends suffering from trauma, whether or not they are conscious of it.

"I am 23 years old and moved to Canada from Israel to work on my career right after I finished my military service. When I heard Gina speak about trauma at a mutual friend's house, I immediately thought of my friend Motshki, who had gone through several horrible incidents when he was serving in Gaza, and who was clearly suffering from some sort of trauma. During the session with Gina, he talked about the events that bothered him, and I was surprised to see how quickly he became at ease talking about and processing his most difficult emotions.

"When Gina suggested it was my turn, I felt embarrassed. I thought that whatever I had witnessed in war was nothing compared to what my friend had suffered. I had witnessed terrible things happen to others, but nothing happened to me directly. I did not think I needed a session; next to Motshki's story, my problems seemed so much smaller. I did not realize the events I had witnessed had marked me, nor did I expect this session to be the first of a series. I realized the way I coped with what I witnessed was to deny; but I had been affected by what I had seen.

"To my surprise, my session helped me discover the deep issues that were affecting my most important life decisions. Feelings and sensations that lay deep in my subconscious mind were, unbeknownst to me, affecting the way I faced and planned for my future. The session helped me bring these issues to the forefront and deal with them. I realized I had coped by denying that I was I suffering from any trauma. Three sessions later, I had much more clarity about the path I wanted to take and I felt much better having the tools and perspective to deal with my experiences. We have to come to terms, whether or not we like it, with the fact that trauma plays a role in everyday life. Sweeping it under the rug will not make it go away but only allows it to build up."

PART I
THEORY OF TRAUMA AND HEALING

CHAPTER ONE

BASICS OF TRAUMA

M ost military personnel find combat to be exciting and even exhilarating, despite the constant physical and emotional exhaustion and the occasional morally troubling situations. Most do not expect to be traumatized by war, believing they have the necessary resilience to come out unscathed and that they will contribute to their country's safety. Yet trauma is part of the personnel's experience.

Most people think of a traumatic event as something that is shattering and extraordinary. However, traumatic events can also be ordinary occurrences. The accumulation of these varied types of traumas leaves its impact on the balance of the autonomic nervous system. Following is a list of the variety of traumatic events that affect people, including soldiers.

"Extraordinary" traumatic events include: natural and man-made disasters and epidemics; homicides, assaults, deliberate crimes; repressive governments; religious and ethnic persecution or oppression; torture, human rights violations and slavery; acts of terrorism, war, pogroms, genocide, holocausts; captivity, refugee status and

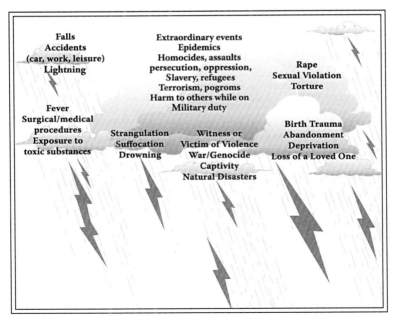

Fig. 1

exile; sudden and violent change of regimes; being in the position of harming others in the line of duty (police, soldiers, and executioners).

"Ordinary" traumatic events include: car crashes, work or leisure accidents, surgical and medical procedures, life-threatening illnesses, high fevers in infants, falls, major injuries, sudden and unexpected losses, exposure to toxic substances, drowning and suffocation, and trauma associated with birth.

ADDITIONAL VULNERABILITIES MILITARY PERSONNEL MAY FACE

- In the application of lethal force in the course of one's duties, a prospect many find harder to bear than being targeted by the enemy

- An on-going risk to their lives, thereby facing more hazards for traumatization than the average person despite their special training

- The increased vulnerability to trauma due to the length and degree of exposure to war: the longer military action is sustained without opportunities for rest and recovery, the likelier for military personnel to develop traumatic symptoms

- Cumulative traumatic stress: symptoms may also manifest if the war has no specific end in sight or if the expected leave or termination of tours of duty gets postponed or there are more tours of duty than expected

ADDITIONAL STRESSORS FOR MILITARY PERSONNEL, OTHER THAN WAR

Some of these stressors are targeted toward the Israeli model, which unlike the present American model, uses non voluntary military service. Most apply to both types of recruitment.

Preparation time: may be too short; may not give enough forewarning (which would decrease stress) or may have unpredictable departure. Many personnel in times of emergency lack training and have to learn on-the-job.

Duration of the deployment: may endure over long periods and require several readjustments on the part of the personnel and their families. The length of the tours seems to be more debilitating than the numbers of tours.

Definition of the mission: may be poorly defined, unfocused, ambiguous or shifting. It may also be passive, with a lot of wait-and-see situations, creating more stress than an active mission. A mission may lack clear progress or regress, or it may be perceived as less worthy than other missions.

Degree of austerity of living conditions: Often living conditions are basic bordering on the primitive, include poor nutrition, improper rest, and overall basic health concerns.

Degree of contact with home, family and personal culture: This includes lack of access to usual communications or when mission requirements dictate secrecy.

Exposure to negative media coverage: Media coverage might be inaccurate, biased by political opinions and lack credibility; additionally and inadvertently adding to stressors to the overall military efforts. It might also express the cultural unpopularity of a war, which unjustly targets military personnel

Exposure to a foreign alien culture: Military experiences might be unpleasant in unfamiliar cultures with significantly different values and mores.

Exposure to extreme trauma: Often military experiences include unexpected degrees of brutality, especially against children and women.

Exposure to the sheer number of dead: Military personnel may witness a large number of casualties, both military and civilian. (*See* Bloody Tarawa Story Chapter 16); first-hand evidence of combat deaths and unexpected brutalities, triggering widely diverse emotions, ranging from horror, sorrow, and regret, to disgust, hatred and a burning desire for revenge; use of cynical humor, later arousing guilt and shame.

Exposure to widespread lack of respect for recognized rules of warfare: This creates a dilemma when uneven respect for accepted rules is at work, putting their lives more at risk.

Perceived inequalities in exposure to risk: Military personnel know they are more at risk than the general population—a knowledge that is reinforced by the widespread media coverage of traumatized soldiers.

DEFINITIONS OF TRAUMA

Traumatic events are those occurrences that challenge and overwhelm our capacity to cope and respond, causing our body/mind to be stuck in survival mode, leaving us unable to recover our equilibrium. The various definitions of traumatic events include:

Shock Trauma: The impact of an unexpected and frightening event, which happens too fast and too soon and is too much for our nervous system to assimilate. It triggers intense feelings of fear, helplessness and loss of control, and disorganizes the nervous system. People in shock trauma feel dazed, confused, bewildered, shaken, and disoriented.

Developmental Trauma: This is defined as the consequence of an ongoing mis-attunement within the child-parent relationship. It can be caused by neglect or physical and emotional abuse in childhood. It is often intertwined with shock trauma experiences and manifests in dysfunctional character traits.

Post-traumatic Stress Disorder (PTSD): Is an anxiety disorder resulting from unresolved traumatic events. Symptoms include intrusive flashbacks, hyper-vigilance, and avoidance.

Somatic Experiencing® Broader Definition of Trauma: This definition includes anything from one's life experience, which remains stuck and unresolved that causes disturbances at the biological, physiological, emotional, mental or behavioral levels. This broader definition of symptoms (in addition to PTSD symptoms), includes a variety of health problems, syndromes and psychosomatic illness; psychological disorders such as anxiety, including separation anxiety, depression and fatigue; behavioral disorders such as substance abuse; eating disorders; angry, impulsive or aggressive behavior; chronic relationships problems and violence. In a wider definition of PTSD, reactions to trauma can range from complete inability to cope with daily life to utter destruction of others.

WAR TRAUMA COUPLED WITH PAST DEVELOPMENTAL SHOCK TRAUMA

When war and developmental trauma overlap, it can be very confusing and upsetting for the traumatized soldier. Traumatic war experiences can push patterns of unresolved earlier conflicts into trauma and/or retrigger past traumas. The good news is that the processing of war traumas can provide opportunities to alleviate earlier traumas and acquire new strengths, even many years later. In the future, it may be desirable and possible to establish a policy of clearing one's early traumas during basic training.

Discharging Developmental and Shock Trauma

Sam was a serious and committed thirty five year-old teacher. On a class outing with his thirteen-year-old students and some of their parents, one of the parents fell and injured herself. The fall was a bad one as the woman had broken her leg and suffered several other bone fractures with a lot of bleeding. Sam took care of her and called the ambulance. Nobody really knew what had happened to her. They imagined she had ventured alone on a side path to take some pictures and had climbed a fence to have a better view; but she lost her balance and fell off the fence, which was quite high above the ground.

Although Sam had attended to her very competently and the woman recovered well, after this outing, Sam shied away from other class trips. He felt responsible for the fall and was terrified that something would go wrong again. His body was tense and he talked to himself obsessively about his guilt and responsibility.

In therapy, he was able to recognize that there was a pattern that had been there all his life, what we call a 'developmental issue' that was retriggered by this shock trauma. As a 'parental child,' he felt responsible for everything.

In the sessions, he was asked to focus on his resources and then notice any constricted sensations in his body and see what happens next. Some of his resources were actually past class outings he had liked very much. When thinking of them, he felt calmer, and could feel his breath get deeper and fuller. He became able to connect his exaggerated sense of responsibility to some past difficulties in his life, and learned to discharge the activation it brought up in him; He was then able to develop the capacity to identify through his felt sense when he was truly responsible for a situation and when he was not. "I did all I could. It was not my fault," was his conclusion after he processed the event through the sensations in his body. After seven or eight sessions he felt fine and could resume all his activities without worry and panic.

Childhood Trauma Revisited

A Caucasian-American from the South and Vietnam veteran, John spent his service time in Vietnam in conflict more with his fellow servicemen than with the enemy. He was immediately involved in interracial fights. When his commander, an African-American officer, wore a Black Panther logo and John wore symbols of the Confederacy, his officer locked up John in a concrete barrack, which later received a barrage of enemy fire. It was a nerve-shattering experience for John.

Upon his release, instead of receiving an expected communications assignment in a military office, he was purposefully assigned to the dangerous task of carrying the radio at the front of the patrols. Outraged by this assignment, he considered deserting while on leave, but out of loyalty to his World War II-wounded father, he remained on the dangerous front lines throughout his service.

John returned with several physical wounds and deep emotional issues. He felt disconnected from everyone around him, including his girlfriend. He mostly lived in isolation and inactivity. Alcohol was his only solace. He was caught in an unending pattern of fighting, alternating with bouts of isolation followed by fleeing to a new city in an attempt to start afresh. He fought and ran for 24 years, unable to ease his pain.

In 1992, he finally began therapy. At first, his body was tense, his eyes glazed and wild. He suffered from agoraphobia, residual pain from a war-related knee wound, and alcoholism. However, soon after, he was able to break his repetitive pattern. He joined a group therapy and felt, for the first time, part of a therapeutic community where he felt heard and could tell his story in a receptive environment.

One of John's earliest and biggest resources was his ability to tell funny stories, laugh, and make others laugh—a talent, which contributed much to his healing. As the pain he had buried resurfaced, he would focus on the tension the memories elicited in his body, and alternated between the sensation of constriction and the sensation of expansion elicited by his laughter, until he released the built-up tension.

Going back and forth between laughter and camaraderie, and the retelling of war-trauma stories, John was able to re-experience and discharge long buried painful events without feeling re-traumatized. He also reconnected with his family and bonded with the veterans in his group, both Caucasians and African-Americans.

During one of the sessions, John remembered the pain he felt when his mother died of stomach cancer when he was only eight years old. As he described how he imagined her stomach barraged by radiation he curled up, his body taking the same posture he held when describing the barrage of incoming fire in the locked barrack. In a flash, John realized these two experiences connected in his mind, amplified the impact of his war experience and crippled him. His new awareness allowed him to uncouple the war trauma from his childhood suffering. He felt tremendous relief when he finally released the traumatic energy held for so long in his body.

John was able to negotiate with the VA for the physical rehabilitation treatment he needed. He also became intent on forming new relationships. One day, he told his therapist: "Imagine this. I finally got a doctor I can trust, and he is Asian. I must have come a long way."

FACTORS INFLUENCING THE MAGNITUDE OF TRAUMA

The magnitude of trauma's impact depends on various factors:

- The length and severity of the traumatic event

- The timing of the event and the developmental stage in which a person experiences it; the earlier the trauma, and the fewer the resources, the more damaging the impact
- Success or failure in coping with previous traumatic experiences
- Genetic resiliency
- Conscious and unconscious cultural attitudes towards trauma
- The type and amount of social support and resources available during and after trauma
- Spiritual balance and faith

THE EFFECTS OF TRAUMA ON THE BODY/MIND

In order to heal trauma, it is helpful to understand that *"the body keeps the score."*

- *Trauma registers in the body.* Trauma is a neurobiological state which results from the response of a particular body to a particular stressful event at a particular time. One individual may respond differently than another to the same event and this same individual may respond differently to the same event at different times.

- *Trauma alters brain chemistry;* it triggers hormonal changes which alter the levels of neurotransmitters and increase adrenalin, cortisol and/or opioids production (unleashing primitive self-protective responses which bypass the neo-cortex even when the current circumstances are no longer a threat).

- *Trauma affects the balance of the autonomic nervous system (ANS);* unresolved threat deregulates the ANS and its autonomic basic functions; it over-activates and unduly prolongs the no-longer needed defensive responses.

- *Trauma leaves excess arousal energy in the body,* which manifests in a myriad of symptoms (see Chapter 3 for multiple and varied symptoms). For many military personnel, in addition to the usual definition of PTSD symptoms, a trauma response takes the form of drug and alcohol abuse as self-medication, or a scary underlying sense of murderous rage.

- *Trauma thwarts the completion of our defensive responses and stores them as incomplete movements in the body,* creating tension and pain leaving us with a profound sense of helplessness, and making us more vulnerable to repeated trauma, such as recurring falls, accidents, etc.

- *Trauma impairs memory function:* Trauma victims who develop the PTSD /dissociation spectrum of symptoms (part of the freeze response discussed in Chapter 2) seem to suffer from memory deficits such as fragmentation of reality perception and gaps in the continuity of their experience, the product of a destabilized amygdala and of hippocampus damage. The initial trauma is not relegated to the past nor integrated in normal auto-biographical memory channels, but invades the individual's present and future.

- *Trauma affects belief structures:* Trauma can affect and be affected by personal, familial, and cultural narratives, values, traditions, mores and meanings. Often it is the result of a rupture between what the individual experiences and what his/her belief system and worldview can sustain.

- *Trauma may manifest at different times:* People may have traumatic symptoms soon after the traumatic event, or years and even decades later.

In other words, in SE®, trauma is simply un-discharged traumatic arousal and incomplete defensive responses around a particular moment of the traumatic event that for whatever reason was not assimilated by the person's psyche, whether at the level of meaning or of sensory containment.

Trauma is in the Body

Seven years after he left his military service veteran soldier Carl went to therapy to work on his compulsive use of marijuana.

After a few sessions, his therapist asked him to show the posture his body took when using the drug. The veteran was surprised to find out it was the same posture he had, when sitting in a bomb shelter in Lebanon, waiting for Hezbollah's bombing to stop. The experience had been a terrifying one, and marijuana was his way of self-medicating to try to calm the terror of that time still held in his body.

Recognizing the connection between his drug abuse and his terrifying experience during the bombing, he was able to release the sensations of terror from his body, heal his seven-year trauma, and give up drugs.

Postponed Trauma Reaction

Avi was on duty in Gaza during the 1987 Intifada. During one of the battles he was assigned to watch over the body of a 16-year-old Palestinian boy. It was night and he was left alone with the smell of burning tires and sounds of shooting all around him, not knowing whether it was enemy or friendly fire. He also did not know when he would be relieved from his duty.

Avi finished his military service as planned and went back to his Kibbutz thinking everything was normal. Fifteen years later, during his reserve service, Avi's PTSD symptoms started to appear. He was reluctant to serve in the reserve Army, but knew he had no choice. He asked to be the regiment commander's driver. Although the job put him in the frontline and exposed him to more danger, Avi felt safer, since his job allowed him to always know what was going on and to never be uninformed about military maneuvers.

In another tour of reserve duty in 2002, Avi started suffering from flashbacks from his 1987 Intifada experience and developed panic attacks. He then realized he had suppressed his experience. He started connecting the anger and impatience he felt in his personal life (especially with his child) to his 1987 war experience.

Haunted by his memories, Avi left the Kibbutz and spent an increasing time alone by the sea. His normal zest for life seemed drained out of him. Previously known to be the life of the party, Avi did not want to do anything but listen obsessively to the news.

His panic attacks grew worse and his anger was triggered by everything. When he learned that one of his commanders was a mental health therapist, Avi decided to talk to him about his problems. The commander helped him discharge the flashbacks and the panic attacks stopped. A grateful Avi made it a point to encourage all his Army friends who were also having traumatic symptoms to seek help.

Like AK in our previous example, Avi became aware that if in 1987 he and his commanders had been fully aware of the impact of extreme events and of the tools now available to address them, he would have been spared countless sleepless nights and years of shame about his angry outbursts in his family.

A HOPEFUL DEFINITION OF TRAUMA

Trauma is a common and normal part of life and our body and mind are naturally hard-wired to cope with it. Most of the time we heal from trauma on our own, but when it is too overwhelming and the energy remains stuck in our system we develop traumatic symptoms.

In order to heal trauma, we need to learn to release the stuck excess arousal and complete the fight/flight responses that we mobilized to meet the threat. It creates hope to view trauma as simply an uncompleted process rather than permanent damage.

Trauma need not last a lifetime. It does not have to leave us devastated and dysfunctional. On the contrary, healed trauma is often transformative. Not only do we feel alive when we resolve our traumas, but we deepen our capacity to overcome devastating situations in the future and have a better ability to handle fear. Healed trauma allows us to feel a greater sense of control over our lives, empowers us to develop a fuller spectrum of responses and experience more zest for life.

CHAPTER TWO

TRAUMA AND THE BRAIN

The Triune Brain

Understanding how the brain functions during trauma helps us better grasp how to heal it.

The following diagram illustrates the different layers of our brain:

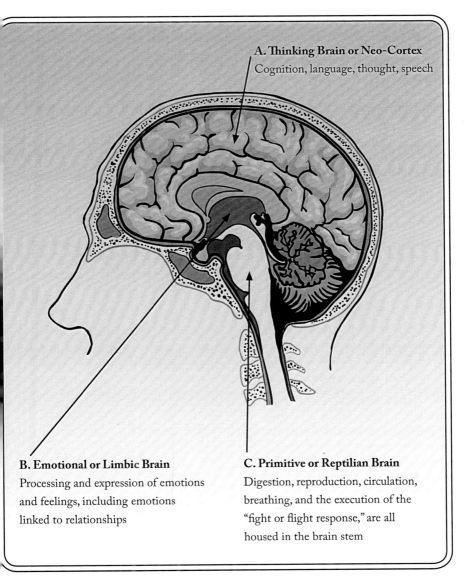

A. Thinking Brain or Neo-Cortex
Cognition, language, thought, speech

B. Emotional or Limbic Brain
Processing and expression of emotions and feelings, including emotions linked to relationships

C. Primitive or Reptilian Brain
Digestion, reproduction, circulation, breathing, and the execution of the "fight or flight response," are all housed in the brain stem

Fig. 2

Trauma and the Brain

OUR THREE-LAYERED BRAIN

The human brain is composed of three interconnected layers, designed to interact with each other seamlessly in an integrated whole. In trauma, these layers disconnect from each other and create a lack of integration, throwing off the nervous system.

A. The **thinking brain,** or **neo-cortex,** controls language and higher cognitive functions, including learning, problem-solving, making choices, reasoning, planning, and flexibility. It also controls voluntary movement and self-regulation as it normally regulates the two other layers of the brain. The neo-cortex uses words, ideas and concepts.

B. The **emotional,** or **limbic brain** governs emotions; it is the seat of motivation, attention, and emotional memory. It registers fear, terror, rage and joy, operating mostly in terms of pleasure or pain. The emotional brain speaks in images, metaphors, and emotions.

C. The **primitive** or **reptilian brain** is instinctive and controls the execution of the fight, flight, and freeze reflexes. It coordinates balance, arousal, action and all vital basic functions, such as breathing, digestion, circulation, sleep, heartbeat and sexuality. The primitive brain speaks in terms of internal physical sensations and sensations generated from external stimuli captured through our five senses. The primitive brain does not know time sequence.

Unresolved trauma impairs neural integration. It causes the neo-cortex to lose its ability to manage or inhibit the other layers' activities, affecting constructive thinking, problem-solving and the ability to be emotionally flexible. The limbic brain remains over-activated, continuing to trigger the defensive response of fight, flight and freeze—even when no longer necessary. The primitive brain remains in a state of constant activation, resulting in impulsive reactions, often alternating between hyperarousal and withdrawal or paralysis.

Healing trauma means re-establishing the lost integration by re-establishing self-regulation (the control over physical, emotional, cognitive and behavioral processes). The reptilian and limbic brains need to recover their balance and be returned to the control of the neo-cortex. Re-integration is achieved by using conscious awareness (neo-cortex brain activity) focused on the body's internal sensations in order to discharge and to complete defensive movements (the realm of the limbic and primitive brains).

THE NERVOUS SYSTEM

The nervous system gathers and stores information about the external environment and the body's internal state. It communicates and controls the body's movements and sensations. Its components include:

- The *Central Nervous System (CNS)*—is composed of the spinal cord and the brain, it controls voluntary movement and conscious thoughts

- The *Peripheral Nervous System (PNS)*—is composed of both sensory and motor nerves (neurons). The sensory nerves receive stimuli from the environment and report them to the CNS. The motor nerves communicate action to the muscles and glands. The peripheral nervous system is composed of two separate systems:

  › The *Sensory-Somatic Nervous System (SSNS)*—which controls our five senses

  › The *Autonomic Nervous System (ANS)*—which regulates all the body's basic autonomic functions

THE IMPORTANCE OF THE AUTONOMIC
NERVOUS SYSTEM (ANS)

In SE®, the focus on the regulation of the autonomic nervous system is particularly important. The ANS is the key to healing trauma because it is the center of survival responses. It operates

The Nervous System

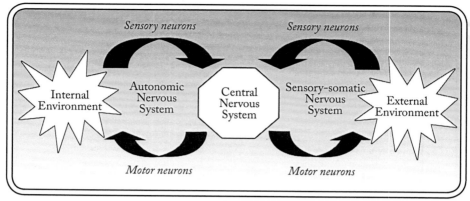

Fig. 3

without our control, and it regulates our visceral system (our guts) and all basic autonomic functions.

The ANS has two branches: the *Sympathetic Nervous System* and the *Parasympathetic Nervous System*. The Sympathetic branch acts like the gas pedal of our nervous system, moving its motor. The Parasympathetic branch is like a brake pedal and helps discharge the arousal of the sympathetic system. They balance each other in a reciprocal fashion, one arousing and one releasing the arousal, depending on the situation and needs of the moment.

When we are relaxed and happy, there is a gentle rhythm back and forth between the two branches, undulating between automatic charge and discharge, and between arousal and relaxation. This gentle rhythm gives us a sense of well-being and success in managing our lives successfully.

NORMAL AND EFFECTIVE RESPONSE TO STRESS

Under normal conditions, the neo-cortex controls the limbic and primitive brains, taking in information, processing it and making decisions. Although the limbic brain informs these decisions with its

Resilient Nervous System

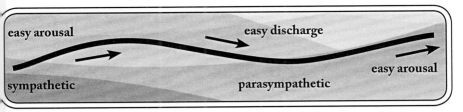

Fig. 4

emotions, ultimately, the neo-cortex is the one in control. However, when we face a threat—whether real or imagined—we operate on an unconscious level. The amygdala—the part of the limbic brain which registers emotion—and the neo-cortex are activated within a split second of each other. If the neo-cortex cannot handle the threat through communication and reason, it withdraws its inhibiting action and the amygdala takes control, immediately triggering an emergency response that releases stress hormones, activating the ANS and shifting resources away from non-urgent bodily functions. At this point, the reptilian brain takes over and organizes instinctive defensive responses outside the realm of conscious thought, deciding whether we should fight, flee, or freeze.

At the level of the ANS, there are two phases of the emergency response to threat. When we are resilient (physically and emotionally balanced) the charging phase (Sympathetic) is followed by a calming phase (Parasympathetic) of equal measure. This gentle, flowing rhythm back and forth between the sympathetic and parasympathetic branches, pendulating between automatic charge and discharge, gives us a sense of well-being and control. When the charge/discharge cycle has completed itself, homeostasis is re-established and the stress response can be deemed resolved.

At the physiological level, the Sympathetic branch is activated in response to threat and several changes take place. The pupils dilate for more acuity. Saliva decreases to conserve body fluids. The heart rate increases to carry the blood and oxygen faster to the muscles.

Role of the Sympathetic and Parasympathetic Branches of the ANS

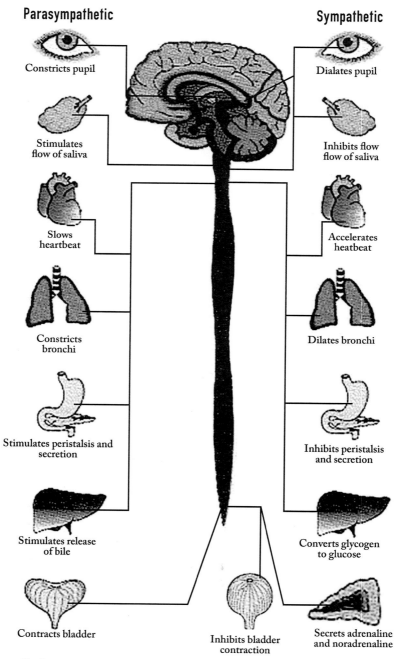

Parasympathetic

Sympathetic

Constricts pupil

Dialates pupil

Stimulates flow of saliva

Inhibits flow flow of saliva

Slows heartbeat

Accelerates heatbeat

Constricts bronchi

Dilates bronchi

Stimulates peristalsis and secretion

Inhibits peristalsis and secretion

Stimulates release of bile

Converts glycogen to glucose

Contracts bladder

Inhibits bladder contraction

Secrets adrenaline and noradrenaline

Fig. 6

The Reciprocal Function of the two Branches
of the Autonomic Nervous System

The Sympathetic Nervous System (SNS)	The Parasympathetic Nervous System (PSNS)
The SNS **gets us ready for action**. It regulates arousal, increasing activity during times of stress—whether positive or negative. It is active when we're alert, excited, or engaged in physical activity but it also prepares us also to meet emergencies and threat by: 1. Increasing our heart rate, breathing, and blood pressure. 2. Shifting blood away from our stomach and kidneys to our muscles to allow for quicker movement. 3. Constricting our blood vessels and draining the blood away from the skin (which turns pale and cold). 4. Dilating our pupils, retracting our eyelids and focusing our eyes. **Hyperarousal of the SNS** results in: • Slowing or shutting down our immune system. • Lowering our libido. • Causing our body to stop secreting eye, nose and genital fluids which can make us more prone to sickness.	The PSNS **helps us relax after arousal**. It helps us unwind and reorganize and regenerate after threat by: 1. Helping us let go of muscle tension. 2. Lowering heart rate and blood pressure, slowing and deepening the breath. 3. Aiding in digestion. 4. Returning blood to the vessels (turning our skin flushed and warm again). 5. Allowing the immune system to function fully again and secreting bodily fluids. The PSNS also oversees feelings of contentment, pleasure, happiness, grief and sadness. In states of emergencies and threat when we can't fight or flee, the PSNS will initiate the freeze response and block sympathetic arousal without discharging it. **A fixed position of the PSNS** results in: • Immobility • Depression • Fatigue and lethargy
*The Sympathetic branch is like **the gas pedal** of our nervous system. It gives us energy for any action we plan, and it helps us prepare for threat.*	*The Parasympathetic branch acts like **the brake pedal** for our nervous system. It helps us relax and unwind as well as discharge sympathetic arousal; and it triggers the freeze response.*

Fig. 5

The Fight / Flight / Freeze Mechanisms

FIGHT

FLIGHT

FREEZE

Original Drawings Courtesy of Soosan Suryawan

The bronchioles dilate to facilitate more energy to fight or flee. The intestinal secretions decrease. The blood vessels at the surface of the body and in the hands and feet constrict to increase blood pressure. When the emergency is successfully resolved, the parasympathetic branch reverses these reactions (see Figures 5 and 6) and brings the system back to homeostasis.

At the hormonal level, this process of preparing to face and escape threat is negotiated by the endocrine system: as the sympathetic branch is stimulated, excitatory hormones are secreted into the blood in large quantities. Once released, these hormones—epinephrine and norepinephrine—travel very rapidly throughout the body in the bloodstream, producing the well-known "adrenaline rush," triggering the physiological responses described above.

Once the threat is over, a complex series of feedback loops tells the body to turn off the stress hormones, which return to normal levels.

EMERGENCY RESPONSE TO THREAT: FLIGHT, FIGHT OR FREEZE?

When we perceive something new in our environment:

- We **orient,** by turning our attention toward the stimulus. Within the emotional brain, the amygdala assesses whether the stimulus is dangerous or pleasurable and whether to void or move toward it.

- If the amygdala is wary of the stimulus, it alerts the whole body/mind by triggering a strong arousal response in the sympathetic branch of the nervous system. Heart rate and breathing increase, blood pumps, muscles tense, and vigilance intensifies.

- The brain assesses how best to respond: flight, fight or freeze.

- **Flight** is our first instinctual response, generally the most efficient for our system.

- **Fight** is the second choice when we cannot flee and have the strength to fight.

- **Freeze** is the last choice when it is impossible to flee or fight. This is an adaptive response that provokes an altered state of consciousness which can spare us from pain and our immobility may also disarm predators. The freeze controlled by the PNS is a protective function against a too intense and potentially harmful SNS response.

Later we will analyze how the freeze response is also at the core of traumatic symptoms.

When we are able to flee from or fight a threat, the very act of running, escaping or fighting enables our body/mind to use up the powerful energy ignited to face danger and return to homeostasis. This natural discharge of the threat-related energy is essential to our health allowing us to avoid and even eliminate the after-effects of trauma.

In addition, the fight, flight, and freeze responses start with innate preparatory action plans to face danger as once a plan has been evoked, it must be carried to completion in order for our bodies and minds to know that the danger is over and for our systems to return to normal. If we do not complete our plan, the excess energy remains fixed in our body and our autonomic nervous system remains off-balance. When we complete our defensive responses and discharge the traumatic arousal, we are able to recuperate normal functions and resolve physical pain.

A Discharged Freeze

An example of discharge in the animal world is given in a National Geographic video from 1997, Polar Bear Alert.

A frightened bear is run down by a pursuing airplane, shot with a tranquilizer dart, surrounded by wildlife biologists, and then tagged. As the massive animal comes out of its shock state it begins to tremble, peaking with an almost convulsive shake—with its limbs (seemingly) flailing at random. The shaking subsides and the animal takes three spontaneous breaths which seem to spread through its entire body. The (biologist) narrator of the film comments that the behavior of the bear is necessary because it "blows off stress" accumulated during the capture. If this sequence is viewed in slow motion it becomes apparent that the "random" leg gyrations are actually coordinated running movements—it is as though the animal completes its running movements (truncated at the moment it was trapped), discharges the "frozen energy," then surrenders in a full bodied "orgiastic breath."

Difference between Releasing and Failing to Release Stress

"Ben" was in a unit which had experienced a difficult ordeal with one dead soldier and two wounded ones during a short battle commanded by "Al." At the invitation of an SE® therapist, Al agreed to help his soldiers process the ordeal. He normalized the chaotic mix of sensations and contradictory emotions they felt, assuring them it was natural to feel that way. He also welcomed their thoughts about what had happened.

Al then asked his soldiers to track their bodies, tuning into the sensations elicited by their feelings and thoughts. He then asked them to give time for their body to release these sensations. This release helped them sort out their fears and their anger.

At first, the members of the unit were uncomfortable speaking to their commanders about their feelings, but once one started to talk, the others followed eagerly. At the end of the process, they felt calmer and better able to "contain" or assimilate the difficult situation they had just experienced.

Ben's friend "Robert," on the other hand, was in a platoon that had seen soldiers killed in the last war and whose commander did not have the skills to help them address their feelings.

Robert reported that he and his comrades were seething with anger. The soldiers in his group acted out and engaged in aggressive behavior. Some were reluctant to serve in the reserve Army. They did not trust anyone and did not understand why they should still be in the reserve Army. "We have already taken part in the war. It is enough." No one realized how distraught they were from their traumatic experience. Their negative feelings about the Army were the outcome of their unprocessed and unreleased traumatic activation.

THREAT RESPONSE GONE AWRY: FREEZE AND STRESS ACCUMULATION

The freeze response—caused by the suppression or interruption of the flight and fight response and which results in "stuck energy"—is a major cause in the development of traumatic symptoms in humans. The reptilian brain is in charge of this response.

At the ANS level, this pent-up excess trauma energy triggers the primitive brain to believe the threat is still present, causing to continually release stress hormones (now toxic to our nervous system) and keeping the chronic threat response. We remain constantly on alert even when we no longer face an external threat. We have internalized the trauma. Our attention becomes riveted on it. We focus intensely on what looks and feels terrible, no longer remembering that we have internal and external resources that can help us heal. Time alone will not heal us.

This chronic and intense level of traumatic activation keeps the ANS deregulated, leading to a repetition of dysfunctional responses. Trapped in alternating cycles of an ANS stuck at "On" and "Off," our basic life processes are impaired, affecting breathing, heart rate, sleep, appetite, temperature, perspiration, sexual function, self-preservation and reproduction.

The previously gentle fluctuations between the sympathetic and parasympathetic systems are now replaced by jagged signs of excessive sympathetic arousal (such as racing heart, thoughts or speech, angry outbursts or panic attacks) and excessive parasympathetic activity (disconnection, shutdown, fatigue, lethargy or depression). Chronic hyper-arousal consumes opioids, depletes our adrenals and makes our body lose its natural rhythms. Our nervous system acts like a seesaw, wavering between hyper-arousal and apathy; between

Going from a Resilient to an
Over-Activated Autonomic Nervous System

Resilient Nervous System

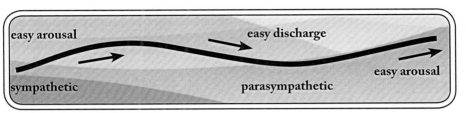

Over-Activated Nervous System

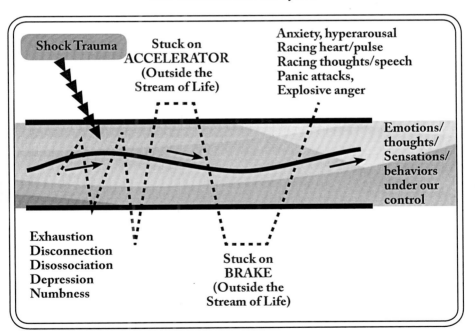

Fig. 7

explosive emotions, numbness and exhaustion. We refer to our nerves as being "fried" or "blown," and live on the edge, convinced that something bad is going to happen to us. (See Fig. 7).

These unconscious responses impair neo-cortex functions and memory and replace rational cognition. We loose our capacity to self-regulate, to process information and memory, and to reason. Intense emotion drives our reactions. We respond impulsively and loose our equanimity. This gives rise to a general sense of unease, the product of our own internal biology, which we tend to blame on external factors such as other people or our flawed character. Dysfunctional behavioral responses to threat become habitual. We become stuck in one type of response even though the situation calls for a different one, e.g., every situation is perceived as a fight. There is chronic avoidance of confrontation or a frozen collapse and resigned response to all challenges, compromising the ability to take future appropriate protective actions when facing new threats.

At the physiological level, it is naturally possible to discharge the freeze response, but frequently we don't. Lacking a neo-cortex, animals in the wild don't have this problem. When the threat is over, they automatically discharge the freeze response through autonomic responses, such as deep breaths, trembling, shaking, and complete the defensive movements. On the other hand, we humans often block this natural autonomic process, either afraid of reliving powerful feelings of terror and rage or embarrassed by the autonomic discharges and fearing rejection for being out of control. We unconsciously override the involuntary impulses of discharge. The frozen energy keeps our nervous system hyper-aroused and unbalanced, continually releasing stress hormones and sending the message that something is wrong, triggering the symptoms described earlier.

At the hormonal level, if trauma is not resolved within three months, the neuro-endocrine changes become chronic, increasing vulnerability to traumatic events in the future. The brain continues to secrete stress hormones to cope with a threat that doesn't exist anymore, keeping the body in a state of chronic biochemical stress. This results in high blood pressure and other symptoms, the consequence of abnormal cortisol levels, responsible for mal-adaptation in long-term memory processing and in the integration of experience.

Undischarged Terror

"Jack" was a veteran who had saved three platoons of his fellow soldiers who were isolated on a barren hill. The troops were under heavy enemy fire and without water. It was strategically imperative they hold the hill from the enemy, who could otherwise block and attack the whole regiment. Jack fetched water from a water hole for the troops.

As the platoons ran out of water, Jack ran back and forth several times under heavy fire to get them water. He came out unscathed. His brave act saved everyone from serious dehydration, allowing them to continue the fight, and the soldiers called the event "the water jar miracle." However, Jack left the Army soon after and disconnected from his friends.

Five years passed. In order to reconnect with his friends, Jack extracted from them the promise to never speak about the incident. Whenever his comrades would say, "We don't understand what happened to you. We have won the battle and you saved our lives. Why would you not talk to us about what happened?" he would just mumble something, keep silent, or walk away.

After much insistence on their part, he finally sought therapy. Asked by the therapist how many times he ran back and forth to the water hole and for how long, he blurted out crying, "I am still running." The underlying terror under the dissociation of his heroic action remained registered in his body and still haunted him. Jack was a hero torn between feeling like a hero and feeling like a coward. He could not relate to his hero image, because inwardly he was afraid he could not do it again if required to do so. The feeling of terror was still so present in his body, that he feared reliving the event, feeling again the terror and the shame of not being able to act heroically again, if he talked about what happened.

The Impact of an Undischarged Freeze Response

During mountain maneuvers, a reserve platoon made its way toward a frontier enemy post. Two of its tanks fired to help the troops maneuver. One tank hit its target while the round from the second tank landed off-target amidst the troops. Luckily it did not harm anyone. As both tanks kept firing, it became clear one of the tanks was misaligned and its rounds were going to fall again amidst the platoon. The commander shouted to the troops to disperse, although this did not guarantee safety because no one knew where the stray rounds might fall.

Two of the soldiers just froze and could not move. The round fell amidst the platoon and again miraculously did not harm any of the soldiers. The frozen soldiers refused to continue the training. This event was much more traumatic for them than for the rest of the troops. They left the platoon, left the reserve Army, and eventually left their country.

Eight years later, one of the soldiers felt compelled to return from abroad to take part in a famous battle. The battle was part of a big operation in the city where a suicide bombing had just taken place. The soldier said his return was a healing experience for him. He deliberately went inside a tank, checked the direction of the mortar to make sure it was right, and went to battle. During the next armed battle his country fought, he served again with the troops with bombs falling near him, but he felt no fear. He was now over his problem, but it had taken him eight years and therapy to realize that his freeze reaction had not hurt nor endangered anyone and that he did not have to live in shame.

The other soldier never returned home.

If the platoon commander had understood then about survival instincts and trauma, knowing how to bring people out of the freeze right on the spot, the two soldiers may not have left the army and their country nor have suffered for so long. When the military can normalize the freeze response, reframing it as a logical biological response to a threatening situation that can be overcome right then and there, soldiers will be helped to discharge and regain control to the benefit of themselves, their comrades, and to the entire military.

DISSOCIATION

Dissociation is a state of internal disconnectedness identified as an extreme form of freeze. Dissociation acts as an emotional and physiological "breaker switch" that turns off to protect the body's nervous system when there is an energy surge. This effectively reduces the impact of the experience and when time-limited, is a healthy survival adaptation. If prolonged, it disconnects us from our body with lasting traumatic symptoms, affecting our normal social and emotional processes. When we dissociate, part of our awareness disconnects from some of the elements of our experience. We may feel confused, numb, agitated, or have nightmares and flashbacks, while forgetting the context in which they belong. We may feel lethargic or heavy and lack energy without knowing why. At the extreme end of the dissociation spectrum, we may lose our sense of self, living a strange and unrecognizable life in a "fog" that separates us from the rest of the world.

Eventually we need to re-associate all the elements of the event, carefully and gently to avoid being re-traumatized and relapsing. If we reconnect with the split-off elements of our experience too quickly, we will feel the unbearable horror and rage that made us dissociate in the first place and freeze again. As the fog lifts and we recover, we need to release the arousal of those strong feelings. We must learn to discharge using the skills presented in Part II.

REACTION TO THREAT AND THE MILITARY IMPERATIVE

Our responses to threat are hard-wired into our nervous system. The decision to fight, flee, or freeze is not generally under our control. Flight is the most logical first response to threat as it protects us the most from being harmed. However in the military, the purpose of battle is to fight and military trainings are designed to override the flight/freeze instinctual responses. The motivation of defending your country or way of life also helps override the flight instinct. However, frontline military personnel are physiologically conflicted between the need to save their own lives and the duty to fight for their country.

Although the decision to flee or fight during battle is made at the higher military echelons, soldiers sometimes cannot override their survival instincts in the heat of battle and they may flee or freeze. Their nervous system simultaneously signals "go" and "stop." The freeze response, possibly adaptive in other circumstances, becomes maladaptive when it immobilizes soldiers in the middle of battle, puts lives at risk, and becomes the habitual response to threat.

Military training with its emphasis on functional military behavior includes overcoming the powerful survival instincts. This leaves military personnel to feel guilty and ashamed when these instincts take over, even if they saved their lives. Moreover, being perceived by fellow combatants as cowards who abandoned their comrades or seen going into a freeze response is devastating for soldiers and can ruin their ability to function.

Soldiers who survive battles during which some of their comrades perish are plagued by survivor's guilt even if they fought with valor. Those who survived because they fled carry worse feelings of guilt and remain haunted by doubts for the rest of their lives about whether they did the right thing, even if they survived because of their decision.

Commanders may fear that if they normalize the flight/freeze reaction it will make more military personnel flee or freeze. However, if the military recognizes these responses as instinctive and out of one's control instead of as a matter of character, it will be easier for them to address these issues on the spot. They could help soldiers get out of the freeze, discharge the fear and recover their self-control. This will assure them of better reflexes, faster recovery and function.

Overcoming Triggers and Avoidance

"David" served as a driver in the reserve army. A remarkable family man and a vice-president of a high-tech company, he regularly and dutifully performed his reserve service. During his earlier military service he had been closely exposed to death and corpses on two occasions. The first time was when his tank killed a terrorist in Lebanon and the body had to be removed. The second time his soldier friend Sal committed suicide and David had to take his remains to the infirmary; a sight he cannot forget.

One day the siren rang and David drove the soldiers to the place of the attack. Terrorists were shooting and had killed an Israeli civilian. The soldiers saw the body and began to pursue the killers.

Designated to drive the pursuit vehicle, David said he forgot his eyeglasses and had to go back to the base. Once there, he vomited until he was exhausted and drank until he was bloated, as if trying to wash away something inside of him. The sight and smell of the civilian corpse triggered the memory of the bodies of the terrorist and of his friend, provoking a violent reaction of repulsion in him.

Using SE®, his commander helped David discharge the energy stuck in his memory and body. He helped him become desensitized to the smell and the subsequent repulsion. After that, David went on with his job. Although in that particular incident he was not able to complete his assignment, David was very happy that he did not have to leave the company and was able to continue his service and function well.

DEVELOPING HEALTHY RESPONSES

Just as we can strengthen physical muscles with exercise, we can strengthen our resilience by developing and practicing healthy responses to threat and trauma.

Somatic Experiencing® (SE®) heals trauma by facilitating the integration of the three levels of the brain. It uses awareness and "the felt sense" (which we discuss in Chapter 6) to regulate the nervous system (the reptilian brain), to integrate emotions (the limbic brain), and restore control to the neo-cortex (thinking brain). SE® is particularly adept at healing trauma held in implicit memory, a type of trauma that can be retrieved mostly through body consciousness, such as movements, and internal physiological states (such as heartbeat, rapid pulse, etc.).

CHAPTER THREE

SYMPTOMS OF TRAUMA
AND SIGNS OF HEALING

If we practice remaining present to our difficult traumatic and stressful experiences without trying to escape them; without labeling, stopping, judging, or criticizing what we feel, we have the opportunity to release and heal from the negative impact of our experiences.

While it seems counterintuitive, focusing for a short period of time one sensation at a time, on the uncomfortable sensations generated by a traumatic experience in fact relaxes these constricted sensations. Rather than amplifying them, it allows the body to shift, change, and re-establish its natural balance—the foundation for our well-being. This symbol of an inverted eight represents the principle of the innate pendulation at work—the back and forth movement of the organism between constriction and expansion, between tightness and openness, between trauma and healing. It is this natural oscillatory process that can bring movement to undue the stuckness and fixity of trauma.

SYMPTOMS OF TRAUMA IN INDIVIDUALS

Trauma's disruption of brain integration throws the body/mind into a state of disequilibrium, generating traumatic symptoms that may manifest immediately or months later, or may take years to appear. Trauma symptoms are innumerable. They often appear disconnected from the original event that provoked them. If you have some of the following symptoms and have not been able to heal, they may be connected to a past traumatic experience. However treating the immediate physical symptoms may help you release unconscious traumatic triggers even if you do not connect them to a particular event.

Symptoms of Trauma Vortex

"Joe," a Vietnam veteran, was successful in business as long as he worked for himself. He had been married and divorced four times. He had three stomach surgeries. There was no medical explanation for his continual pain.

"For some unknown reason, my gut reacts to all my emotional ups and downs," he explained. Therapy helped him connect his stomach problems with his 30-year-old war traumas.

Indeed, Joe had been continuously on the frontline throughout his entire tour of duty in Vietnam. He shot many enemy soldiers and witnessed the deaths of many comrades. On the surface, he seemed to have adjusted well to the horrible conditions of war, but his stomach registered the chronic hyper-arousal, with the associated shut down of the digestive system.

Symptoms of trauma include:

Physical

- Chronic pain, including chest or back pain, headaches
- Dizziness, vertigo, fainting, elevated blood pressure
- Muscle tension, twitches, pain in the joints; numbing; nausea
- Hyper arousal signs—faster pulse rate, heart palpitations
- Hyperventilation, with rapid breath or difficulty breathing
- Increased sweating, chills, cold, clammy skin

- Hyper-alertness, being "on-edge"
- Flashbacks and nightmares; hallucinations and delusions
- Panic attacks
- Hypersensitivity to light, sound, smell, touch, and taste
- Fatigue, insomnia, loss of appetite and loss of sex drive
- Physical weakness and paralysis
- Worsening of prior medical conditions

Emotional

- Recurring, intense, unpredictable and irrational emotions
- Dramatic and abrupt mood swings, irritability, anger, rage
- High states of anxiety with panic; agony
- Uncontrollable fear/terror long after the event is over
- Profound helplessness; despair, depression, and fatalism
- Disruption of the usual sense of self, family, community and society; safety, predictability, and trust
- Loss of sense of adequacy
- Loneliness, isolation, alienation from others
- Loss of confidence, hope, faith; traumatic guilt and/or grief

Mental

- Confusion and disorientation
- Inability to concentrate or learn, short attention span
- Forgetfulness, loss of skills and of memories, carelessness
- Paranoid beliefs, racing, obsessive or negative thoughts
- Tendency for radicalism, polarization; intolerance
- Loss of ability to reason and be reasonable, to make decisions
- Loss of spontaneity and trust in one's instincts
- Vulnerability and suggestibility, suicidal thoughts
- Loss of interest in one's families, work, passions, and interests

- Cynicism, disenchantment
- Projection of difficult feelings and thoughts unto others
- Tendency to blame, judge, and criticize the self or others
- Inability to face life or death in a normal way; disruption of the normal illusion of immortality, specially for youth
- Inability to be happy; haunted by a fierce loyalty to the dead

Behavioral

- Restlessness, inability to sit still, tapping hands and feet
- Exaggerated startle response
- Repetitive (or pattern of) immobility and freeze; passivity
- Inability to function and to fulfill duties
- Impaired speech, changes in speech pattern
- Acting out, outbursts, impulsive or risky behavior, erratic actions
- Regressive or anti-social behaviors, affecting work and career
- Meeting one's needs at the expenses of others
- Reclusive, withdrawn or strange behavior; cutting oneself off from one's resources; keeping a stony silence about their war experiences and their feelings in general
- Addictive behavior—use of drugs and alcohol—slow suicide
- Dysfunctional communication, domestic violence
- Fear of loss of control, leading to perfectionist or obsessive compulsive behaviors to recuperate the sense of control

On the battlefield

- Eschewing all accepted rules for battle
- Deep hatred and loathing for the enemy
- Mutilation of the enemy dead
- Killing enemy prisoners or non-combatants
- Engaging in torture and brutality; killing animals

- Loss of sense of responsibility and control over one's actions
- Looting, pillaging, raping
- Refusal to fight, self-inflicted wounds, malingering
- Going AWOL, desertion
- Combating allies and threatening one's own leaders

Social

- Feeling powerless/isolated in the social order; challenged sense that life is meaningful and orderly
- Turning anger, rage, and hatred against society
- Adoption of the role of pariah
- Mistrust of or hatred of humanity
- Joining extreme movements or destructive cults
- Shame for protecting oneself while others remain in danger
- Stockholm Syndrome, devotion to perpetrators of violence

Spiritual

- Hopelessness; meaningless; loss of humanity
- Misplaced pride resulting in callousness/lack of compassion
- Deep feelings of shame in relation to life and to God; feeling of being punished by God; disbelief in and rejection of God; withdrawal from religious life; or conversely, adopting an extreme form of religion

At the family level

- Strained relationships; co-dependent behavior
- Domestic violence—spousal and child abuse
- Family breakups, separation, and divorce

At the collective level

- Polarized beliefs and emotions against groups or nations
- Distortion of collective narratives

- Intolerance of religious, cultural, and ethnic differences; genocidal violence
- Use of the media to promote intolerance; incite violence
- Xenophobia

TRAUMATIC BRAIN INJURY

Labeled as the Iraq and Afghanistan wars' "signature injury" or "invisible wound," traumatic brain injury (TBI) is caused by these wars' signature weapon—IED blasts. This has resulted in an epidemic of concussive injuries not seen in previous wars and affecting up to 20% of exposed military personnel. These explosions create shock waves of over-pressurized air and other electromagnetic phenomena, which enter the skull of anyone within proximity to the blasts.

Symptoms of TBI often overlap with and parallel PTSD symptoms. They include:

- Dizziness, excessive fatigue, sleep and balance problems, headaches, hypersensitivity to noise and light, vision change
- Anxiety, irritability, depression, mood swings and anger
- Impulsivity, agitation, aggression or apathy
- Impaired memory, learning, speech and problem-solving
- Isolation, avoidance of people and crowded places

There is also a cumulative effect from added exposures, especially if symptoms from previous blasts are not fully resolved or there was delay in treatment.

Scientists are studying the chain of events that happen during an explosion—including the shockwave of compressed air, the electromagnetic pulse, the electric and magnetic fields that can produce surges in current and voltage—to determine how they might affect the human brain. Previous research on brain injury has focused mostly on blunt trauma to the skull.

MILITARY-RELATED RISKS OF TRAUMA

Military personnel weather traumatic events far better when their personal values are congruent with military ones and when they perceive war actions as necessary and justified. They are more vulnerable to traumatization if they are at odds with military authority or if they oppose the war they are fighting. They are affected differently when their families and country are in danger and/or under duress from war. This stands in contrast to military personnel fighting a war while their countrymen lead normal lives that are untouched by the far away raging destruction, oblivious to its consequences.

They are also susceptible to secondhand trauma from helping wounded or dying comrades, and hearing about or watching war tragedies through the media. Because they develop a special bond on the battlefield and identify with their fallen comrades, soldiers are much more affected when they see comrades die in battles they deem to be (or that are portrayed by their countrymen and media) as immoral or avoidable.

Military personnel risk more stress when military authorities make the wrong decisions regarding their safety and endanger their lives unnecessarily, or when they order battles perceived as futile, which bring no military advantage or are subject to failure.

You may recognize yourself or others in this symptoms list. Symptoms can occur occasionally, frequently or chronically. If you or your military colleagues have several symptoms ranging from frequent to chronic, seek professional help and choose therapists who specialize in trauma. Also be aware that many of the physiological symptoms described above can derive from organic health issues as well and will require medical attention.

The House without Doors

"Dan" was a married veteran with three children. He had never talked about the war and had never sought any help. However, to protect his shattered and hyper-aroused nervous system from any trigger of the sounds of war, Dan made sure that his house had no interior doors. Slamming doors sent him into a deep rage. His children were forbidden to shout or play loudly and everyone tiptoed around him. Despite all his family's efforts, Dan could not handle the stress in his body. He tried to commit suicide. His 13-year-old daughter found him in time and he survived the attempt. For her sake, 17 years after the war he sought therapy for the first time.

When questioned about Dan's lifestyle, his family described a life of withdrawal, lack of interest in their activities, and a father simply not emotionally available. His daughter said she could never count on his presence or his opinion. She had left school at 16 and her father never reacted. Her mother was mentally ill and very weak. She knew her parents loved her, but she could not rely on them. Therapy helped Dan heal and he was able to be more emotionally available for his daughter, who now spends most of her free time with him.

THE SIGNS AND JOYS OF HEALING

Recovering the balance of our nervous system after the onslaught of trauma can transform our lives and be an extraordinary gift. When we heal our traumas we not only get rid of our symptoms but access unexpected benefits. We develop a more cohesive sense of self with a renewed energy to engage passionately with life. Healing from trauma is transformative. Our ability to triumph over life's difficulties helps us lose self-doubts, inhibitions and surrender to the mystery and enchantment of the unknown. Healing trauma frees us to reach our higher potential and take an active instead of a passive role in life.

The list of benefits includes:

Physical

- Better orienting, more openness to good stimuli
- Sensations of expansion, spaciousness, lightness
- Sensations of centering, grounding; sense of deep integration
- Capacity to sense the internal experience easily; the felt sense
- Capacity for full breath, experiencing flow, rhythm, and a sense of settling; for better body care and hygiene

Emotional

- Good access/control over emotions; wider emotional range
- Ability to feel calm while knowing danger is possible
- Capacity to feel calm, joyful, loving, compassionate, optimistic, hopeful, and trusting; feel healthy anger, fear, grief, or guilt without being overwhelmed
- Feeling empowered, stable, strong and connected to ourselves, others, and nature; in control of ourselves and our environment

Mental

- Capacity to recognize our level of activation and the need for release; to recognize and find new resources
- Clarity of mind; ability to weight decisions with ease
- Capacity to tolerate and even enjoy differences
- Thinking realistically and positively; being curious and capable of insights
- Ability to concentrate and learn; good memory
- Capacity for humor and to encourage ourselves and others
- Renewed interest in family, work, pleasure, and self-discovery
- Ability to see all sides of a problem or conflict; to see different options and choices and to accept reality
- Finding positive meaning in one's traumatic experiences

Behavioral

- Release stress through the breath and discharging techniques
- Free flowing movements; good coordination; focused action
- Peer-sharing and feedback
- Capacity to self-regulate, manage anger and conduct positive self-talk
- Building social networks; building unit and military cohesion
- Controlling rumors; flow of correct information
- Rewarding and praising ourselves and others
- Engaging with different people and situations, having loving and harmonious relationships; meeting basic needs in healthy ways while attending to the needs of others
- Using resources, laughing and being creative
- Being available to others and their talents
- Conducting constructive negotiations

Social

- Feeling connected to the larger community and to the world
- Participating in and contributing to different circles
- Caring for humanity and working towards the general good
- Engaging in civic duties

Spiritual

- Drawing on spiritual and ethical resources
- Connecting with the deep self, awareness of our true nature and capacity to see ourselves objectively
- Developing our spiritual sensitivities; higher consciousness and compassion for ourselves and others
- Engaging in non-judgmental, compassionate religion
- Showing humbleness and gratitude

- Feeling connected to God and the sacredness of life; ability to feel awe and ecstasy
- Seeing the good and the bad in ourselves, people, and life and choosing to focus on the good
- Being generous and having the desire to give and help
- Making contributions

Family

- Harmonious and stable relationships; familial harmony
- Healthy gender and generational roles
- Good boundaries between children and parents

Collective

- Assisting refugees and survivors of atrocities
- Interacting positively with foreign allies
- Working with NGOs in efforts of relief
- Healthy nationalism balanced with universal values
- Sense of belonging in the family of nations, aware of the good and the bad, and choosing to see the good
- Having a balanced collective narrative
- Deepening of pluralistic values, tolerance of religious, cultural, ethnic, and economic differences
- Peaceful resolution of conflicts

Additional Healing Benefits for the Military

- Realistic understanding of life its preciousness
- Development of a deep sense of compassion for others and for oneself
- Capacity for leadership; commitment and deep friendship
- Ability to handle life's stresses with increasing tolerance to discomfort, pain, injury, and hardship
- Capacity to overcome fear and the harshest conditions of life

- Capacity for heroism, courage, and self-sacrifice embodying the hero archetype
- Sense of mission and purpose; taking actions that benefits veterans, their offspring and society
- War experience as an initiation rite; learning wisdom at an early age—usually acquired after the mid-life crisis
- Better acceptance of self and more realistic sense of what life is about.

CHAPTER FOUR

TRAUMA AND THE MILITARY

THE STIGMA OF TRAUMA

Until very recently, the effects of trauma continued to be unaddressed for many soldiers, because of the widespread and erroneous belief that receiving help, makes a soldier less worthy to himself and/or others.

Today's warfare in some forms is more dangerous than before. Because of the widespread media coverage of military trauma, we might imagine that most military personnel realize they are vulnerable to trauma.

However, because they are brave, "disciplined, physically and mentally tough, trained" and the best of the crop (see the Soldier's Creed) most newly enlisted personnel believe they are above injury. They repress thoughts of vulnerability that come up, because it will require that they seek help and thus risk being stigmatized. Even admitting to these thoughts will make them feel less worthy. Thus, despite all the new literature about war trauma and the increased awareness about the subject in the military, seeking help for trauma still remains a stigma in the military.

The Soldier's Creed

I am an American Soldier.

I am a Warrior and a member of a team. I serve the people of the United States and live the Army Values.

I will always place the mission first.

I will never accept defeat.

I will never quit.

I will never leave a fallen comrade.

I am disciplined, physically and mentally tough, trained and proficient in my warrior tasks and drills. I always maintain my arms, my equipment and myself.

I am an expert and I am a professional.

I stand ready to deploy, engage, and destroy the enemies of the United States of America in close combat.

I am a guardian of freedom and the American way of life.

I am an American Soldier.

Returning military personnel, on the other hand, know that war experiences can profoundly hurt them and they want to beat the stigma. They know that in the brutality of today's warfare, where terrorism blurs the rules of engagement, war trauma is particularly devastating.

Most know that panic attacks, nightmares, sleepless nights, uncontrolled anger and impulsive behavior, the drive for revenge and violence, or the inability to lead normal lives are symptoms of trauma. Many who experience these symptoms do not consider the root cause may be an underlying emotional disorder because of their overwhelming desire to return to "a normal life."

"I want to go home, and I don't want any symptom to stop me from reentering normal life."

In addition, when there is no mechanism for release, cumulative stress may produce traumatic symptoms. It may take months or years for the traumatic symptoms to manifest.

Therefore, military personnel faced an imperative to normalize traumatic symptoms as a predictable reaction to events of extreme stress—a reaction that is dependent on the state of the affected nervous system. It is not a character flaw or a character disorder. Soldiers must be able to feel safe to explore their levels of traumatic activation when they come out of battle and/or a tour of duty as a matter of return to routine health. Such characterization will allow them to minimize the experiences they suffered and prevent future reactions. They must not fear losing their position in the military nor fear their peers' scorn if they admit to having symptoms of stress. Many soldiers suffer from trauma and more are vulnerable to developing PTSD. No one can afford to let trauma remain unrecognized and untreated at any time.

Overcoming the Trauma Stigma

Ilan Bahar, a renowned journalist who works for the Israeli newspaper *Maariv*, broke his silence about the trauma that shattered his youth and drove him for more than 30 years to lead a double life when he wrote his 2005 book, *Ze Ma She Ani Zokher* (*This is What I Remember*). The trauma he revealed took place in 1974 when he was driving with five other soldiers along the Suez Canal. They drove over a mine and everyone was killed except Bahar.

His wife and children were the only ones aware of his agonizing sleeplessness, hair-trigger anger, and incapacity to connect deeply with people. He finally collapsed into a nervous breakdown. Only then did he go to therapy.

In his book, Bahar wrote that if he had known about *"helem krav"* (battle shock) and what to do about it, he would not have lost his emotional and physical health for so many years. In addition, he wrote how he could not save his house from foreclosure. When he received a bank notice announcing the imminent sale of his property, he realized it was better to put it up for sale himself. He did so with a heavy heart and much agony. While he was fighting for his national homeland and helping to save it, he was losing his private home.

Bahar talks about how his therapy allowed him to regain his sanity. He recovered from his PTSD. His book and interviews opened the door for many soldiers and others who suffer from trauma to address their emotional trauma and war-related problems.

AMERICAN MILITARY PTSD STATISTICS

According to the National Center for Post Traumatic Stress and the U.S. Department of Veteran Affairs, acknowledging trauma remains a stigma for veterans and the military. They still perceive seeking help as a sign of character weakness and lack of manhood. Although 80 percent of the American military with significant mental health problems have recognized they have problems, only

40 percent wanted treatment, and only 26 percent reported actually receiving treatment.

Studies indicate that the more frequent and the more intense the involvement in combat operations, the more the risks of developing chronic PTSD increase. Recent evidence from the present Iraq war confirms that with the intensity of combat operations in Iraq, more soldiers are returning with PTSD. It is believed that 18 percent of those serving in Iraq and 11 percent of those in Afghanistan will develop PTSD. We believe that many more will have traumatic arousal in their system, but which may only manifest years later, if and when they are exposed to stressful events.

Trauma: Iraq War

The following statistics show American soldiers' depth of exposure to combat and the ensuing traumatic situations in the Iraq war.

- Soldiers in Iraq reported receiving small-arms fire. . . 94%
- Soldiers in Iraq reported knowing someone who was injured or killed 86%
- Reported seeing dead or seriously injured Americans 68%
- Reported handling or uncovering human remains. . . 51%
- Reported shooting or directing fire at the enemy. . . . 77%
- Reported responsibility for the death of enemy combatants 48%
- Reported responsibility for the death of a non-combatant 28%

Most of these soldiers were thus exposed to first or second-hand trauma. A recent analysis of data about veterans of the Afghanistan and Iraq wars who sought help from the VA system, confirmed that many returned from their service with

---

serious psychological problems such as anxiety and adjustment disorders, depression, substance abuse and PTSD. When "other" mental health disorders were added (including psychoses, schizophrenia, neurotic and personality disorders and sexual disorders), the report showed that over 32,000 veterans were affected. It indicated that the "single most common mental health diagnosis was PTSD, coded in 13,205 [...] veterans, representing 52% of those receiving mental health diagnoses and 13% of all [...] veterans in our study population."

Source: National Center for Post-Traumatic Stress Disorder and the U.S. Department of Veterans Affairs, 2007. www.stliraqwarvets.wordpress.com, 7/12/07

HISTORICAL STATISTICS FOR WAR-RELATED PTSD IN AMERICAN MILITARY PERSONNEL

Trauma: Vietnam, Afghanistan, and Iraq

According to the National Center for Post Traumatic Stress and the U.S. Department of Veteran Affairs in March 26, 2007, 15% of Vietnam veterans still suffer from PTSD decades after the war ended with recurring flashbacks, nightmares and re-enactment.

Statistics show a poor resolution of war trauma, despite the widespread awareness of the ravages of war on soldiers and other military personnel. While the number of homeless veterans from all wars totals 194,000, the number of beds available in VA shelters and hospitals is 15,000 in the U.S. The number of traumatized veterans who move back with their families is significantly larger than the number of those without trauma, at a ratio of 1:4 instead of 1:12.

Other studies have shown 15%-30% of Iraq and Afghanistan veterans returning with mental health issues, including PTSD. The numbers are significant. From the two million American Army personnel who fought in Iraq and Afghanistan, with 4,500 dead and

35,000 injured, a sizable number of traumatized returning veterans will develop all kind of symptoms.

Furthermore, two million children with a parent in uniform have their lives deeply affected by their parents' traumatic symptoms. Vietnam veterans with PTSD, for example, are three to six times more likely to divorce compared to Vietnam veterans without PTSD. Many have been arrested or jailed, at least once; 11.5 percent have been convicted of felonies.[1] (Source: National Center for Post-Traumatic Stress Disorder and the U.S. Department of Veterans Affairs, 2007.)

Referencing the US Army statistics released in June 2009, a CNN report confirmed the continuing upward trend for a second straight year of suicides among soldiers. In 2008, the Army recorded 133 suicides, the most ever. The Army has implemented a service-wide effort to combat the problem, recognizing that soldiers were working long hours and not spending time with their families between deployments. The Veteran's Administration estimates that 5,000 vets commit suicide annually, in higher numbers than the general population.

In the same month the experts at the Wounds of War conference at Columbia University reported that the wave of addiction and mental health problems among returning US veterans of the Iraq and Afghan wars could be greater than that resulting from the Vietnam War. Prescription drug abuse was a concern at the conference, but most participants noted that excessive drinking remains a huge problem among soldiers, sailors and airmen despite alcohol being banned from combat zones in Muslim countries.

Statistics from the Armed Forces Health Surveillance Center reports one in eight troops returning home from Iraq and Afghanistan were referred to counseling for alcohol-related problems. The Army reported the rate of soldiers enrolled in alcohol-related programs nearly doubled in the past five years.

The VA has identified 20,000 homeless vets in the Los Angeles area alone that have served in Vietnam, Iraq or Afghanistan and the number is growing. They sleep in Los Angeles' alleyways, and have a problem returning to civilian life after living out of rucksacks and eating out of tins.

Department of Veteran Affairs Assistant Secretary Tammy Duckworth, herself a double amputee from the Iraq war, states there are particular problems with returning vets who return home and don't go home to a military base with a full Department of Defense hospital. They live in small towns across America and need to be able to access help, which is why it is crucial for families to be involved in the healing process.

INTERNAL COLLECTIVE TRAUMA IN THE MILITARY

Racial Issues

In addition to cultural differences with the external enemy, racial issues are also brought to the forefront within the ranks of the military. The dominating importance of hierarchy can make soldiers particularly vulnerable to racial stereotyping and scapegoating.

Although much bonding occurs in the military among soldiers from all racial and ethnic backgrounds drawn by a common purpose and enemy, racial stereotyping and scapegoating are still common, military camaraderie notwithstanding. It is the nature of highly traumatic situations to adversely affect racial relations and further polarize already existing differences.

Stereotyping within the U.S. military was particularly acute during the Vietnam War. Many returning veterans talked about having to confront racial prejudice among their own compatriots and believed this heavily contributed to their war trauma symptoms. Besides incurring the horrors of a guerilla war, the Army's efforts were further marred by several incidents of racism among the various racial groups in the military, sometimes even resulting in harm done to American soldiers by their own comrades.

However, the American military has taken leadership in dealing with racial issues within its own ranks by giving trainings in organizational diversity. It has provided opportunities for leadership to Americans of all backgrounds. It is an important initiative that needs to continue in order to diminish the internal traumatization of military personnel.

Racial issues exist in other militaries as well, with more or less virulence. Some countries do not have such a wide variety of ethnic and religious diversity as the U.S. However, even countries with a broad ethnic mix can have a very different experience with racial relations, due in part perhaps to a deeper bond provided by some common factor such as religion.

In the Israeli Defensive Forces, racial relations constitute a different experience. Soldiers begin their service with pre-existing racial prejudices—each generation has its groups discriminated against according to the group's order of entry into the country and its level of education. However, hierarchy in the IDF combat units is almost non-existent, and the Army, because it plays such a major socializing role in the social and political structure of the country, has made a serious effort to become the social leveling force in Israel. Of course, incidents of racism do exist but the military deals with them more quickly and with more assertiveness.

Sexual Assaults in a Dual Gender Military

Just like racial bias, gender prejudice and misogyny are also part of the problems existing in the military. Many women have complained of sexual assault by some of their male comrades during their tours of duty. In addition to the pain of the assault, they have to face shame, guilt, and disapproval for reporting fellow soldiers, if it results in disciplinary action against them. Military women who suffer from sexual assaults-a military-related PTSD—are also prey to sleeplessness, nightmares, panic attacks and agoraphobia, as well as suicide ideation.

Hushed in the beginning when women started serving in the military, the problem is now more in the open. There are many more treatments run by the Department of Veteran Affairs and new legislation has been created to allow receiving help without having to press charges.

VETERANS AT HOME

> Trauma is contagious and the pull of the
> trauma vortex is magnetic

The information about trauma should be widely spread among military personnel during their trainings and most certainly at the end of it. Trauma's impact is profound, with serious economic, physical, psychological and mental consequences for soldiers and their families. Additionally it has serious economic and political consequences for society.

Trauma is mysterious, being expressed in so many different and seemingly unconnected ways. Thus veterans' families often suffer the repercussions of their soldiers' emotional troubles without knowing what to do. They are left befuddled by the pervasive symptoms they witness and without the necessary information or skills to help their loved ones. Easily-triggered anger and sensory hypersensitivity are among the most common and salient symptoms of veterans. These symptoms often manifest into violence that pervades family life, terrorizing children, alienating wives, and discouraging the empathy of friends and families. Traumatized veterans also re-enact the violence they encountered on the battlefield in their communities. Families and communities can be caught in a cycle of reactive responses, perpetuating the trauma cycle without helping the veterans. Disseminating the information about how to recognize and heal trauma to veterans' families and communities will minimize veterans' somatic illnesses, emotional turmoil, divorces, child/spousal abuse, cycles of violence, and suicide rates.

Wanted: 2min film to change Veterans' Image to the Public

Posted on www.CraigsList.com, December 11, 2007, 11:28 am, Los Angeles, California. Original URL: http://losangeles.craigslist.org/lac/vol/506038979.html

A disabled veteran Army sergeant wanted to create a TV commercial or Web video that would familiarize the public with soldiers' combat-related emotional traumas and change the image Americans seem to have of veterans. He wanted people to understand that veterans' problems are real and that veterans are treated at the VA for symptoms connected to their service in the war. He wanted the public to know that veterans "...don't want a free ride. All of us wish that we had no wounds or memory of our combat service. Then we would be just like you with a clear mind and body."

He wanted the public to imagine how it is possible for soldiers to be deeply affected "forever" by the traumatic situations they face, and how hard it might be for them to re-integrate into a society that did not suffer from the war. He wanted America to care about itself by caring about its veterans.

He sent a pressing appeal for people truly to help and "to do some good for our veterans that's more than a yellow ribbon on your bumper; if not maybe someday we won't step up. Our men and women now in uniform are hearing everything being said about the treatment of veterans. Do you think they will re-up? Something has to be done and now. America has PTSD."

BEATING THE STIGMA

Military personnel must be reassured that powerful and negative reactions to extreme situations are normal. They need to realize that events of this magnitude can so overwhelm their body/mind that they may get deregulated and lose their emotional balance and capacity to respond appropriately. They need universal acceptance that it is normal to be deeply affected by the war without being considered physically weak or emotionally disturbed.

A large part of training—such as that of the U.S. Navy SEAL Teams—is the attempt to ascertain how an individual will respond to extremely harsh conditions. Failure to respond at a certain level during those times of extremely harsh conditions is considered just that: failure period. Individuals who fail to respond are taken out of training. At that time they are given counseling. They are told that they are not failures as humans. However, the psychological ramifications or traumas are most likely not fully addressed. SE® can help military trainees to better cope with the stress as well as to help those who have "failed" military training to cope with their situation.

Beating the Stigma during Service

"Aaron," a soldier in active duty, summarized the general attitude in the military:

> "The military thinks that only cowards suffer from PTSD. I would never have gone to the Army's psychiatrist. It is only when I discovered that my commander was a therapist that I allowed myself to request a private conversation with him."

Aaron told his commander about his insomnia, his inability to have sex with his girlfriend, the bouts of rage that suddenly overtook him, the deep sense of shame and intermittent fear that gripped him. Worst of all, he felt that these feelings kept him apart from his friends and made him feel he did not belong to his unit anymore.

Aaron's commander quickly applied SE® principles. He asked Aaron to choose two friends and in his mind's eye to run the scene of talking about his problems with them.

He asked him to notice if he could "feel his emotions and thoughts in his body." Aaron ran the scene in his mind and felt a strong sensation of discomfort in his chest and stomach. His commander helped him discharge until he was comfortable with the scene. He then asked him to go talk to his friends in person, which allowed Aaron to feel he was part of the unit again. In talking to them, he found out that while he was ashamed of many things, his friends actually considered him a brave soldier.

They told him how his readiness to say, in the middle of battle, that he missed his dead friend, touched them. They respected his courage to request from his commander that he gives water to an enemy prisoner left to suffer from thirst. They admired his courage to take his canteen of water to a comrade caught under enemy fire, when Aaron had felt that if he were a "real man," he would shoot the enemy instead of helping his friend. He had also been very ashamed that he vomited when he helped another friend look for his missing finger, forgetting that none of the other soldiers had even gone to look for the missing finger.

Traumatized personnel must realize the following: trauma is the result of uncompleted instinctive defensive responses and of undischarged traumatic arousal stuck in the physiology. This arousal can be released and the defensive responses completed. They can heal and be ready to better cope with the next traumatic arousal.

Most military personnel and their families do not know that trauma is curable. They don't know that it is possible to exercise and strengthen their resilience and that they can be trained to maintain their emotional health just as they are trained to maintain and care for their equipment and their physical bodies. They can learn the tools that help them cope with war traumas and lessen the effects of PTSD. They can learn to deal with difficult emotions and maintain a connection to their communities. Active duty personnel and veterans can be cared for by society in an effective way.

Although today there is more acceptance of trauma both in society and in the military, military personnel helped to cope with their traumatic reactions by their commanders is still a rare occurrence.

WAR TRAUMA, DOMESTIC VIOLENCE AND SUBSTANCE ABUSE

For many veterans and their families, violent behavior towards their loved ones or within their communities, were some of their most feared trauma symptoms. For example, according to the Israeli Policethe percentage of domestic violence went up immediately after the 1987 Intifada took place. Recently, there has been a spate of spousal murders by traumatized veterans in the US, which has alerted the military and clamored for public attention. More literature is devoted to the stress of families and military personnel with each return home. Returning personnel first have to face "re-entry issues."

There are the usual difficulties confronting anyone returning home after a period of time, during which each family member has a new role. The family has managed to cope without the contribution of the person who was away, and different family members have adapted to new roles, etc. Returning personnel face additional burdens. Many of the details of daily life have changed during the soldiers' service. They are likely to feel insignificant or even a burden to their families. This creates a strain on the family and on relationships, often resulting in divorce. According to Susan Storti, Ph.D., the project director of Synergy Enterprises which provides mental health and substance abuse consulting services, one unit in Rhode Island had 85% of its soldiers with mental health issues upon return, while 80% eventually separated from or divorced their spouse.

War Trauma and Spousal Abuse

"Sam," a war veteran, came to the Veterans Hospital rehabilitation center, crying and complaining for the twentieth time: "It happened again." Sam had hit his wife and his son again.

"My son came home very late tonight and slammed the door. I jumped out of bed and shouted at him. He answered me angrily and I could not contain myself. I saw a red screen then and there."

What Sam did not say, was that he had hit his son badly this time.

"Then and there" was the battle that had taken place more than 30 years ago, for which Sam was cited for valor and given the medal of excellence. Sam was then serving in the armed forces and half of his platoon members were killed. He fought the entire war, and when he returned home, he never talked about his experiences until 15 years later.

In 20 years, Sam had held 12 jobs and gone bankrupt twice. He had always been a very soft and gentle man before the war, until the day "I saw red. The red curtain came down." At those times, Sam would feel a terrible anger rise in his chest and he would lash out, but he never remembered what he did. He had one session of therapy in which he relived the war episode so brutally that he was reluctant to do any therapy again.

In the past, trauma therapy included fully reliving a traumatic situation and feeling its impact all at once, without discharging it at the body level, thus often deepening the traumatic reactions instead of relieving them.

Substance Abuse by Veterans

It is now well-documented that substance abuse—drugs and alcohol in particular—is a coping mechanism used by many returning veterans. Alcohol is a self-medicating and palliative therapy that has costly consequences.

Several aspects of today's armed struggles contribute to an increase of PTSD cases. In addition to returning to a civilian world unfamiliar with the difficulties they confronted, returning military personnel who have served several tours of duty, are exposed to a greater likelihood of traumatizing experiences. The climates they faced were extreme, the culture and religious dissonance tremendous and the brutalities of war unusually severe. The nature of the enemy fire was disorienting in addition to suicides bombings and IED which were difficult to predict as well. Others simply recoiled at the bad name that media coverage of the treatment of prisoners at Abu Ghraib and Guantanamo Bay had given the American Army.

As Dr. Barbara Van Dahlen Romberg, the founder and president of Give an Hour, explains, the organization provides free mental health services to redeployed troops and is dedicated to educating Americans about the issues affecting our returning warriors, getting the word out to veterans that services are available outside traditional channels like the Veterans Administration. Dr. Romberg, a Washington psychiatrist, started her nonprofit organization in 2006. According to Dr. Romberg, three thousand providers have committed to offer at least one hour of counseling a week for a year. Since then around 5000 hours were offered. Military personnel and their families looking for help can find volunteer providers in their area by searching by Zip code and receive once-a-week counseling for a year.

Safety Compromised for Political Considerations

At the beginning of the El Aqsa Intifada in late 2000, a Druze Israeli soldier, Madhat Yusuf, was trapped at Joseph Tomb in Nablus with several comrades of his unit. In the ensuing fight with the Palestinians, Yusuf was gravely wounded. The national media broadcasted his eight-hour agonizing death, anguishing his family and the entire nation. It also traumatized many soldiers. The media covered the story at length and an investigation committee was formed later.

The soldiers in Yusuf's unit were trapped with him. Yusuf was bleeding to death but no one came to the rescue. While the reason for holding back the rescue may have been that there were too many commanders involved but no one to take responsibility, the real reason for Yusuf's death seemed to be a thorny political situation—the fear of breaking an armistice with the Palestinian Authority. This fear paralyzed the Israeli Army and stopped it from executing the core motto that characterized its success: *lo mafkirim hayalim* ("you do not leave a wounded comrade in the field"). The fallout of this tragedy reverberated throughout the nation.

Right after the Joseph Tomb incident, a regiment of reserve soldiers sent to Nablus was reluctant to go into battle. They were not averse to serve, but they were afraid that they might be the next ones to be abandoned in the field. They had previously been certain they could always count on their comrades to take care of them and protect them, but the sight of the Army letting a soldier bleed to death in the attempt to safeguard a political agreement with the Palestinians showed them that they might not be able to count on help in all situations.

These soldiers confronted their commanders and asked them if the Madhat Yusuf incident might happen to them as well. Luckily, their commanders really listened and arranged a group discussion at the platoon level. They invited the soldiers to talk things out together, work in groups on the negative impact left on them by the soldier's death and the sensational and obsessive media coverage of it. One commander familiar with SE® was sufficient to help the soldiers resolve their fears and concerns.

Currently, there is no formal structure in military culture to explore such difficult issues without placing blame and condemnation, which often turns such issues into unnecessary catastrophes. The need for a formal structure to address such psychological situations becomes more necessary with every collective traumatizing event.

POLITICS AND COLLECTIVE TRAUMA'S IMPACT ON SAFETY IN THE MILITARY

Political considerations and expediencies often increase the risk to military personnel, making military personnel and their families lose confidence in the military decision-making process. An entire nation may be collectively traumatized as a result and lose trust in its military. The story of Madhat Yusuf illustrates such a situation.

The Yusuf tragedy was a collective trauma for both the Israeli military and the Israeli public. The soldiers' belief in the Army's absolute commitment to their safety and rescue at any cost was deeply shaken. The Army's autonomy in securing the safety of its soldiers had been compromised by the political process, but for the nation, "the Army (had) lost its way; it stopped working according to the core values that built its strength."

The conditions of Yusuf's death marked many groups and made them change their world views, revisit their most cherished beliefs, and question their leaders' and their military's ability to protect them. They felt anguish and anger about the lack of safety. The incident remained in the memory of the Druze community. When the Army Chief of Staff responsible for the decisions surrounding Yusuf's death ran for political office years later, the Druze community did not support him.

For the Druze community, the feeling of neglect and sacrifice was palpable. For the "peace process," perceived partners were found to be false partners, and the psyche of the country was split in half—those who mistrusted their adversary and those who wanted to trust at all cost.

Such events are likely to happen, especially in countries under chronic traumatic stress. No one can predict when and if they will happen. No one can promise to protect military personnel from these situations.

However, unfortunate events like Yusuf's death do not have to turn into collective traumas. Each of the affected sectors needed to be addressed. Their worries and concerns needed to be validated and soothed. Their questions needed to be answered with candor, patience, and compassion. In other words, the collective nervous system needed help by discharging the deleterious impact of the event on the different sectors.

In addition to the impact of political considerations on military decisions, the military must face another type of trauma vortex.

Military and political leadership need to understand how the pull of collective trauma can change the direction of war as populations let their fear or anger dictate their political decisions during elections. This pull can lengthen or shorten war or stop it too abruptly, risking the appearance of weakness and generating more violence. Alternatively, such an event can provide an opportunity to explore and process the fault lines uncovered.

Collective trauma needs to be addressed, whether it is a nation's own collective trauma or the trauma of its neighbors spilling into its borders. Today, many nations are forced to deal with both types of collective traumas at the same time.

COLLECTIVE MILITARY TRAUMA VORTEX

The impact of a collective military trauma vortex on the conduct of war can be enormous. A military trauma vortex is a collective phenomenon in which battalions—or the military as a whole—respond in dysfunctional or unproductive ways (engaging in war too fast, too slow, too strongly, too weakly, or withdrawing at the wrong moment based on unresolved past experiences, or perceived failures, battles with ambiguous results, making people question their ethics), hurting military goals and efficiency, and possibly encouraging the aggression of the enemy.

Furthermore, the conduct of military personnel has a great impact both on the resolution of a conflict as well as on the state of the country afterwards. Although the military does not play a political role, it is essential that it understands the nature of personal and collective trauma, how to identify its beginnings, and how to limit its destructiveness. The live media war coverage and its manipulation to influence public opinion put the conduct of the military under such scrutiny that it can hurt their cause, forcing military personnel to take risks that endanger them.

Although in Chapters 14 and 15 we cover all issues, dilemmas, and benefits related to ROE, we address it in this chapter when it relates to pertinent issues.

OTHER ISSUES

Controversial Previous Wars

Military personnel who are currently engaged in wars that follow previous controversial wars are particularly at risk for trauma. They are likely to be deeply affected by their country's previous traumatic war experience, e.g., the Vietnam War experience affected the American experience in the Iraq War, and Israelis in the Lebanon War II in 2006 were fearful of repeating the "Lebanese quagmire" of 1982. Beyond their own already difficult war experiences, soldiers may encounter a recalcitrant nation afraid of re-enactment, and even face a hostile home media. The international media often hold a very critical position towards powerful militaries and their operations irrelevant to the justness of their cause. Even if justified, the display of powerful weapons unleashed on an apparently weaker opponent, is instinctively repulsive to people, who will react emotionally without engaging in a deeper analysis of the situation.

Pressure from the Media

As previously noted, the media unwittingly can play a significant role in creating or amplifying trauma, affecting military personnel, their families, their communities, and the public as a whole.

We will cover more at length the relationship between the media and the military, in Chapter 13, The Media's Role.

Orders and Dilemmas

Even when military personnel believe in and can justify their participation in a war, there will be occasions when orders go against their values. An example would be searching for weapons depots placed in civilian areas or homes. The requirement to fire before entering in case there is an entrapment for the unit is a particularly distressing dilemma for many soldiers. Indeed, if the order is not followed, and people in the house shoot and kill personnel in the unit, soldiers will be responsible for the deaths of their comrades.

Many preemptive actions may create this dilemma as well. Pre-emptive actions produce casualties on both sides but the assumption behind the pre-emptive action is that there would have been more casualties if it action were not taken, or that a favorable outcome would have been limited. On the other hand, one can rarely be sure that casualties might not have been avoided without the pre-emptive action.

Orders and Responsibility

Another dilemma for military personnel is in following military orders where they may later be held accountable for actions committed under orders. Regardless of the rule of military obedience, in politically charged international actions, individual soldiers and officers may be held responsible for their actions.

Soldiers may sometimes find themselves in situations when they have to go against higher military orders to save their own life or the lives of their comrades, producing guilt or the fear of punishment for breaking an important military rule.

The search for new guidelines that keep war as human and ethical as possible, while still allowing countries to protect their populations against aggression, is becoming more pressing every day. Yet war is alive and well. Megalomaniac autocratic leaders in search of glory and power still abound, and the struggle for equality of power among the nations of the world is still with us.

In Chapters 14 and 15 we address the healing vortex in modern warfare and outline examples of military leaders who are struggling with many of these dilemmas and searching for ways to transform war.

CHAPTER FIVE

STREAM OF LIFE WITH THE TRAUMA VORTEX AND HEALING VORTEX

STREAM OF LIFE EXPERIENCE

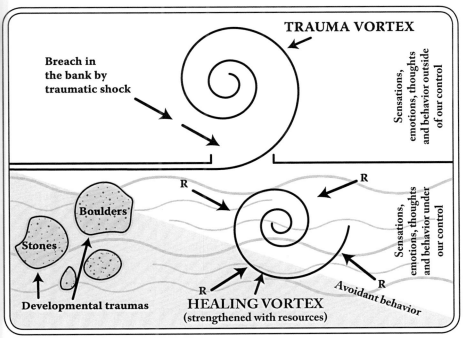

Fig. 8

At the same time that a trauma vortex is triggered, a healing vortex—or counter-vortex—takes shape, allowing the traumatic event to be assimilated into the stream of life. However, when traumatic events are too overwhelming, the innate ability to heal is too weak to process the event on its own. It needs resources, attention, and awareness.

The "Stream of Life" metaphor describes *our emotional life, which flows like a river within its banks.* This river contains all the sensations, feelings, thoughts and behaviors that are under our control. There are also stones and boulders in the riverbed—difficult situations we have faced in the past that may account for some of our personality quirks, but that are still part of the river and are under our control.

When traumatic shocks are too overwhelming, they cause a breach in the banks of our river creating an abrupt rush of energy outside of our control: *a trauma vortex*. The pull of a trauma vortex whirlpool reduces the flow in the river and diminishes our capacity to manage our sensations, feelings, thoughts and behavior. If this vortex is undischarged, it becomes fixated in our body/mind, making us easily re-triggered and hyper-aroused. Alternatively, we learn to fear that whirlpool so much that we spend all our energy trying to steer away from any possible triggers or links to it, thereby creating artificial barriers and limiting the scope of our lives.

THE TRAUMA VORTEX

The "Trauma Vortex" describes a self-perpetuating spiral of pain and confusion that exists outside of the stream of life, outside of our control. The word vortex evokes the dynamic and ever-escalating nature of trauma's impact. The metaphor is shorthand for the pull of haunting and intrusive traumatic memories; of helplessness and hopelessness; and of the loss of control over our physiology, emotions, thoughts and behaviors that plague the traumatized.

- When we are stuck in the trauma vortex, all sense of normalcy disappears. We disconnect from ourselves, our bodies and from other people.

- The nervous system often retains memories longer than the conscious mind, causing us to overreact to or avoid (without understanding why) people, places, foods, smells and sounds that unconsciously retrigger the traumatic event.

- In addition to altering the biological, psychological, and social balance, trauma can also destroy our prior sense of fitting in, having a place in the world. When this happens the world sometimes starts to seem immoral and unpredictable, and violence becomes acceptable.

- A trauma vortex can develop quickly or over time. It may go dormant and be re-triggered months or decades later. Situations where people already have difficulty meeting their basic psychological needs aggravate this vortex.

Although we know that trauma can affect us at anytime, we are just learning that resolution and healing can follow right behind.

Re-triggered Trauma: June Blues

"Alexa," a casualty officer who looked after wounded soldiers at *Ktzinat Nifgaim,* told of her symptoms:

"I became a vegetarian after the First Lebanon War. I could not (and still cannot) stand the smell of burned flesh. For four years, I did not do anything. Even though I went to therapy, I just sat on the floor and did not talk. The images of removing personal effects from the wounded or killed soldiers, placing the effects in bags and delivering them to their families or to the hospital still haunted me.

Even after twenty years, when June 5th approaches (the beginning of the 1987 Lebanon War), I feel terribly sad, cannot eat, sleep, or work. I have to take a leave of absence. I am haunted day and night, by all the soldiers' bodies I escorted to their grieving families, or the soldiers I escorted to hospitals or for rehabilitation."

THE HEALING VORTEX

The "Healing Vortex" refers to our innate capacity to cope and heal from tragedy.

Recent research confirms that healing trauma is possible, that the human brain is flexible and can regenerate itself at any time and bring the organism back into balance. Most significantly, it can form new neural connections inspired and shaped by relationships and new experiences throughout life.

Resources are used to strengthen and remind our nervous system of its ability to self-regulate and to cope. With a strengthened healing vortex, we are able to process the traumatic experience and integrate it into the stream of life. Resolving our traumas reinforces strengths and even helps us discover ones previously never identified.

There are techniques to help us reverse the spiral of the trauma vortex, engage the healing vortex, and return our nervous systems, bodies, and brains to a sense of well-being and safety. They help us self-regulate and heal our symptoms by discharging the excess energy still trapped in our bodies long after the difficult event has passed.

Once we discharge this unused energy, our bodies stop releasing the hormones that prepare us for defense. We stop internalizing the threat and expecting the trauma to repeat itself. We can truly move on, both in our bodies and in our minds.

We use these concepts to remain conscious of the power we have to activate the healing vortex and resist the pull of the trauma vortex towards negative reactions. Knowing the different characteristics of a trauma vortex can help us better resist its pull.

The next few pages describe different aspects and examples of the trauma vortex that will allow you to identify it more quickly. The next chapter introduces tools to engage the healing vortex and gives an easy blueprint to move from trauma into healing and coping.

From the Trauma Vortex to the Healing Vortex

At age 17, "Michael" served in Iraq during the Gulf War. As a front-line combatant in a tank, he felt the overwhelming strength of American firepower and witnessed thousands of dying or fleeing Iraqi soldiers. Memories of all the Iraqi corpses he had to put into body bags haunted his dreams.

Two years after his return from Iraq, Michael was living dangerously, addicted to methamphetamines. He had fantasies of pursuing drug dealers on the streets and obtained weapons to do so, not realizing that in his addictive state he was continuing to re-enact the hyper-arousal of the war battles. His body was full of tension and his eyes were wild. He was completely alienated from his family and had no friends. Michael was caught in a chronic "fight" response, which gave him a sense of power similar to when he was on the front lines in Iraq. In reality, his response only endangered his life and the lives of those around him.

After a few months in a local VA therapeutic community, Michael was able to process his war experiences and learn how they had affected him. He learned that his reactions to his experience in Iraq were normal responses to traumatic situations that subsequently affected every aspect of his life. As he processed his experiences in therapy and was able to discharge his hyper-aroused nervous system, he recovered his clear thinking and realized he had choices in life other than re-enactment. He quit using drugs and stopped pursuing drug dealers. His family's willingness to attend therapy was a precious resource that also contributed to his recovery. Michael became assistant manager of a sober living home. He also found a new job and married.

A few years later, he visited the VA and brought pictures of his wife and children. He had maintained his clean and sober lifestyle and seemed relaxed. He offered to help other veterans in the community. Recovery from trauma had given him a positive self-image and resilience. It also reinvigorated his joy of life.

VARIOUS ASPECTS OF THE TRAUMA VORTEX

Unconscious Triggers and the Pull of the Trauma Vortex

In its swift response to a threat, the primitive brain takes a snapshot of everything going on at the time—individuals, animals or objects, colors, sounds, smells, location, weather conditions, and even the time of year. Any one of these elements can later become an unconscious cue of danger and re-trigger the same old fear(s). When we become fearful, we feel perplexed or foolish about situations we know to be benign but in which our body memory is still stuck in the old trauma reality. As it continues, we feel despair, crazed, embattled, and easily defensive, or alternatively we simply become numb and withdrawn without knowing why.

The Urge to Repeat

In order to understand the frequency and severity of veterans' problems with trauma re-enactment, we must understand what research has shown about brain mechanisms.

Our bodies drive us unconsciously to repeat traumatic events in the attempt to manage a better outcome and finally discharge the traumatic energy it stores. However, every time we revisit the traumatic event without discharging the excess energy, more energy becomes stuck in our systems, actually deepening the impact of the re-enacted trauma.

A Tragic Re-enactment

During his tour of duty in Vietnam, "Tom" witnessed a fellow soldier raping a Vietnamese woman. He became violently agitated and killed the soldier who committed the rape. His sexual abuse as a child and the fact that he was married to an Asian woman triggered Tom's rage reaction. Witnessing the rape reminded him of his own childhood pain, of his wife's humiliation and the distainful and racial comments she was subjected to in the U.S. Her vulnerability and his frustrated need to protect her, as well as his unresolved childhood trauma, triggered a rage he could not contain.

Upon his return from Vietnam, he was hired as a highway patrol officer. His duties included responding to domestic violence complaints. One night, as he responded to a house call, he again became so agitated and enraged by the woman's complaint of sexual abuse that he killed the woman's husband.

Tom was never charged with either of these murders. According to him, he even received a verbal commendation for the murder of the rapist soldier in Vietnam. However, his own difficulties with his rage impulsive killings left him with unmitigated guilt. He cycled between bouts of unbridled alcoholism followed by despair, long periods of recovery with gainful work and rebuilding solid friendships.

Tom eventually committed suicide. At the time of his death, the understanding of trauma's tragic impact was still nebulous and many of the newer trauma-healing methods were unknown and unused in veteran-care settings. These methods have contributed to healing trauma at unprecedented levels, even if they may not be able to help all cases. An earlier knowledge of these cutting-edge methods for trauma treatment may have prevented many tragic outcomes.

An Example of Positive Re-enactment

Sometimes, war experiences help soldiers develop the ability to work under intense pressure and successfully deal with highly stressful situations that otherwise would be traumatic to people not exposed to combat zone life-and-death circumstances.

"Doris" was a female military nurse who served on the front lines in the Vietnam War. She nursed the wounded and witnessed an endless stream of war casualties. When she returned to the U.S., she was dissatisfied with regular nursing assignments. She recognized the origin of her dissatisfaction and began to process her war traumas. However, even after processing the shock and terror of the war, she still did not feel satisfied with routine nursing assignments.

She asked to be placed in an infant ICU, working with premature or otherwise compromised babies struggling to stay alive. Doris was satisfied once again to be on the frontlines of life-and-death situations, working to help infants survive or help families deal with the grief and trauma of losing their babies. As in her wartime ICU experience, Doris was once again in situations where she could mobilize her compassion for people in highly traumatic situations.

Common examples of trauma repetition with veterans include:

1. *Repetitive acts of fighting and violence:* Traumatized veterans may repeatedly be involved in fights and shooting incidents. Some end up in jail. However, most veterans do not engage in violence, but may often seek occupations that continue to serve and protect the public.

2. *Repetitive failures of relationships:* Many veterans go through multiple divorces or marital crises that occur on the anniversaries of their military trauma. Exaggerated emotional responses or the need to avoid emotions—common signs of PTSD—impair successful communication in relationships. Again, it is important to remember that most veterans are able to maintain long-term marital relationships.

3. *Repetitive injuries to the same area of the original war wound and resistance to medical treatment:* There are scientific reasons for what many veterans call "being addicted" to dangerous situations. By taking into account the role of our brain chemistry—adrenalin, cortisol and endorphins—in the initial trauma and in its reenactment, we can begin to understand why repetition occurs. Each of these hormones is addictive in a different way.

While endorphins reduce pain, they also are associated with patterns of hyper-arousal, commonly called an 'adrenalin rush.' At low levels, endorphins assist pleasure, but at high levels they block the perception of pain and promote a sense of euphoria to allow survival efforts to be at their highest. They also become a reward to the body and a motivation to repeat traumatic scenarios. The system repeats the hyper-activated situation because it wants to feel good again. We should think of re-enactment not as a sign of a flawed or irresponsible character, but rather as an unsuccessful attempt to heal old wounds.

Trauma re-enactment still is not easily recognized. At the individual level, we often seek treatment only after a series of traumas has forced us to recognize a dysfunctional and painful pattern. At the collective level—groups of people, societies, or nations—the compulsive and unconscious urge to re-enact trauma is deeply disturbing and extremely dangerous.

Unresolved traumas keep us in a chronically activated state. Future exposure to traumatic triggers (e.g., the noise of a helicopter or the smell of burning tires) causes the brain to release high levels of adrenaline and endorphins with every trigger.

Applying the Stream of Life Metaphor

"Abe," a commander who uses SE® with his soldiers, recounts how he finds the stream of life metaphor very useful when he works with soldiers who don't know anything about the theory or about trauma and healing vortices.

"The metaphor identifies symptoms of trauma and the process of healing. They incorporate the metaphor's language immediately and use it to create images of healing from within.

"I first tell them that the language I am introducing may sound 'new age' but that it works.

"You should know that when bad things happen, we have two vortices present. You have sensations of constriction and their opposite—sensations of openness and expansion—right here in the stream. Resources are memories of places that make you feel calmer or stronger. Think of them as the healing vortex. Think of a resource and think of a traumatic image and go back and forth between the two until you sense the release of the tightness."

After the second Lebanon War, Abe used the metaphor to train his soldiers in the Golan Heights. All had served in this last war and were standing at the border, practically in the same place where they had previously fought. The soldiers referred to the place as "The War." When Abe asked them about their experience, several admitted they still felt troubled by it. He asked the group to imagine a place that was "safe" and then to picture in their mind's eye the exact place where they fought in Lebanon. Each soldier was to tell the group about his safe place.

Abe drew on the ground a large recumbent figure eight with one loop representing the healing vortex and the other the trauma vortex. He broke down the experience in small steps to help them "digest" it at an easy pace. He instructed his soldiers to imagine the resource image in the healing vortex loop and the battle location in the trauma vortex loop. Then he asked them to think of a safe place in the healing loop, and of the long hours spent preparing to go up the hill in the trauma loop, and focus their attention back and forth between the two. Next, he had them go back and forth between the safe place and the moment when they received their orders of where to go. He then chose one of the soldiers and worked with him in front of the group.

"Go back and forth between the two," he told him. "What do you feel?"

"My stomach tightened, and then it released," said the soldier.

Abe continued to work with him through the different stages of this experience, until the last image of being in Lebanon felt neutral and completely manageable. The soldier felt much better. After that exercise, all the soldiers who had worked on their activation vicariously through their comrade agreed they felt less preoccupied with the war. Their commanders noticed they talked less about it.

Trauma Re-enactment: Weather, Time, and the Anniversary Syndrome

Like animals, we have internal clocks based on the variations of seasonal light and the phases of the moon that are quite sensitive to the passage of time. Subtle external conditions such as temperature or light at the time of a traumatic event are stored in our subconscious memory. When these conditions recur during the natural change of seasons or years, they unconsciously activate the trauma vortex—a cyclical reactivation often drives repetitive reenactment.

Military personnel and the families of dead personnel are particularly vulnerable around certain times of the year, such as Memorial Day, dates of remembrance of specific wars, or specific dates when tragedy hit them. Even newspaper articles, news coverage, or relevant documentaries and movies can act as triggers for their traumatic experiences. Some Israeli soldiers, for example, refer to rain only like "the rain in Kabatya"—where the lack of visibility from the heavy rain made easier for them to be ambushed by the enemy. One Vietnam Veteran reacts to the idea of any jungle as a death trap and reacted strongly to an invitation to visit the Amazon: "There is nothing great about the Brazilian jungle; for me any jungle is the jungle in Vietnam." Others react on the anniversary of traumatic events.

Anniversary of the Têt Offensive

Many Vietnam veterans become activated on the anniversary of the Têt Offensive of 1969, a series of operational offensives during the Vietnam War that coordinated the efforts of the Viet Cong with the North Vietnamese People's Army of Vietnam against South Vietnam's Army of the Republic of Vietnam (ARVN), the United States, and the other ARVN-allied military forces. The operations were called the Tết Offensive as they were timed to begin on the night of January 30–31, 1968, *Tết Nguyên Đán* (the lunar New Year Day). The offensive began spectacularly during celebrations of the Lunar New Year, with sporadic operations associated with the offensive continuing into 1969.

The Tết Offensive resulted in a crushing operational defeat for the South Vietnamese. It is widely understood as a turning point of the war in Vietnam, in which the Viet Cong and the North Vietnamese won enormous, mostly psychological and propaganda, victories. These victories led to the loss of popular support for the war in the United States, and the eventual withdrawal of American troops. The Tết Offensive is viewed frequently as an example of the use of propaganda and of media influence in the pursuit and fate of military objectives and interventions.

Every year on January 30-31, many Vietnam Veterans who have left their treatment programs relapse into drug or alcohol use. It took years for therapists to become aware of this repetitive behavior and relate it to this momentous trigger date.

This pattern can be broken when expressed in a positive manner. A touching example of this is "Marc," a Native American Vietnam veteran who worked in the VA as a janitor. Every year on the anniversary of the Tết Offensive, the stairwells and hallways of the VA were scrubbed and cleaned impeccably, due to the janitor's diligence. Marc used his job to work through the agitation that the trigger date aroused in him.

During one weekend of the anniversary of the Tết Offensive, "George," another Vietnam veteran, started shouting and screaming, then suddenly withdrew from any contact. Marc, realizing this was a reaction to the Tết anniversary, approached George and spoke with him calmly. His soothing voice calmed George, helped him recover his control, and spared him from another in-patient hospitalization that had demoralized him every year. The understanding, validation and empathy that Marc felt for his fellow veteran enabled George to break the pattern of trauma and live through the Tết Offensive anniversary for the first time without it escalating into another disheartening breakdown.

Trauma and Projection

If an activated state remains unresolved, we seek an explanation for all that traumatic energy troubling our body/mind. Unfortunately, we often resort to seeing the cause of the repetitive trauma as originating from outside ourselves. We project this energy onto others, blaming them as the source of our terrible discomfort and attacking them in order to "protect" ourselves. This, of course, creates unnecessary interpersonal conflicts, perpetuating and deepening our cycle of pain. This also translates into conflicts between groups and nations.

Trauma and Validation

Trauma's powerful grip on military personnel leaves their loved ones bewildered or judgmental, often demanding that the traumatized individuals, "Just get over it. Why keep wallowing in it?" they wonder. However, this fundamental lack of understanding about trauma's biological foundation only adds to the suffering of the traumatized. Military personnel caught in the involuntary and repetitive re-enactment of trauma are already berating themselves for a behavior they know is destructive, but over which they have no control.

Military personnel, who do not understand the origins of their malaise and project those bad feelings onto others, blaming the world for their own suffering, end up carrying a triple traumatic burden—

their own suffering, the suffering they provoke with the blame, and their alienation from the world. When criticized, labeled, or judged by the people who are affected by their trauma, including military personnel, traumatized people feel even more of the pain and chaos that trauma brings into their lives. Lack of validation of traumatic experiences is common both at the individual and at the collective level.

The story of "Vera," a policewoman who was working at the junction of Dizengoff and King Georges in Israel during the second Intifada is a good example.

The Need for Validation

"Vera" survived two suicide bomb explosions, both on the Number 5 buses that exploded at the same junction a few months apart. Overwhelmed by her experiences, Vera developed several symptoms of trauma. She could not work or even go near the place where she saw the bombs explode. She was unable to care for her children and could not bear to be near anyone wounded. Loud voices and frightening stories made her tremble all over.

Both explosions had taken place on the Jewish holiday of Purim. Each year on this holiday she shut her doors and would not leave her house. Vera did not allow her children to wear costumes to the Purim parties because of the images of the maimed and dead children in costumes she witnessed on those two fateful days. Many Israelis actually share Vera's agitation around Purim because of the pictures in the newspapers and on the television. Vera's family, unable to handle the stress and limitations of her symptoms, finally told her, "You survived. You are alive. What is the matter with you?"

Vera was upset that no one around her understood that what she saw was horrifying and impossible to forget. The more they told her to get over it, the more Vera dug in about her symptoms and refused to go see a therapist.

One day, Vera's child complained their home was unlike any other child's home. Terribly embarrassed, Vera finally decided to go to therapy. Her whole family came to the clinic for a session to learn about the nature of her symptoms and learn how to help her with her traumatic reactions. Once they had the chance to talk about and discharge their feelings of anger, frustration and powerlessness about the limitations her trauma had inflicted upon their lives, they were able to empathize with her suffering and to be supportive of her healing.

———————

In the same vein, validating the horrors of military experiences and the subsequent suffering, however illogical and unnecessary the continuing suffering seems, paradoxically helps military personnel let go of their need to feel understood and believed, and allows their own healing vortex to begin.

This same principle applies as well to groups and nations perceived as wallowing in suffering decades and even centuries-old, but who never really received a full validation for their terrible experiences. It must also be applied to people whose trauma vortex manifests in aggression, terror and war. Sometimes century-old traumas are retriggered by apparent similarities, and move people into fear, rage and revenge, to fight the failures and humiliations of the past, mirrored by present conditions.

Veterans' Stories

VIETNAM WAR VETERANS
(1) After returning from Vietnam, many veterans found civilians were unfriendly and that they had to defend themselves for having served in the military. A number of veterans began using weaponry in their own neighborhoods, getting into battles, protecting their "turf" and creating areas that were dangerous for everybody.

(2) The term "going postal" refers to several well-known incidents in which employees of the U.S. Postal Service, unable to adjust to the routine and drudgery of civilian work and with the adrenaline still running in their bodies, took out their frustrations (at their jobs) by going on killing sprees. Many of those involved in post office-related crime were Vietnam veterans.

(3) One Vietnam veteran, who had trouble sleeping, would awaken with a startled response, striking out at anyone within reach if he was disturbed during his rest. Even though his son and daughter-in-law had warned their four-year-old son against going into the room when Grandpa was sleeping, the child entered the room. The veteran jumped out of bed and struck the child, throwing him across the room. Fortunately, the child was not badly hurt and the family had been educated regarding the veteran's PTSD problems. They did not blame the grandfather for his behavior, but continued to instruct their son not to enter the room unexpectedly. Only the understanding of the veteran's symptom allowed the family relationships to remain intact.

GULF WAR VETERANS
After the first Gulf War, veteran "Carlos" got a job working for the federal government in the Department of Immigration. As a member of a minority, "Carlos" took offense to the derogatory comments made in jest by a colleague. Still activated from the war, and with untreated hearing damage from driving tanks, Carlos responded by threatening his colleague with a weapon, over which he lost his job.

The Oklahoma City bomber, Timothy McVeigh, was a Gulf War veteran. His destructive behavior may well have resulted from the high-intensity trauma experienced by many veterans of the Gulf War, and which may have retriggered childhood traumas. He had also found refuge in the collective trauma vortex of a white supremacy group that recreated and perpetuated inter-group histories of traumas of several of the minorities in the US.

"Samuel," a veteran of the first Lebanon War, roamed the streets after dark, looking for fights with anyone, especially with Israeli-Arabs, who in his mind were substitutes for Palestinians or other enemy Arabs. The police psychiatrist rejected Samuel's request when he wanted to join the Border Patrol because the psychiatrist judged Samuel too aggressive. A previously gregarious fellow that had gotten along with everyone, Samuel had turned violently anti-Arab after his best friend was killed next to him in Lebanon. His animosity towards Arabs became notorious and his aggressive behavior continued, resulting in repeated jailing.

TRAUMA, SHAME, SECRECY, AND ANGER

Shame has a powerful grip on traumatized personnel and it seriously impairs their ability to seek help and to heal. Traumatic shame is different from the natural socializing shame that most people learn to process, helping them to mature. Traumatic shame is a bottomless well of suffering that disconnects military personnel from any self-compassion, from the belief that they belong to humanity, and from the belief that God is on their side.

Shame makes people keep their traumas secret, and secrets keep the trauma festering, adding to the pain and deepening the feelings of alienation trauma generates. Anger is a particularly difficult issue for military personnel. It is normal to feel anger when one lives through a traumatic event. Although people are often afraid of it, anger is a biological imperative. It is the way they know something is wrong and that their sense of self is being compromised. Anger can indicate different things—being hurt; needs are not met adequately; rights are being violated; being used; loss of friends; seeing absurdity and the waste of many battles and wars; or ignoring some important issues and not living with integrity. Some, schooled in spiritual systems, view anger as shameful or as a sign of weakness. For others, anger serves as a mask that covers more unbearable or unacceptable feelings. "Rage-aholics," for example, find it easier to get angry and vent than to feel powerless, incompetent, or shamed—feelings that are often masked by anger.

But anger does not carry an automatic moral implication. It is simply something that is felt; an emotion that indicates that there is an area requiring one's attention. However, because when they express anger, people risk rejection and disapproval, they tend to repress it, letting it build up until they vent it in aggressive ways.

Traumatic anger is still more problematic. It is anger coupled with helplessness, which turns into rage; it is the anger of a hyper-activated nervous system that is unable to release its excess energy. This type of anger feels so powerful that people are terrified of loosing control, fearing they will become destructive. Fear of a powerful traumatic anger is so primal that it becomes paralyzing. One must avoid anything that may bring it up, and try repressing it at any cost. Repressed anger can trigger strong headaches even uncontrolled spastic movements. Repressed emotions, including fear of out-of-control anger, may be the underlying factor behind many chronic pain or immune disorders, migraines, peptic ulcer, spastic colon, irritable bowel syndrome, fibromyalgia, and asthma.

Many people, especially veterans with nervous systems highly wired by their repeated exposure to horrible occurrences, cannot control nor repress their anger and become ostracized for it. Indeed, many people view anger only as destructive energy, responsible for all the aggression and violence in the world today. Anger is often associated with hurting others and blamed for all the atrocities people witness or hear about in the news. It is true that driven by anger, people have done great physical and emotional harm to themselves and to others.

Anger and the Military

Anger is a most common legacy for military personnel and veterans. Many war veterans have talked about being troubled, not only by their continuous fear of being harmed, but even more by their fear of harming others. Many veterans face multiple medical procedures with extraordinary bravery and endurance; yet they are haunted by the raging anger they feel burning inside of them. They are terrified of their lack of control over their emotions and actions, especially when their anger explodes so quickly and powerfully that they don't have any chance to rein it in.

They fear that frustrating interactions with others, whether their families, staff at hospitals, other veterans, or civilians, will trigger rage responses. They know that when they react, they will "blow it," and do something that will further disconnect them from others, get them in trouble with the law or cause them terrible guilt. They talk about being simply horrified by their own anger.

Some veterans re-enact aggression while asleep, as many veteran's spouses have confirmed; they report being struck during the night. These veterans generally rate their own triggers to violence at the top of their worries.

The fear of losing control becomes so fundamental that some veterans will avoid anything that may elicit this response. Other veterans, fearing their anger will expose them to rejection, try to repress it and end up expressing it in dysfunctional ways, including psychosomatic, or "physical traumatic symptoms." Still other veterans can use anger as a mask to disguise unacceptable and stigmatized fear, terror, and shame. For "rage-aholic" veterans, anger is more acceptable than feelings of helplessness, inadequacy, and shame.

An Example of Unresolved Traumatic Anger

"Mooli" served for three weeks in the Gaza Strip as a reserve officer of the Israeli Army. Upon his return, when he was walking down the kibbutz road to his apartment, several young boys suddenly ran up to him, approaching him from his left side. He automatically reached for his gun and almost fired before he realized they were his brothers and their friends running towards him, happy to see he was back, and not the stone-throwing youth from Gaza.

Mooli was very upset with the incident and returned immediately to his unit on that same day, saying he could not handle civilians at this time. He was very frightened, and spent the whole Sabbath taking several showers and baths, reluctant to go back home because he was afraid that with his anger, jumpiness, and impulsive reactions, he might kill somebody.

Mooli's fears were rooted in his past experience during the first Intifada, when children aged 8, 10, and 13 (his younger brothers' age) had thrown stones and Molotov bottles at him during one of his patrols. One of the bottles had hit him on the head, and he still carried a small scar. Outraged, Mooli had fired his gun in the air, even though his orders were to never shoot at stone throwers. He felt that he had been carrying his anger for a very long time.

After the incident, it took many months for Mooli to learn to relax in his kibbutz. Eventually, he felt he was able to resolve his problem somewhat, but he still talked about the unfortunate incident as one of the prices of war. He also declined to take the officers course because of this incident. Mooli's fears controlled his career.

UNIVERSAL BASIC NEEDS

The understanding of the concept of universal basic needs sheds much light on what happens to us in trauma. People all have psychological basic needs for:

- Safety and security

- Autonomy; for appreciation, respect and positive self-image
- Having our experience and reality validated
- Competence and efficiency
- Having meaning and a role in the world
- Trust in others and to be seen as trustworthy

The healing vortex allows us to meet one's basic needs in a healthy way, while the trauma vortex pushes us into destructive ways of meeting these same needs. If you are caught in a trauma vortex, it is helpful for you to be able to differentiate between feeling suffering and expressing it in destructive ways. Make sure to meet your basic needs in constructive ways. Allow your family and friends to alert you when they notice you are acting in negative ways.

Remember that in trauma feeling bad feels right, and feeling bad often seems to justify acting accordingly. Ask and explain to your family the importance of their validating your suffering while cautioning you on the possible destructiveness of your responses. Be aware that trauma distorts narrative, and allow friends and relatives to help you identify how trauma has distorted your narrative of life. It is helpful to give them this book to read, or the parts that seem most meaningful to you.

Because traumatized people in general are convinced that the actions they are taking to fulfill their needs are the only ones possible, people around them—their peers, family and medical staff—can help them to identify they are in the trauma vortex by asking the questions about fulfilling their needs, such as: Are you achieving real safety? Do your actions support your own self-esteem and command the respect of others? Do your actions inspire people's desire to validate your suffering? Are your actions earning you the trust of others and facilitating your ability to trust others? Is your behavior giving meaning to your life?

A Story of War Trauma and Somatic Experiencing®

"Ben" was a combat veteran who sought treatment for his alcoholism 30 years after the war. His presenting symptoms included a longstanding crippling pain in his hands and arms, which he had not related to psychological issues. He eventually underwent four reconstructive surgeries in his arms and hands to recuperate their normal function. A lifetime of alcoholism had cost him his wife and children. Nevertheless, he was gregarious with friends and business colleagues, and he thrived, working as a salesman.

When he started Somatic Experiencing® therapy, he realized for the first time that his war traumas had affected not only his mind, but also his body. During the sessions, he was able to process and discharge some of the traumatic energy still frozen in his nervous system. He summarized the changes he noticed in himself in one sentence: "I have begun to get myself back."

Now that he "had himself back," he realized that, although he appeared to be outgoing and well-adjusted, it had been only at a superficial level. He reckoned he had not felt alive since before his service in the Army, before the war. After he discharged the traumatic energy stuck in his system, he felt his emotions spring from within his deepest core. He expressed sorrow for not having received this kind of help sooner (which may have spared him the painful syndrome that affected his arms and hands and the loss of his family), but he was grateful to be able to re-enter a vibrant world.

THE TRANSFORMATIVE POWER OF THE TRAUMA VORTEX AND THE HEALING VORTEX

The paradox implicit in the metaphors of the stream of life with its trauma and healing vortices teaches that while the experience of trauma has incredible destructive power, it also has the power to make one stronger and to give a renewed appreciation for life. In addition, overcoming trauma teaches more empathy for the suffering of others.

People do have an innate capacity to rebound from extreme experiences of threat. However, certain experiences are so challenging and traumatizing that they become too overwhelming and people can no longer instinctively cope and rebound from them alone. It is during those times that it is necessary to engage the healing vortex consciously and reconnect with one's innate capacity to heal.

When trauma overwhelms and deregulates the nervous system, we need support to reconnect with our healing vortex. Simply knowing that the healing vortex exists already establishes a blueprint of the path to recovery. Our strides on that path may be tentative and tortuous, our steps small and slow or fast paced and energetic, depending on the conditions surrounding our traumas, but it is the path that is important and not the speed.

It is possible to transcend the most abject and terrifying circumstances when we access the healing vortex. It allows us to survive instead of succumb, to keep our reason and not go mad, overcoming bitterness and reach wisdom.

The therapeutic tool presented in this book is most helpful in these circumstances when we need to heal and transcend horror and tragedy.

A Healing Vortex in Action during Combat

"Albert" was a Vietnam veteran whose life alternated between cycles of success in his construction business and periods of despair and alcoholism. When he entered therapy, he repeatedly asked, "What is wrong with me?" He felt ashamed and guilty about his lapses.

Later in therapy, he was able to bring up marvelous childhood images, when asked to think of a resource from his childhood. He had lived in a small village full of magnificent rolling hills, old trees, and was happy to be in nature, where he was free to roam the countryside with his friends, protected by the older kids. With the help of this resource, he focused mainly on his lack of self-esteem over his relapses.

In group therapy with other veterans, he began to share his war fighting experiences. When asked for positive moments during his Army years, Albert revealed that his worst fear was to let himself reminisce about his pleasurable experiences in Vietnam because the thrill of escaping was mixed with the distressing pleasure of killing the enemy. Helped by the therapist to separate the two experiences, he was able to feel again the pleasure of running in the hills of Vietnam, sometimes on his own and sometimes with others in his squadron. Then he connected the thrill of running freely in his childhood town to his running in the jungles of Vietnam; he was able for the first time, to enjoy the sense of pleasure and freedom without it being marred by the high that came from killing an enemy. He was then able to pendulate between the positive and the negative experience and to release the anxiety and guilt connected with the pleasure of killing.

One day, Albert described in group one of his most frightening yet pleasurable experiences in the war. While on patrol on the edge of a river, he was separated from his platoon and was almost caught by the Viet Cong. He ran and ran until he could jump in the river and hid among the trees.

His group members knew the landscape and had the same experience; they could relate to his thrill of running, fleeing and hiding. They vicariously shared Albert's sensory experience of mastery of escaping danger. Albert's innocent and conflict-free childhood pleasure helped them all connect again with the feeling of uncontaminated joy that had been so hard for them to experience since their military service.

From this resourced space, they were able to address their feelings of deep shame and anger for the double bind that overwhelms so many war veterans: asked to fight an implacable enemy, they kill and survive; they enjoy the triumph of their survival, and the powerful high that sometimes comes from killing. When they return, they are ashamed of the pleasure they felt, left with tumultuous feelings and images about their battle experiences and ordeals they feel they cannot share with anyone.

For the first time in years, these veterans were able to process and integrate their unspoken feelings of fear, the thrill to survive, the high from the power to kill, and the shame that their country made them feel because of its later opposition to the war. They untangled their mixed emotions and processed them one at a time.

With their renewed capacity to feel such joy themselves, it was easier for them to get into the deep grief of having had to kill and connect to the self-compassion that allowed them to understand and forgive themselves. More importantly, they touched for the first time the possibility of living a normal life—one that was no longer haunted by their war experience.

As for Albert, he finally understood why he had not been able to enjoy his successes in life. He had sabotaged his own efforts. Feelings of triumph were unconsciously linked to the thrill of survival, the high of killing in war, and the guilt that comes from it.

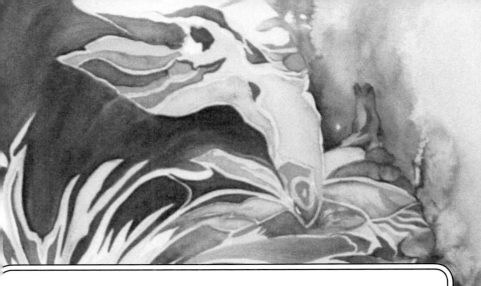

PART II
TOOLS FOR HEALING

CHAPTER SIX

USING THE LANGUAGE OF SENSATIONS
AND THE FELT SENSE TO HEAL TRAUMA

A HARD-WIRED HEALING VORTEX

The healing vortex is also contagious

It is good to remember that the healing vortex is also contagious, and that the innate ability to heal is universal and hard-wired in all. When in traumatic situations, remember to shift focus from the trauma vortex to the healing vortex. Your awareness helps you remember that your body knows what you need to heal. When we are too deep in the trauma vortex, we need the help of others to get out of it.

Somatic Experiencing® heals trauma by helping to integrate the three levels of the brain. It uses awareness and the "Felt Sense"—the ability to focus on one's inward experience—to regulate the nervous system and re-establish a healthy flow of energy in the body, integrate emotions, and restore control to the thinking brain.

SE® works by itself as a tool for healing trauma, but it can also be integrated into other trauma-healing techniques. Often, the combination of a method called Eye Movement Desensitization Reprocessing (EMDR) in addition to SE® is a very powerful mix for healing trauma. There are more and more therapists trained in both techniques, as well as many others that can add their helpful tools for trauma healing. Each technique can also stand on its own. Whether with cognitive behavioral approaches, EMDR, prolonged exposure, debriefing, the energy therapies, or simple anger management, SE® adds the element of the autonomic nervous system, allowing the release of traumatic energies to happen at the somatic level. SE® is also uniquely adept at healing trauma held in implicit memory, a type of trauma, which is retrieved mostly through movements and internal states, such as heartbeat, rapid pulse, etc.

Just as military personnel strengthen their muscles with exercise and discipline through repetition, they also can strengthen their resilience, using the tools presented in the next three chapters. These SE® tools will help them to develop resiliency, regulate their nervous system and integrate their thoughts and emotions.

THE FELT SENSE

The Felt Sense as the Basic Tool for Self-Knowledge

The Felt Sense is the language of the body/mind and one of the most important tools for engaging the healing vortex. It informs us instantly and simultaneously of both our external and internal environments.

The Felt Sense tells us things like the position of our body, when it is moving and where it feels tense or relaxed. It uses our awareness of what is going on inside of us to tell us how we feel about what we are experiencing at any given moment. It informs us even when we are not conscious of it.

The Felt Sense has more to do with what we feel than with what we think. It is a body/mind energy that involves a deeper intuitive knowledge, giving us different information than what our thinking brain can provide alone.

Research has confirmed that our ability to connect with our Felt Sense determines how quickly we rebound from trauma. In order to heal trauma, we must focus our awareness on our physical sensations, and allow instinctive and autonomic processes to be completed. We become better integrated when we combine our animal instincts with the human capacity for awareness.

Using the Felt Sense as a tool for healing means shifting our focus from emotions and thoughts, to their physical bodily expression, and which are called "sensations." Sensations allow us to read our experience in terms of pleasure or displeasure, comfort or discomfort.

The Felt Sense helps us also tune into our subtle instinctual impulses and resources, which is crucial for healing trauma. As you will see in Chapter 8, a "resource" is any person, place, object, memory, positive experience, action or personal quality that evokes soothing, calm feelings or a sense of strength. Resources elicit pleasant sensations in our body. Even so, sometimes we move quickly from a resource to a constriction. When this happens, we need to keep our attention on the constricted sensation until the resource comes up.

Because we are used to focus on our thoughts and emotions it may seem difficult sometimes to keep our awareness focused purely on physical sensations; at times, also, the sensations may feel too intense. However, when we understand that a sensation has a short life span and that the Felt Sense helps us move through difficult sensations quickly yet gently, it is easier to allow ourselves to focus on them, however unpleasant they might seem in the moment.

Just holding our focus on the Felt Sense allows constricted sensations to dissipate. Tuning into our Felt Sense is a bit like meditation. We do it gently and without force, focusing our awareness on what we experience and not on what we think. When words, images, thoughts and emotions come up, we notice them but stay focused on our sensations. We keep a curious and detached attitude, without trying to explain or interpret what we notice.

The ability to reason provides us with the ability to argue two sides of a single issue. Both might seem equally valid. However, when we focus on the information that the Felt Sense gives us regarding this same issue, we can bypass our mind's ability to play the devil's advocate and touch what is unique about us, the essence of our own personal and unique truth.

The Felt Sense allows us to gather and extract all kinds of subtle, vital and enriching information, and to reach a deeper sense of knowledge. Unlike the slower work of sifting through emotions or complex thoughts, focusing on sensations moves healing faster. The answers we need come to us intuitively.

The Felt Sense as a Flow

If thoughts or images come up, do not attach meaning to them. The best information for stabilizing the nervous system comes from sensations, rather than from words, pictures or insights. Move through your Felt Sense as you would flow through a stream.

You may choose to stop and do Exercises 1 and 2 now or come back to them later. For your convenience, we have also grouped all of the exercises together at the end of the book.

Getting Acquainted with Your Felt Sense

Feel your feet on the ground and feel the way your body makes contact with the chair. Feel your body in as many details as possible: feel how the chair is supporting your back. Sense the way your clothes feel on your skin; how the collar of you shirt touches your neck. Feel where your pants or skirt touch your legs, and where your hair touches the nape of your neck.

Now, sense the sensations inside the walls of your body. What sensations do you feel when you sense underneath your skin? Take all the time you need to notice the subtle (and not so subtle) sensations. Notice your breath, your heartbeat, and the feelings in your chest and stomach and in your limbs. Notice your jaw, your face and your head. Notice if your body feels comfortable. Allow your body to move until it feels comfortable.

How did you know that you felt comfortable or uncomfortable? How did you know your body wanted to move? Which sensations contributed to your feelings of comfort? Did your sensations get more or less intense when you focused your attention on them? Did you feel more or less comfortable? Did your sensations eventually change? What part of you noticed the sensations? What part of you noticed the change in the sensations?

In summary, the Felt Sense is the ability to focus inwardly and get a quick appraisal of how we feel about our environment and how we want to respond. Focusing on our internal sensations with our Felt Sense allows us to assess our level of comfort or discomfort, giving us a measure of our experience.

———

Practicing the Felt Sense

It is possible to exercise and practice the Felt Sense like we exercise a muscle.

Take one minute only to look around you, making a mental note of every single detail in your external environment. Notice all the details you may not have noticed before.

Then take another minute, close your eyes and notice every sensation inside of your body. Notice your breath and heart-beat, and the muscle tone of your arms and legs. Notice your jaw, your face and your throat. Notice if there are any sensations in your stomach. Notice if and where there is flow or tension in your body. Just take a mental note, without doing anything about it. If you do this exercise twice a day for two weeks, you will have your Felt Sense at the ready.

———

SENSATIONS

The Language of the Primitive Brain

The reptilian brain speaks in the language of sensations, images, and metaphors. In order to enter the healing vortex, it is important consciously to physically experience our internal sensations. Healing trauma needs neutral awareness focused on our sensations—on their subtlety, variety and rhythm—not on rational logic or thinking.

Focusing on the sensations in our body can intensify our experience at first. But because sensations have a short lifetime—a beginning, middle, and end—and are always changing and flowing, focusing on them moves our healing more quickly than focusing on the more complex processes of emotions and thoughts.

We also approach traumatic material tiny step-by-tiny-step, including resources, because trauma work is so sensitive.

In addition, we can break down our difficult feelings and thoughts into their physical expression to move more easily through them.

We speak to the primitive brain in the opposite way than we speak to the neo-cortex. We do not ask: "What do I think?" instead we ask: "What do I sense and feel? What are the characteristics of my sensations?" Where do I feel them?

The simple act of identifying the specific elements of our sensations helps them move and change. This is the incredible power that awareness, focused on the Felt Sense, has on our body/mind.

A LIST OF SENSATIONS

CONSTRICTION / TRAUMA	EXPANSION / HEALING
Disconnected; Numb; Hollow	Flowing; Fluid; Free; Streaming
Knotted; Tight; Contracted;	Aware; Expansive; Floating;
Cold; Icy; Frozen; Wooden	Loose; Breezy; Bubbly
Blocked; Congested; Heavy	Tingly; Electric; Energized
Trembling; Shaky; Wobbly	Full; Warm; Smooth; Calm
Queasy; Dizzy; Empty	Thick; Light; Deep
Suffocating; Achy	Balanced; Secure; Open
Twitchy; Itchy; Butterflies	Stable; Firm; Solid, Steady

To access better the Felt Sense, we need to familiarize ourselves with the language of sensations, the language of the body (see list above). It is a vocabulary we know but are not accustomed to applying to our internal experience.

Read the list of sensations above a few times to familiarize yourself with sensations.

You can do Exercise 3 now or later, using the list above.

Tracking and Interviewing Sensation

When you notice a sensation inside your body, "interview" it: notice where it is in your body; notice if it has a shape, color or temperature. Notice if it is solid or hollow, and if it has a texture. Use the list above to describe four sensations you are feeling right now, giving two or three characteristics to each one. Try to choose sensations of tension and of comfort. Example: my breath is calm, deep and flowing; my jaw is tense, tight and achy. I feel a pleasant tingling and warmth in my chest; or tightness and butterflies in the stomach.

Time for Sensations and Movements

Time is an important element when releasing traumatic energy. We are usually not focused on the Felt Sense and we don't listen to our instincts. It takes some time—though just a couple of minutes—to tune into our internal landscape. It takes time to become aware of what our body/mind needs, and time to practice speaking the slower language of sensations and imagery.

It takes time to feel sensations and release excess energy; time to complete interrupted defensive movements engaged in response to threat, time to notice the details that escaped us during the traumatic event, and to respond now in ways that were unavailable then.

POLARITY AND PENDULATION PRINCIPLES

Somatic Experiencing® bases trauma healing on the principle of polarity—everything in life comes in pairs of opposites.

SE® relies on the polarity of contraction and expansion, our body's natural life rhythm of contraction followed by expansion, expansion followed by contraction. If we focus our attention on the constriction—the trauma vortex—this will naturally engage an expansion, moving us into the healing vortex.

Trauma naturally causes us to contract: to become the tightest and smallest target in an attempt to stay safe. However, if the contraction becomes chronic and our nervous system stays fixated in it, we lose the benefits of the inherent polarity, which naturally brings expansion and relaxation. Our reality narrows and we become fear-based. We avoid relationships and new experiences. In healing trauma, the goal is to get our nervous system unstuck so that it can go into expansion again. We do this by relying on the polarity principle.

With awareness, expansion always wins over constriction; without awareness, constriction wins and is responsible for the contagion of trauma.

Pendulation—swinging like a pendulum—describes our capacity to move the focus of our attention between the sensations of constriction and the sensations of expansion in our body in order to help release the traumatic tension. For example, we move our awareness back and forth between a sensation of tightness in our throat and a sensation of solidity in our legs until the constriction releases. Although this process of looping is naturally available to us at anytime, often our neo-cortex overrides the release process and we need to use focused awareness in order to reinstate it.

DISCHARGE

This section will briefly introduce the concept of discharge in the exercise, as it happens automatically in the pendulating process. More details are given on the discharge process in the next chapter.

Again, you may choose to stop and do Exercise 4 now or later. It will allow you to experience the polarity between constriction and expansion and the sensations of discharge.

Experience of Constriction, Expansion, and Pendulation

This exercise will help you understand and feel what sensations of constriction, expansion and discharge are and how to pendulate.

CONTACTING YOUR FELT SENSE AGAIN
As in the Felt Sense Exercise #2 above, sit comfortably in a chair, close your eyes, and scan your body. Scan your face, head, breath, heartbeat, back, neck, shoulders, arms and legs. It is easier to focus inward with your eyes closed. Notice how your clothes feel on your skin and sense how the chair holds your back. Notice where you feel most supported physically; where it feels most comfortable in your body. Take the time to just sit and feel for a few minutes. Take inventory of your sensations without judging, analyzing or interpreting what you notice and without trying to change anything.

CONTACTING A CONSTRICTION
As you are checking your inner landscape, see if you notice sensations of tension or constriction in your body and "interview" them. Focus on one of these sensations at a time and identify its size, shape, texture, color and temperature. Just notice the tension without doing anything about it yet.

If you do not notice any tension, think of a mildly unpleasant occurrence that happened to you and see if this thought elicits constricted sensations in your body. Notice the different dimensions of these sensations.

DISCHARGING: MOVING FROM CONSTRICTION INTO EXPANSION
As you focus your attention on this one constriction (always take only one constriction at a time) notice what happens next. Notice when it releases. Notice what happens when it releases.

Does a deep breath come up; do you feel a gentle shaking, trembling or vibrating in your hands and feet, or down your arms and legs? Maybe you noticed a heat wave cross your chest or your back. Did you feel a warm sweat in your hands, face, or chest? Did you hear the gurgling sounds in your stomach, or started yawning? Notice what discharge feels like for you and allow it to happen, giving it all the time it needs. You may feel different signs of discharge at different times.

CONTACTING AND DEEPENING EXPANSION
Notice the signs of expansion in your body as you discharge. Does your breath feel deeper and calmer? Does your chest feel expanded and more open? Do your shoulders feel released? Do you feel a pleasant sense of flowing in your body?

CONTACTING CALMNESS IN YOUR BODY AND PENDULATING
If the tension you focused on does not release and you feel no signs of discharge, focus your attention on a part of your body that feels most comfortable. Notice if it feels calm, stable, or grounded and whether there is a sense of flow.

If you can't identify a calm place, imagine a pleasant experience and notice the sensations that the image brings up in your body. Now take your attention back and forth between the sensation of constriction and the sensation of calm and expansion, back and forth several times until you feel the discharge. Do you now notice that you are taking deeper breaths, or feeling heat waves, or warm sweat? Do you hear your stomach gurgle? Notice then the sensations of expansion in your body, a sense of more openness and integration.

Sometimes, sensations of constriction release and keep coming back.

Often, there are thoughts, beliefs, emotions or images connected with them, which need to be addressed. In Exercise 5 we show you how to work with these thoughts, emotions and images that are attached to constricted sensations and release them.

THE SIBAM

The SIBAM and the Felt Sense

SIBAM is an acronym used in SE® to describe the five channels of experience that inform our Felt Sense. Each channel gathers the appropriate information to give us a sense of our external and internal reality.

SENSATION: all of our internal experience

IMAGERY: all the information our five senses provide

BEHAVIOR: actions and movements, conscious, unconscious; voluntary or involuntary

AFFECT: all our emotions, both subtle and obvious

MEANING: anything having to do with the thinking process

When we feel good, there is an ever-changing flow between the channels. Trauma causes us to constrict the flow of information between two or more of these channels, keeping us stuck in patterns of fixed responses.

The following are examples of constriction in the different channels of the SIBAM.

Examples of Constriction in the Different Elements of the SIBAM:

Sensations: muscle tightness, or muscle numbness; headaches, dizziness.

Images: inability to take in the whole environment or hypersensitivity of the five senses.

Behavior: agoraphobia; obsessive-compulsive behavior; avoidant behavior, or trauma re-enactment behavior such as a series of accidents, or fights, or going into freeze albeit we had the possibility to defend ourselves.

Affect: emotional numbness, depression, anxiety, rage, shame, narrow range of emotional response, exaggerated emotional responses.

Meaning: obsessive negative thinking, no tolerance for differences, narrow view of the world, polarized thinking, generalization, and lack of range and nuances.

The SIBAM helps us organize information regarding both symptoms and resources along its different channels. Once we learn to re-establish the flow between its five channels, we can heal trauma.

In order to work with deeply ingrained traumatic symptoms, you may need a more involved process and the help of an SE practitioner. You will then be helped to move back and forth between all the elements of the SIBAM and their corresponding sensations. This process will allow you to gather the various and subtle aspects of an event that are stuck in your memory, as well as to release the excess energy it left in your body/mind.

However, if you are working with symptoms you can handle, Exercise 6, below, shows you how to work with negative thoughts and emotions with SE® by transforming them into sensations and discharging them.

In order to process the information that the different channels of the SIBAM provide, we need to understand how to translate them into the language of sensation.

Image: We convert the images that come up—from any of the five senses—into sensations.

Behavior: We convert movements into sensations.

Emotions: We convert emotions into sensations.

Thought: We convert thoughts into sensations.

You may do Exercise 5 now or later

Transforming the SIBAM Elements into Sensations

In order to quickly release traumatic stress, it is useful to learn to identify signs of stress in our senses, emotions, and thoughts; and to transform them into sensations, which allows us to discharge them swiftly.

TRANSFORMING IMAGE INTO SENSATION
Imagine an unpleasant sound, smell, taste, touch, or image, connected to a traumatic event. Notice what sensations come up, focus on one at a time and allow it to discharge. If the constricted sensory experience keeps hold of you, you can go to the opposite sensory experience by asking yourself: "What do I feel in my body when I imagine the opposite image, smell touch, taste or sound?" Then track the sensations that the question elicits in your body, and pendulate between the two. Notice the discharge and release in your body.

TRANSFORMING BEHAVIOR INTO SENSATION

As you start paying attention to the involuntary movements of your body, such as your arm stiffening, your leg moving incessantly (restless leg) or your hand tapping on the table, what do you notice happening in your body? These movements may be related to an uncompleted survival response that wants to come through or it may be that your body is giving you more information on what happened during the event. In the first case, you focus your attention on noticing whether an organic movement wants to complete and allow it to happen slowly and then see how it feels in your body. In the second case, you may ask yourself: "What does this part of my body want to do?" If you could put words on that movement, what would it say? Do you notice anything else happening in your body? Keep tracking the sensations that arise, and discharge the constrictions that come up.

TRANSFORMING EMOTIONS INTO SENSATION

If you have any recurring intense negative feeling, such as fear, rage, despair, sadness, or shame, notice where you feel these in your body. What kind of sensations do you experience? You may feel cold; your breath may get shallow or you feel you stopped breathing. You may feel paralyzed, frozen or constricted. Notice the sensations underlying the emotion and focus your awareness on one sensation at a time until the constriction dissipates.

TRANSFORMING THOUGHT INTO SENSATION

Focus on a negative or obsessive thought (about yourself or the world) that bothers you, such as "I can't do anything right." "I cannot trust anyone," "Nothing ever works for me," etc. Notice what sensations of constriction come up, whether tightness in your belly or a collapse in your chest, etc. Again, focus on one sensation at a time, until it discharges or call on the opposite thought—"I am efficient," or "Some people are trustworthy, some are not." Or simply recall a time when your life seemed to flow and focus on how that mempry registers in your body. You may then feel a sense of grounding and stability in your legs, strength in your back, warmth in your belly or expansion in your chest. Then pendulate between the two sensations until the constricted one releases.

AWARENESS

In order to heal our past, we need only to be aware of our internal experience, and focus on our present feelings, sensations, thoughts and images, without judging or evaluating them.

Awareness is a powerful and accessible tool for alleviating traumatic suffering in most of us. It can help us stop the feedback loops of tension in our bodies before they snowball out of control into traumatic anxiety. It allows us to track signs of bodily tension such as tense muscles, tight abdomen, or shallow breathing; and track the signs of healing vortex that arise spontaneously in our bodies, when we focus on one sensation at a time. This process prevents these sensations from ricocheting into each other. Instead, it promotes healing through the ability to digest one's difficult experiences, one little piece at a time.

Awareness in SE® means observing what goes on within our inner landscape with a special kind of consciousness, different from ordinary every-day consciousness, that unlocks our unconscious. It allows many of our lost, forgotten, or repressed experiences to come up, some painful, some pleasant. They are memories, actions, and wishes that may be difficult to accept at first or gratifying to discover. Our unconscious is full of hidden treasures and old unresolved memories that keep us prisoners.

Healing comes from our ability to witness our inner processes and reactions by looking at them from above with "the third eye," a special awareness that carries no judgment. Our willingness just to be present to what happens in our body/mind frees us from whatever has a negative hold on us. It allows us to reclaim the parts of ourselves that we had disowned. Being present to our internal experiences actually allows us to release whatever pain is still attached to our past experiences and to engage with life in a more conscious way, giving us more options to how we choose to respond to our present experiences.

We simply focus our awareness on our current internal sensory life, with detached curiosity and close attention to subtleties, giving our nervous system all the time it needs to manifests itself to our consciousness and time to reorganize. It is a gentle process; we follow the rhythm our body dictates. We do not focus on logic or on evaluation though we take note when those functions come up and we integrate them in the sensory motor realm. We just tune into the instinctual responses that emerge, allowing us to connect and integrate our powerful primitive impulses with our rational brain so that we can feel whole again.

We heal in a gentle way when we merely move our attention back and forth between a constricted and a non-constricted sensation, allowing time for the discharge to take place. Focusing our attention on our inner sensations, we look for the discharge signs that our awareness must elicit. As we noticed before, once we become conscious of their characteristics, sensations quickly transform into something else.

Of course, in the midst of battle, there is clearly no time or place for this kind of focused awareness. However, even during combat there are times of waiting. Every military person knows the expression, "hurry up and wait." That would be the right time to track the sensations and discharge whatever tightness and tension there is. Certainly, at the end of the day, or whenever there is a lull, one can take stock of one's nervous system and help it discharge in order to keep it balanced.

During military firearms training, in order to have a good aim, military personnel are taught to monitor their breath and relax right in the middle of battle, helping them center and steady themselves, to be able to shoot with precision. They learn to exhale completely—

"coming to zero point of exhaling," before taking the next inhalation getting to the "point of silence." They can easily add the discharge body-centered exercises presented here, if they receive the support of their commanders to take the time to track and discharge activation.

Healing Awareness

The ability to bring curious and neutral awareness to a difficult sensation, emotion, or issue allows the psyche to face the difficult sensation, emotion, or issue with equanimity, mobilizing its capacity for self-healing and bringing creative resolution.

CHAPTER SEVEN

DISCHARGING TRAUMATIC ENERGY

F aced with a threat, animals in the wild fight or take flight, and if those options do not work, they freeze. When the danger is over and they are safe again, they discharge the excess energy caught in the freeze as described earlier in the instance of the polar bear, by shaking, trembling, breathing, and completing running movements.

Our autonomic nervous system also normally discharges and regulates itself without our conscious control, returning to a balanced equilibrium if we are not overwhelmed. We need to re-activate this healthy discharge mechanism to consciously remind our body what it unconsciously does when we are not overwhelmed. When trauma disrupts the normal discharge process, we need time to settle and surrender to the involuntary nature of discharge.

As military personnel you know when you have discharged the traumatic energy and moved out of the trauma vortex into the healing vortex, when you notice that you remain calm and that your habitual agitation is gone when you recall the traumatic event. You recover your basic functions: sleeping and eating disturbances disappear; your emotions stabilize, and fear, shame, and anger take a back seat. You no longer feel the need to be isolated, but feel connected to your body and life now feels normal and exciting again.

Discharging Traumatic Energy Helps Fulfill Military Duty

"Avner," an officer in the reserve Army, was serving in a fighting unit in 2003 at the Beit Ilma junction near a refugee camp when he and his soldiers were attacked by enemy fire. Nobody was injured in his unit. Avner stayed calm under fire and gave the correct orders, following Army's rules. His superiors complemented him on his appropriate response and lack of casualties in the incident.

However, when Avner was asked to go back to that same junction on another occasion, he and two of his soldiers refused, saying they did not feel safe there and preferred not to serve in the next reserve service.

They were asked to meet with a commander, who used SE® with them. The commander asked Avner and his two friends to go back in their mind's eye to the incident at Beit Ilma, describe the event and notice the physical sensations they felt in their bodies when they remembered the event. Each of them felt different symptoms of arousal. Avner and one of his soldiers felt tightness in their chests and stomachs, while the other soldier felt his heart racing and his temples throb.

The commander asked each man to focus on one sensation at a time and "notice what happens next." The three of them discharged and released their constricted sensations. Avner took several deep breaths and felt a l bit of trembling; one soldier trembled and shook, and the other yawned several times and felt heat across his chest. Asked to notice again what happened in their body when they thought of the Beit Lid incident, Avner and one soldier felt both calm. The third needed one more round of focusing on his internal sensations and more discharging to release the anger he still felt.

At the end of the session, Avner and his soldiers reported much relief. When they were called for their service, they did not have a problem going back to their post in that same junction. From then on, Avner led discharge sessions for his team after each military excursion, "Because," he said, "even when nobody is hurt, it can still leave a scar."

SIGNS OF DISCHARGE

Recognizing and familiarizing yourself with the signs of discharge will help you when you need to release the trapped excess energy, surrender to the discharge movements and give them the time necessary for their completion.

Discharge movements such as trembling, shaking, or vibrating may feel odd and uncomfortable at first because they are unfamiliar and involuntary. However, once we understand that these are signs that the nervous system is slowing down and calming, discharge will start feeling comfortable and even pleasant. After the discharge, we may feel tired, but a tiredness with a deep sense of relief and relaxation.

Signs of discharge include:

- vibrations, trembling, and shaking
- deep diaphragmatic breaths
- warm sweat or sensations of heat waves
- gurgling in the stomach
- goose pimples
- spontaneous outbursts of crying or laughing
- yawning
- impulse for movement—such as running, laughing, etc.

RECOGNIZING ACTIVATION: THE FIRST STEP TOWARDS DEACTIVATION

In order to discharge the traumatic excess energy in your body, it is helpful to recognize signs of hyper-activation of the sympathetic nervous system and to focus your awareness on them. This allows you to move through them toward ultimate discharge and release. You may need to also identify the signs of hyper-activation in your comrades in order to help calm them.

Signs of hyper-activation include:

- Faster heart beat
- Shallower, faster, or more constricted breathing
- Dilated pupils
- Increased blood pressure
- Cold, pale skin

- Tight stomach and chest
- Digestion stops
- Increased blood flow to the muscles
- Intensified muscle tone; and hands ready to fight and feet ready to run

DISSOCIATION

Recognizing signs of dissociation is very helpful to help comrades.

Signs of dissociation:
- Feeling cold; pale face; skin is blue
- Eyes are dazed, staring into the distance, or vacant
- Apparently calm, but expressionless and speechless
- Having a hard time moving and following directions, or moving like an automaton
- Confusion and disorientation

RELEASE: A PARASYMPATHETIC RETURN TO CALMNESS

By knowing and recognizing the signs of release—the opposite signs of activation—you can know when you have returned to normal again.

Signs of release:
- Slower and deeper respiration
- Slower heart rate and pulse
- Decreased blood pressure
- Constriction of the pupils
- Blushed/flushed skin color
- Skin warm and dry to the touch

- Increased digestion and peristalsis
- Relaxed muscle tone
- Feeling grounded, clear-minded, and present

TITRATION—TAKING IT SLOWLY:

Titration in SE® means working with trauma in the smallest "digestible doses." To relieve trauma, we do not need to relive it in its full strength, but process gradually, with awareness and in small, digestible pieces.

At its essence, trauma is an overwhelming experience over which we feel we have no control, which our system cannot digest. Thus healing requires us to titrate the stuck energy, i.e. discharge it slowly, a little bit at a time, to avoid feeling overwhelmed again and being re-traumatized. Approaching this energy in small doses avoids feelings of overwhelm and allows it to be "digested."

As we focus on a particular traumatic memory, we may feel several different sensations of tightness and constriction such as tension in the neck and jaw, tightness in the stomach, and a headache all at the same time. Titration means focusing our awareness on only one sensation at a time (for example, tension in the neck, but not the tightness in the jaw, or stomach that comes with it) until it releases, taking all the time we need. This allows the constriction to discharge and release, helping us avoid feeling overwhelmed again; only then should we move our focus to the next constriction.

Too many sensations at once overwhelm our system and override its natural capacity to self-regulate, causing us to miss the subtle information for reorganization that our internal landscape provides us. This possibility of discharging traumatic energy without going into overwhelm makes the healing of trauma much less scary and SE® one of the most gentle and compassionate techniques. If you need to slow the pace of discharge, you can whisper "easy, easy," to yourself. This helps the emotional and primitive brain respond and decelerate.

Discharging Traumatic Energy

"Steve" served in active combat during the First Gulf War. When the war was over, he returned home to his work and his three-year marriage. However, he was restless, anxious, and within two years, he was divorced and unemployed. He complained of severe panic attacks and was unable to complete the simplest of tasks. He had terrifying nightmares and woke up screaming almost every night. He often shook violently and dreaded going to sleep. Whenever he started his dreaded shaking attacks, he withdrew and stopped all communication, or became more and more agitated, angrily exploding at people, followed by immediately apologizing and feeling ashamed.

He felt doomed because he had killed many Iraqis. He also believed that his damnation would contaminate his family and friends and ruin their lives.

In therapy, Steve communicated his anguish through his drawings of bloody demons and images of death. After a few sessions of SE®, during which he discharged some of his traumatic arousal, he became more able to verbalize his fears and to release them by using his imagination to create safe places that helped calm his anxiety.

He revisited the images that harmed him, one-by-one, and released them using the SE® technique. As he focused on each image, he felt at first the constriction and tightness in his body, focused on the sensation and then felt the release, the gentle trembling and shaking or deep breath. He allowed the shaking to take its course until it subsided on its own.

Progressively, he felt a deep sense of calm come over him. His panic attacks decreased in frequency and soon after, ceased altogether. He left the VA rehabilitation program and returned to live in his hometown near his mother and stepfather. A few years later, he started a new relationship, got married, and raised a family.

TRAUMA PREVENTION

Exercise 6 takes you through an example of using the SE® tool as Emotional First Aid in everyday life to avoid the development of traumatic symptoms.

Preventive Emotional First Aid after Injury

If you are injured and you are being taken to a hospital in an ambulance still conscious. If you were in a car accident or just suffered a bad fall, there are things you can do for yourself that will help you get better faster and help others take care of you. Remember all you now know about the nervous system, SE®, and emotional first aid. Focus on helping your body discharge the energy triggered by the threat of being seriously hurt.

Give your body the space, time, and stillness it needs to regain its balance. Focus inward and scan your body, noticing sensations of activation such as a rush of adrenaline, quickened breath, faster heart beat, tensed muscles, feeling hot or cold, or general numbness. Stay present to your sensations, choosing to focus on one sensation at a time. Allow each sensation to move through you, keeping your awareness on it until it discharges and releases the shock.

You can use any of the tools and resources available to you to help your body return to normal. Simply experience what is happening without interpreting or trying to make sense of what you are feeling and sensing. Observe the memories, emotions, or thoughts that may come up without lingering on the meaning attached to them. The best information for stabilizing the nervous system comes from sensations rather than thoughts, pictures, or insights. Move through your Felt Sense as you would move through a stream, the stream of life.

At the same time, you may notice several signs of discharge: shaking and trembling, feeling a wave of heat, taking one or a series of deep breaths or hearing your stomach gurgle. *While you track the discharge, take all the time you need to allow the shaking and trembling to subside.* You may notice a slow and progressive release of muscle tension. The adrenaline dissipates, your breath will return to normal, your hands and feet will become warm again, and you will feel a general sense of relief. Once your nervous system has settled and returned to its normal rhythm, you can then give your attention to the people trying to help you. If you have released the traumatic energies that otherwise would result in symptoms long after the incident, you will have more strength to focus on recovering from the injury.

If the people around you are unfamiliar with the tools you are using, just tell them you need some time to relax your body, which is full of tension and fear, and reassure them that you are aware and conscious. Ask for all the time you need to bring your nervous system back to normal and allow your body to re-adjust. You can explain, "I am discharging the arousal of the event, trying to catch my breath," so that they do not worry or attempt to rush you. Remember, it is important to encourage your mind not to interpret or explain. This is not a thinking matter; it is not for the neo-cortex.

After discharging the energy from your nervous system, you may focus on the meaning that the memories, emotions, or thoughts evoke and finish processing them by integrating them in your sensory-motor experience. Concentrate on the emotions aroused—whether it is fear you may have been seriously injured, or feeling rage at the injury and at what was done to you. Take each emotion into sensations in the body and attend to it one sensation at a time. Focusing on thoughts and emotions that come up before you have fully discharged the traumatic energy may only add to your activation and feeling of trauma. However, once your nervous system is balanced, allow yourself to make connections that help you recognize patterns of thinking, emotional reactions, or behavior.

Even if you are able to do all of this, sometimes a traumatic incident leaves such a profound impact that you cannot fully discharge its energy on your own. If you are too activated and cannot bring your system down—the event may have re-triggered deep old traumas—ground yourself immediately (see exercise below). Look around the ambulance or the hospital room and count 10 to 20 different textures or the primary colors in the room, bringing yourself into the "here and now." Ask a nearby friend or relative to help you come back to the present by talking to you. If your symptoms persist, seek professional help. Our hope is that in a near future, all medical personnel will be aware and trained to help trauma sufferers lower this kind of hyper-arousal.

GROUNDING

Because entering the world of inner sensations is very powerful, we want to give you an "insurance policy" against being drawn into the vortex before you start with the exercises. Sometimes, when you try to work on a difficult and upsetting issue, you need to focus on the sensations of tightness and constriction this issue brings up. You may be overcome by the power of these sensations and dive into the trauma vortex without keeping your dual awareness, which is your ability to witness your sensory experience without being engulfed by it.

The following grounding exercise will get you quickly and immediately out of the trauma vortex and help you recuperate your dual awareness. Grounding does not discharge the traumatic energy, but it gives us back control over our process in daily life. Grounding is also useful with other people when they are too upset to focus their attention enough to discharge traumatic energy. After you ground yourself, you can continue with the exercises. However, if you find yourself diving into the vortex and needing to ground yourself too many times, or being unable to keep your dual awareness every time you focus on the same issue, it is better to seek appropriate professional help.

You may want to do Exercise 7 now or later.

Grounding yourself when you feel too agitated

If you start feeling more and more constriction, without being able to get out of it, you can "ground" yourself immediately and bring yourself into the "here and now" by feeling your feet on the floor and pressing them softly against the floor. If you are sitting, feel how the chair is holding your back. Look around the room, and notice 10 different textures in your environment, or 6 same color objects.

If you still feel agitated, look around the room and count how many different colors there are.

Slowly, you will feel yourself calm down and regain control over your body. You cannot be in the "here and now" and be in the trauma vortex at the same time. Notice how your breath gets deeper and calmer. You may want to go outdoors and find a peaceful place to sit on the grass. As you sit on the grass, feel how your bottom is being held and supported by the ground.

After you ground yourself, you can re-engage in the exercises. If, however, you are still agitated, call a family member or a friend, and ask them to talk to you until you calm down. Try again, and if you feel drawn into the trauma vortex every time, seek the help of a professional.

_____

BREATH

An organic process allows us to restore full breath. If our breath is too shallow or too fast, all we need do is bring attention to our breath and it will naturally slow and deepen on its own. We keep our attention on our breath until we start breathing from the diaphragm in an organic and involuntary way. We do not need to take voluntary breaths to accomplish this.

Threat, fear, and rage bring a dramatic, abrupt shift in much of our physiology, especially in our breathing. Breath becomes rapid and short as it shifts to the upper chest. The abdomen stiffens, the neck and shoulder muscles tighten, and the heart rate increases as we prepare to defend ourselves from threat. However, rapid, short breaths reduce the level of carbon dioxide in the blood, leaving less oxygen for the brain. Low oxygen further tightens muscles and blood vessels, making the hypothalamus send an emergency signal that triggers yet more tightening, panic, and immobility. This cascade of events can lead to dizziness, faintness, and a sense of loss of control. This loss of control can feel terrifying and easily turn into panic attacks, gaining a life of their own.

However, diaphragmatic breath can help us regulate arousal and calm the body by bridging our conscious and subconscious—the neo-cortex and the primitive brain—both of which control the breath.

We restore full breath organically. All we need do is to bring our attention to the breath and it will naturally slow and deepen on its own. We start breathing from our diaphragm in an organic and involuntary way. We keep our attention on the deep breaths that come up and track the space opening they create in our chest, shoulders, head, and face, allowing the whole body to relax and discharge tension. This organic manner of re-establishing a healing breath enables you to avoid hyperventilating or over-charging your body with energy when it is already too charged.

NATURAL DISCHARGE AFTER BATTLE

Some creative military personnel know instinctively how to balance their nervous system and release war activation. They have introduced some of these tools on their own, in their work with soldiers, without necessarily being aware of the theory behind them.

Discharge after Battle

While debriefing in a group session, "Ben," an Israeli soldier who fought in Lebanon said, "When we used to come back from the 12-36 hour ambushes in Southern Lebanon, we had a long walk back to Israel. But even though we were thoroughly exhausted, we would run the last kilometer because we felt we needed the run in order to relax." Without knowing about SE® theory, these soldiers were instinctively completing their flight response from danger, discharging and releasing from their system the excess adrenaline their body generated to meet the threat.

They did not know why they always ran, but they did so, even when one of them was badly injured and they had to carry him. "Those who didn't run" explained the soldier "were not part of our group. They never had coffee or chatted with us and they did not come back to reserve service. The running transformed us and allowed us to get back to normal. It made it possible for us to go on those military missions one more time."

Fight, Flight, Freeze

RECUPERATING THE INSTINCTIVE FLIGHT RESPONSE
Think of something or someone that makes you feel threatened and provokes fear, terror, anger or hurt in you. What sensations does the situation bring up in you body? What do you feel?

You notice that it is possible to run away to escape the threat. What are the different sensations in your body as you notice that you can run away? What are the movements that your body wants to do? What parts of your body would start moving first when you run?

Imagine yourself running. Notice the first part of your body to move. Imagine allowing your body to move the way it wants. Imagine running and getting to a safe destination. What do you notice now? Do you feel your body vibrant and energized, or fatigued in a good way, with a sense of calmness and safety? Keep imagining escaping the situation until your body feels calm and capable of defending itself.

RECUPERATING THE INSTINCTIVE FIGHT RESPONSE
Maybe you notice that there is nowhere to run to, but you can fight your way out of danger. As you imagine yourself fighting, what parts of your body want to move? Which one wants to move first? As you imagine yourself moving your body to fight, what sensations does the image of fighting elicit in your body? Where do you feel the strength, the flow of energy? As you imagine again the scene that frightened you or angered you initially, what do you notice now in your body, after you imagined fighting your way out of the situation?

OVERCOMING FREEZE, THE OBSTACLE TO A SUCCESSFUL FLIGHT RESPONSE
The first part is the same as the exercise above. You are confronting a situation, with events, people, animals, thoughts, images, dreams, etc., that really upset you; frighten you or disgust you. You want to get away from the upsetting experience. Feel the sensations that come up in your body. How do you feel in your body? What do you notice? Concentrate on the sensations that come up in your body. This time you notice that you want to run, but you can't; you feel frozen. What's the inner force that prevents you from running away, or from avoiding the situation? Notice the thoughts of more fear, shame, guilt, even fear of hurting someone, or loos-

ing their love, that may come up and which stop you from defending yourself by running away. Focus on the paralyzing thought or emotion that came up, and notice the sensations this thought or emotion brings up in your body. Focus on one sensation at a time, and notice the discharge signs that come right after. Is it a breath, a trembling, a warm sweat? Allow the discharge to take place. Give it all the time it needs. Then go back to the previous negative thought or emotion. What do you feel now in your body? Can you run away from the difficult, fearful or hurtful situation?

The following is a more detailed example of how to use SE® Emotional First Aid during battle.

SE Emotional First Aids on the Spot

An IDF tank was covering an Army watch post in the mountains of Hermon in Lebanon. The soldiers in the tank were using night vision, surveying the hills and scanning the roads that the enemy could use. They where exhausted by the repetitive tasks and frustrated they had leave only every 30 days. That night, the tank driver and tank commander missed a turn on the road and the tank rolled over. The soldiers remained inside the tank according to usual safety procedures as they were drilled to do.

Three of the four soldiers got out of the tank unharmed and radioed for help. The fourth soldier, "Avi," was trapped in the tank with a fractured hand. "T.," an SE® practitioner and commander serving in Lebanon, quickly arrived at the scene and saw that Avi was upside down, his leg pinned above his head and his uniform caught by shrapnel. Despite the morphine given to him by the paramedic, Avi was moaning and screaming from pain and panicked at being trapped upside down.

T. attended first to the group's safety against enemy attacks by calling a circle of security troops around them and sending a surveillance tank to survey the territory. He then turned his attention towards freeing Avi, touching him and reassuring him, "I'm here to help you; we will get you out. You are hurt but you are okay, and all the others are alright," which immediately calmed Avi. T. then asked Avi to focus his attention on his ankle, while he was touching, and asked him if the touch was light or strong. This helped keep Avi's focus off his hand, while the other soldiers were prying open the tank's screws to free him.

T. was concerned about the emotional well-being of the unharmed soldiers and of the tank driver who was already moaning, "What did I do? I wounded my friend." He left the tank only after asking the paramedic to stay with Avi to make him feel safe while T. was out of the tank. Indeed, in the 10 seconds it took for T. to come out and the medic to go in, Avi was already screaming, "Don't leave me alone."

T. reassured the soldiers, telling them "You followed the rules and saved your lives. You are not to blame." He insisted they remain to see Avi was out of danger. T. also requested that the three soldiers be left alone, without being immediately questioned about the incident.

T. then returned to Avi and resourced him by asking him to imagine where he would rather be. "At the seashore," Avi answered. T. expanded on the resource of seashore images, while he also explained that it would take another ten minutes to get the proper tools needed to pry Avi out. He asked Avi to describe the seashore, where he snorkeled, and the pleasure he got out of snorkeling. Avi said, "I feel it in my chest," while touching it. T. asked him to keep his hand there while he had him focus on the sensation of floating. He also reassured Avi, telling him: "You all followed the rules and saved lives; you just had the bad luck of hurting your hand." He then asked Avi where the closest point was that he could touch without hurting him and Avi directed him there. Because Avi could not see his own hand, T. described all the cutting and tearing the soldiers were doing to free him so that Avi would not be surprised by their movements.

T. asked Avi to describe the pain in his hand. "It is a burning pain. I am trying not to move my hand because the pain will get worse." T. reassured Avi "Your hand is ok. It hurts you, but it is only broken and we will be able to free it. Can you think of anything that would help with the pain?" "Yes, ice to freeze it," answered Avi. "Do you like cold things?" asked T. "Yes, the snow and the cold weather." "Imagine putting a snow ball in your hand." "Yes. That is great. The snow ball would melt in a minute." "So we'll get another one" "And it's August." "So? It's an August snow." They both laughed. Avi then asked T. to hold his other hand because he felt an intense pain as they were releasing his broken hand. T. kept talking about snow and scuba diving, and Avi had stopped screaming when they finally freed his hand.

T. turned next to the soldiers to reassure them that Avi would be all right. He had noticed the road had collapsed. He helped them focus on their sensations and remember the rolling over while discharging. "It was like a rollercoaster." "Do you like roller coasters?" "I like roller coasters, but not this one." They laughed at the idea of having a Luna Park in the Army. T. had them support each other, feel their feet on the ground and slowly free up any constriction or freeze let in their body. Lastly, he had them hum until they felt the vibrations created by the humming all over their bodies. He knew they felt guilty and reassured them, "Remember, this is the middle of the war; you are asked to do things you are not used to doing. You actually got out of this without much cost; without long-lasting damage." He then suggested they should be present when they rolled the tank over and he asked their commander to have them drive their tank together right away. When he saw them two days later, they were all doing fine.

CHAPTER EIGHT

USING RESOURCES TO HEAL TRAUMA

Resources are used to engage and empower the healing vortex as well as to remind our autonomic nervous system of its innate capacity for self-regulation.

A resource can be any person, place, object, memory, positive experience, action, or personal quality that evokes soothing and calm feelings or a sense of strength. Resources can elicit pleasant sensations that feel like tingling in the limbs; expansion in the chest; warmth; relaxation of the face, neck, or shoulder muscles; or deep diaphragmatic breaths.

Merely thinking of a resource causes physical changes in the body and jumpstarts the self-regulation and relaxation process. Thus, resources help the nervous system discharge when it is over-charged.

We all have resources. Resources can be internal, such as a sense of humor and intelligence, or external, such as friends, a good job, or pets. The body can be the best resource in healing trauma. It knows exactly what it needs. If you learn to listen to its signals and tap into its wisdom, it can help you recover your innate capacity, lost in trauma, to handle your emotions, regain control over your actions, and get back your sense of self-worth.

Resources and the pleasurable sensations they generate are available to anyone at any time.

Trauma, however, can disconnect us from our resources and turn our attention away from them. It takes conscious awareness to reconnect with our resources in trauma.

Grounding a Resource in the Body

You can call up a resource in your mind whenever you need to counteract the effects of trauma. However, for it to be truly effective, you need to "ground the resource in the body," feeling the sensations the resource elicits in you at the physical level. The more often you "ground" your resources at the sensation level, the more resilience you will develop.

Grounding a Resource in the Body

Think of a resource—a time, place, situation or being with someone—when you felt relaxed and safe. Notice the details of that image: what are the sounds, smells, colors, and temperature associated with it?

What do you notice happens in your body when you think of that time, place, situation or person?

When you think of the safety and calm it makes you feel, where do you feel the relaxation in your body? What are these sensations like? Does it feel like an opening, an expansion, or a stream flowing down your limbs? Does your breath get deeper? Do your muscles relax? Is there a sensation of warmth around you? Is there a gentle flow down your arms?

Each person will feel these sensations of safety and relaxation in different ways. Allow yourself to connect with and enjoy the sensations that this memory elicits in you.

MAKING A RESOURCE INVENTORY

Since resources can assist in developing layers of resilience in the nervous system, it is helpful to make a list of them and ground them in the body on a regular basis.

- Simply compiling the list can help you assess and develop areas of strength.

- As you ground your resources, you spend more time feeling the parasympathetic release, the calming sensations each one elicits; it expands your sense of well-being and helps you feel more alive, open and available to the beauty and love that exists in the world.

- As you continue adding to your resources, you will realize that the world is an endless source of resources.

- Once you are aware of what resources do, your psyche becomes naturally oriented towards the healing vortex, conquering stress and avoiding illness, despite all the negative situations and hurtful people you have encountered.

RESOURCES ALONG THE SIBAM

This list of resources can guide you in compiling your own.

Internal Resources

SENSATIONS: feeling grounded and centered; having a sense of balance; having physical strength, a healthy body, a sense of boundaries, a sense of control, the ability to feel sensations, a continuous Felt Sense and intuition.

IMAGES: having acute senses—seeing, smelling, tasting, hearing and otherwise sensing—having the ability to imagine

BEHAVIOR: persistence; competence; good coordination; talents; ability to relax and let go, to relate to others, and to lead

AFFECT: calmness, joy, anger, containment, warmth, caring, compassion; lovingness, trust and courage

MEANING: humor, imagination, intelligence; sense of spirituality, purpose, integrity, and morality; curiosity, dream life; ability to make meaning, to be grateful, to be conscious, to understand, and to positively reframe; will power; aesthetic sensibility, appreciation of beauty, words and art

External Resources

SENSATIONS: time; exercises involving breath, muscles and balance

IMAGES: colors, nature, patterns, beauty, perfume, music, art

BEHAVIOR: work, hobbies; worthy causes and charitable work; dance, reading, music, all the arts, sports, rituals; ability to make money, friends, and to make things happen

AFFECT: friends, family, children, community

MEANING: spiritual practice, mentors, religion, knowledge

MILITARY-RELATED RESOURCES

Internal Resources

Courage and bravery; capacity for risk-taking and adventure; capacity for teamwork; feistiness; sense of honor; love of freedom; knowledgeable; resourceful; loyal, strong, capable and daring; empowered , physically and mentally skillful; good survival skills.

External Resources

Weapons; nature; camping; family; friends, especially close friends from the military where they covered each other's back and shared war experiences; house of worship, or other religious affiliation; food; drinks (alcohol and drugs are considered resources by some soldiers); planes; boats; equipment; technology; computers, computerized weapon systems; educational opportunities; medical resources and access to modern medicine; and finally, the respect of the public and the media when the country approves of the war.

Exercise 10 teaches how to make a resource inventory and ground it in the body.

Making a Resource Inventory

Make a list of:

- At least 10 external resources (hobbies, travel, pets, family members)

- Ten internal resources (sense of humor, imagination, determination, etc)
- Five missing resources (not having people, money, friends, or love as a support system).
- Make sure to add to your resource list every day. It is useful to include resources that can be available daily (such as flowers, pictures, textures, smells, sounds or food we like, meditation, etc.), weekly (time of rest or the Sabbath), monthly (rituals for the new moon), or yearly (vacations).
- List items from each time category.

Resources can be small and fleeting or major and long term—from a flower that just bloomed to being in a life-long supportive relationship.

PENDULATING BETWEEN A CONSTRICTION AND A RESOURCE

Most often, awareness alone will allow the constricted sensation to dissipate. When we focus our attention on one constriction at a time, an organic response will often arise on its own in our body and help discharge the constriction—what we called a natural pendulation.

If the constriction lingers and no resource comes up on its own, focus on a pleasant or calm sensation somewhere else in the body and go back and forth between the constricted and the calm sensation—between the trauma vortex and the healing vortex—until the constriction releases.

If it is still difficult to find a resource in the body—a place that feels calm or comfortable—think of an external resource and pendulate between the constriction and the sensation of calm or expansion elicited by thinking about this resource.

Using Pendulating to Diminish Pain

Go into the Felt Sense, your capacity to tune into your inner experience, the sensations within the walls of your body. Sit and feel both of your feet on the floor and focus your awareness on your internal sensations.

The first sensation that grabs your attention may be the place that feels painful in your body. Notice the sensations of pain, but also find some place in your body that feels comfortable and relaxed. Focus on where you have pleasant feelings in your body, even if your attention still goes to the painful spot. Keep your awareness there; notice the size of the area that feels pleasant; notice it spread.

After you spend time becoming acquainted with the relaxed spot, focus your awareness back on your pain. Working to stay at the edge or periphery of the pain is an important concept to help release pain.

Now move your attention back to the spot that feels good. The going back and forth between the sensation of activation and the sensation of resource helps discharge the activation. We call it looping. You can repeat it as many times as it takes for the pain to clear, at first only touching into the edge of the pain.

We do not try to relax the pain by directly focusing on the tight spot because it may create more tension. We break the pain into the smallest components of sensation, focus on one sensation at a time, and pendulate between this constricted sensation and a relaxed area until the constricted sensation subsides.

SE on the Spot: Healing through Resources

Several Israeli soldiers were trapped in a temporary base half a kilometer inside Lebanon, under fire from mortar bombs (*Katyushas*) by Hezbollah. Although protected by an Israeli artillery unit near the border, they could not see it from their location.

These soldiers were asked to hold the hill without any explanation. Although none was injured, they felt extremely frustrated because they were under constant fire without being able to flee or fight; they also did not feel they were contributing to stopping Hezbollah. Although the *Katyushas* kept falling, Hezbollah seemed nowhere in sight. The soldiers felt powerless, under-utilized, and too vulnerable. They had only small guns against Hezbollah's artillery and were dependent on someone else to protect them against an enemy they could not see.

They had to go up the hill five times in one week. They had nightmares of being trapped and became very agitated, shouting and screaming at each other. They had little patience with their families when they called them and stopped taking good care of their hygiene.

"T.," an SE®-trained reserve commander, went up the hill with them twice to help them deal with their nervousness and recommended several discharge movements on their way back to Israel. He asked them to run all the way back, despite their exhaustion, in order to complete the flight response, which they were forbidden to do when they had to walk up the hill. He also insisted that they use the pool and exercise that same day.

T. asked the commanders to debrief their unit in groups of 10 and spot those who were most angry. He met with 15 who were angrier than the others. They were angry about everything: the food, the fighting conditions, the fact that they had to go into Lebanon, etc.

Working with them in groups of five, he validated their frustration about five trips up the hill, being fired at without the ability to respond, and depending for their safety on people they could not see. He showed them how to discharge the sensations of anger from their bodies. He told them he understood how wasteful it was to walk around being angry and how much better their communication with their families would be if they discharged their anger.

They confided how difficult it had been for them to keep their experience back from their families, answering their questions about why they were so angry and impatient with short statements: "You just don't know what I have to do" and "I can't tell you. Don't worry, but it is frustrating," when all they wanted was to reassure them that they were all right and need not worry.

In 70 minutes, T. took the soldiers through the entire process, showing them how to discharge their negative feelings. He had them sit comfortably against trees around a campfire, offering them mint tea and biscuits in the morning at a time he knew the *Katyushas* were less likely to fall, and when the sounds of bombings they heard came from the Israeli Army. He explained the model of the trauma vortex and the healing vortex by drawing on the ground a reclining figure 8, what to do to get out of the trauma vortex, and how they could rely on the innate healing vortex to help them recuperate their balance. He showed them how to track their body sensations and pendulate, going back and forth between sensations of tightness and sensations of expansion.

He asked them to remember something they liked, or something that made them feel calmer or stronger. He normalized their experience, explaining that the stronger the traumatic experience they go through, the more consciously they had to access their resources to activate healing. He helped them "ground" the resources in their bodies, asking them to notice the sensations the resources triggered in their bodies, until they felt better and less angry.

He then asked them to think in their mind's eye of going up the hill again, and had them notice, a little bit at a time, the constricted sensations that came up until they felt them release through slight shaking and trembling. He resourced them some more, and worked with one soldier in front of the group, asking him to think about the hill again, notice what sensations came up with the thought, and watch for the discharge. All his comrades were vicariously releasing their own activation while watching him go through his process.

They tracked and discharged several times until they felt good. He reassured them: "You know that you are not sick. Your reactions are normal, but next time you are up on the hill, just notice if you get activated, focus on one sensation at a time,, resource again, remember where you feel good in your body, pendulate, and track the discharge.

RESISTING RESOURCES

Trauma causes us to focus only on what is wrong and to cut ourselves off from our resources. In fact, it can make it difficult for us even to remember that we have resources and it can cause us to reject the very resources that might help us heal.

If we understand that trauma has a paradoxical pull away from the resources we need in order to heal, we can consciously remember and reconnect with our resources, even when we feel more inclined to dwell on the difficulty. The more resources we ground during our difficult experiences, the more resilient our nervous system becomes and the faster we heal.

There may be times after a traumatic event when we become so disconnected from our healing vortex that we cannot think of a single resource. If this happens to you, ask a friend or relative to help you reconnect with the resources they know you had prior to the trauma. If the pull of the trauma vortex is so strong that you feel you have no friends or resources at all, it is better for you to seek professional help.

You may notice that the resources that come to your mind turn out to be of a "mixed" nature—they relax and worry you at the same time. For example, your children or parents will evoke love as well as concern for their safety or their health. If a "mixed" resource comes to mind, focus solely on the part that strengthens you and ground that feeling in your body. You can even tell the body/mind that you will focus on your concerns later. It is interesting to see how much control we can have over our body/mind.

THE POWER OF FANTASY RESOURCES

Simply thinking about resources helps regulate our nervous system. But quite amazingly, scientific research has shown that resources do not actually have to be real in order to generate healing benefits.

In trauma, an activated amygdala works outside the parameters of logic, time, and space, because the hippocampus, which is the part of the emotional brain that helps us register time and space, shuts down. Even after the threat and actual danger are long past, the amygdala continues signaling "threat" to the primitive brain. This feature of the brain can cause us to relive the terror of long-ago traumatic experiences as if they were still happening today.

However, this lack of grounding in time and space can work to our advantage. Using the imagination, we can import resources into the present or use fantasy resources to release the stuck energy of old traumatic memories.

Indeed "fantasy resources" can evoke the healing vortex in the body as well as real resources. The amygdala can't tell the difference between sensations caused by real situations or imaginary ones. In both cases, the amygdala will read the situation as being safe and will send a message to the primitive brain to discharge the old, stuck traumatic energy.

An Artistic Resource

"Kevin," a combat soldier during the Vietnam War, spent 20 years after the war as a homeless veteran, roaming the streets with long, unkempt hair and deteriorating health. An alcoholic artist, he became friendless and out of touch with his family. They worried about him but were powerless to help him. One day, while selling some of his art at an open-air market, he met another veteran who convinced him to go to the VA hospital to get medical attention, sober up, and pull his life back together.

Much of Kevin's artwork during his time in therapy depicted demonic scenes full of blood and gore or lifeless simple patterns. His night terrors and night sweats worsened when he began to sober up, and during the day he was flooded with flashbacks of horrible war images. During one of the sessions, he commented that the red blood he used to see had now turned to pink and he wondered whether sobriety was worth the loss of the powerful images in his art.

He noticed that hawks flew over the VA grounds, and he started spending hours watching and drawing them. In the newer artwork he showed to his therapist, a bald eagle, a symbol of America, appeared in all of his drawings. During an SE® session in which he was dealing with some combat scenes from Vietnam, he thought of the bald eagle of his drawings as a resource that helped calm his nervous system. He pictured the eagle's huge wings wrapping around his body and protecting him.

During that same period, he reconnected with a comrade from his old Army unit. They each had assumed the other had died and they rejoiced at finding one another alive. Together with this old friend and some newer friends, Kevin could now mourn the loss of his buddies who had fallen in battle. He also visited the Vietnam Memorial in Washington, D.C.

Kevin's sculptures and other artwork began to change. The bald eagle was just one of many figures that now animated his sculptures and drawings. His artwork became vibrant and alive as he recaptured his own life under the symbolic protection of the great bird's expansive wings.

A MENU OF FANTASY RESOURCES

Fantasy resources can be used in several ways to heal trauma. Although this might still seem illogical and even silly at first, fantasy resources have an undeniable impact on coping and healing.

Imagine Corrective Experiences

Corrective experiences help us imagine a different, healing outcome to the traumatic event—bringing to mind constructive and helpful changes in our thoughts, beliefs, emotions, expectations and behavior or in the people instrumental in our traumatization. We focus on the pleasant or empowering sensations the corrective images elicit in our body to help "dissolve" the residual energy trauma left in our nervous system and create new corrective neuropathways. The following sentence allows the psyche to open up to its most creative healing: If anything were to be possible, what would you like to have happen? What would the situation look or feel like? What would be different?

You can do Exercise 12 now or later.

Inviting Corrective Experiences

Think of a situation that still feels painful and unresolved.

- As you imagine the situation, ask yourself: "If anything were to be possible, what would have helped me in this situation? What would I have liked to see happen?"

- Allow time for your mind to elaborate on the scenes with the best outcomes, then focus on the positive sensations that theses outcomes elicit in your body; allow the positive sensations to "wash out," or "digest" the negative ones.

Notice and enjoy the amazing creativity of the images your body/mind brings forth to evoke your innate healing vortex. It is an endless source of pleasure.

Importing Resources from the Past, Present or Future

Importing resources involves bringing present resources into the healing of past traumas. Ask yourself: What would the situation look like if at the time of the traumatic event, I had the resources (strength, knowledge, friends, money, etc) that I have now?

You can also import past resources to present difficult situations. If, for example, you are dealing right now with an unfeeling, uncaring boss, you may imagine bringing in the help of an elementary school teacher who had paid special attention to you. You may also import future resources (imagining your children will be grown, or that you will finish college and get a good job) into the healing of either present or past traumatic situations.

You can do Exercise 13 now or later.

To Facilitate Importing Resources

Imagine again a situation that left you feeling overwhelmed and helpless.

Ask yourself:

"What would the situation look like if the resource I have today was available then?"

- "What would I have done differently? What might have happened differently?

- "Knowing that I will have this resource in the future, how can this help me in my present difficulties?"

- Notice the soothing effect on your body when you bring these resources to mind while thinking of a difficult situation. Give yourself time to discharge.

The Amazing Power of Resources

"Sandra," an attractive African-American woman, already abused sexually as a child, was raped while she was on duty in the military. Although she had frozen during both incidents, Sandra was a strong and determined young woman. She recovered from both traumas on her own. She was a dedicated social worker, working on her doctorate at an excellent university. She also had a wonderful circle of friends who gave her considerable support. However, after Sandra had a routine surgery, her earlier traumas re-surfaced and she started having frequent nightmares, intrusive thoughts and flashbacks of both rapes, along with a desperate need to isolate herself from other people.

This time, Sandra decided to enter therapy. While addressing her rape in the military, Sandra imported resources from her present situation as a student, surrounded by her circle of friends, into her two experiences of abuse and she felt that this time she had definitely resolved her sexual traumas. She went back and forth between the image of herself as a student surrounded by her friends and the haunting images of her past sexual traumas, one image at a time. Gradually, her symptoms diminished and the nightmares and the flashbacks stopped.

To deal with the most recent trauma of her surgery, Sandra used a current resource—a safe place she had on a beach near her university—to help discharge the activation of her medical trauma.

While she was in therapy, an incident occurred that allowed her to see that she had definitely conquered her sexual traumas. She used her present resources to bring a different resolution to her experiences of abuse.

Subsequent to her recent surgery, her doctor's assistant harassed her sexually, with inappropriate advances while she was in treatment. This time, Sandra did not freeze and responded very differently. At her next medical visit, without saying anything, she videotaped the assistant making sexual advances and used the video to press charges against him. Several women had complained of the medical assistant's inappropriate sexual conduct, but there had never been enough evidence to bring charges.

Sandra's therapy helped her have more choices, and freezing no longer was the automatic response when she faced threat. The therapeutic resolution of the traumatic energy in her nervous system restored to Sandra her sense of empowerment, and her assertive action prevented the perpetrator from harassing other women.

Creating Protective Allies

The fantasy resource of "protective allies" can be particularly helpful for military personnel who were physically overpowered either by a group of enemies or powerful weapons. Here again, the images that come up may be fantastic, yet they still help the nervous system regain its balance. One beaten soldier imagined five bulldogs jumping on his assailants. A military woman, who was raped, imagined a gigantic vacuum machine sucking up her rapist.

You can do Exercise 14 now or later.

Inviting Protective Allies

Think of a situation that you feel is still unresolved for you and which left you feeling helpless and unsupported.

Ask yourself: "If anything and everything were possible right now, who or what would my body call upon to help me and to protect me in that situation?

Think of people you know, as well as imaginary entities, whether mythical, spiritual, or religious figures; angels, dragons, ferocious animals, or a squadron of one's companion soldiers. As you think of any of them helping to protect you, notice the sensations of release.

Imagining the Opposite

If a constricted sensation does not dissipate with awareness but instead gets tighter, you can imagine the opposite image. Focus on the sensations the opposite image elicits and the relaxation it generates. Thinking of the opposite sensation breaks the fixed pattern, creating internal movement and lighter sensations in the system, allowing whatever is stuck to dissipate.

The same technique can work for ridding yourself of an obsessive thought or emotion that continues to grip your mind or create a horrible sensation in your chest. Focus on the constrictions that the thought or emotion generates, and in your mind's eye, bring up the opposite sensation, image, or thought.

Each of us has a unique imagination. No two people have ever imagined the same opposite image to a given word.

You can do Exercise 15 now or later.

Antidote Resource—Inviting the Opposite

Ask yourself:

- "What image do I have of this constriction? What is the opposite image?"

- "What do I feel in my body, when I think of the opposite image?"

- "What is the negative thought that occupies my mind and what are the sensations this thought elicits in my body? What would the opposite thought be? As I think of that thought, what sensations come up in me?" Now pendulate between the sensations the negative thought elicits in your body and those the new positive thought elicit, and feel the discharge and release.

- "What is the negative emotion that grips my chest, and which sensations does it elicit? What would the opposite emotion be? As I think of this opposite emotion, what sensations come up in me?" Pendulate between the sensations elicited by the negative emotion and those elicited by the new positive emotion, and track the release.

Using the Body as a Resource

At times, you may feel that your body is tight all over and you cannot find any calm place in it. However, in reality, you can always find some part of your body that is free from symptoms, even if it is your little toe or the tip of your nose. You can expand this little island of calmness by focusing your attention on it; it will slowly help dissolve the tightness.

Focusing our awareness on resources allows our nervous system to discharge, relax, and slowly regain a sense of safety.

Feeling Disconnected from the Body

There may be times when you feel totally disconnected from your body or you might feel that you are "out of your body."

In these cases, you need to track your experience from wherever your awareness is. It may feel too scary at that moment to be in your body if your sensations are too intense. In these instances, your mind takes you away from your body in order to protect you from the intensity.

As you observe your experience from this "out of body place," your attention will gently come back to your body and with time, as you continue noticing your sensations and discharging the energy they contain, your sense of connectedness will increase. If it does not, and you notice that you have a tendency to disconnect, we recommend that you see a mental health professional trained in trauma-healing techniques.

Other Resources

There is also a wide variety of activities or resources, that help discharge traumatic energy, including keeping a journal, meditating, using breathing and relaxation techniques and exercising. Exercise, in particular, can help you get more in touch with the sense of tension and relaxation in your body.

CHAPTER NINE

OBSTACLES ON THE PATH TO INDIVIDUAL RECOVERY

The first step to recovery is to recognize that reactions to events of extreme stress are normal and that access to the appropriate tools will allow healing.

Do not waste time thinking you are weak or that something is wrong with you because you suffer from traumatic symptoms. Reactions to trauma are universal and not even military training is an absolute protection against it.

Recurring thoughts, dreams, or flashbacks of traumatic events are normal and may fade over time. If they do not, professional help that specializes in events of extreme stress is necessary. With today's cutting-edge healing technology, based on a solid understanding of the brain, most traumatic symptoms can be resolved.

As you engage in the process of resolving trauma, you may encounter other issues that impede healing. It is equally important to recognize and deal with all of the following:

GRIEF

Respect the healthy grief that follows the losses that occur and understand the different stages—such as denial, anger, grief and acceptance—of the grieving process. It is also helpful to remember that people grieve in different ways and at a different pace, and that grief comes in waves of sadness.

Healthy Grief about Loss

When traumatic wounds are healed, a deep relief mixed with a sense of grief for the losses incurred along the way may be experienced. It is normal to feel angry about the lost time and lost opportunities. Respect this type of grief and simply give it space.

Here again, just notice without judgment the sensations that the feeling of grief triggers in the body, focus on the resources that come up and allow the constricted sensations to move through.

Traumatic Grief

Traumatic grief arouses more than the pain of loss—it leaves us terrified and dysfunctional. The experience of traumatic grief may include:

- Refusal to talk about the loss
- Deep sense of powerlessness; paralysis
- Loss of safety
- Rage, or anger that feels dangerous
- Self-blame: "It's my fault; "It should have been me instead;" and consuming guilt
- Seeing ourselves as potential victims too
- Flashbacks and startled reactions
- Obsessive thoughts: asking over and over: "Why wasn't it me?"

If you recognize that you suffer from traumatic grief, seek professional help.

BLAME AND REVENGE

Often the difference between seeking revenge and seeking justice lies simply in whether we have regained control over our nervous system or not.

The need to place blame for misfortune or tragedy on someone is a normal response to a traumatic event, regardless of whether we blame the right party. Initial reactions of blame allow us to feel more control over the helplessness we feel when confronted by the suddenness of tragedy. However, the need to blame often is coupled with the need for revenge. If we allow blame and revenge to dominate our reactions to trauma, the traumatic energy will remain stuck in our nervous system. Revenge only perpetuates our trauma and adds to our problems as we turn into perpetrators and attract more violence against us. It also limits our capacity to have a peaceful inner life.

Seeking justice is different from seeking revenge. Expecting people to take responsibility for their actions is different from blame. We also have the right to ask for validation of our suffering and the right to seek justice.

Only a balanced nervous system allows us to choose justice over revenge, to give control back to our thinking brain and take actions based on rational thought instead of impulsive reactions driven by our traumatic emotions. Thus, discharging traumatic energy and completing our survival responses can be crucial for inner peace.

SURVIVAL GUILT: "WHY DID I SURVIVE?"

> During the first Lebanon War, the Israeli Air Force mistakenly attacked an IDF convoy, killing dozens of soldiers. Many of the survivors developed PTSD. Almost all of the survivors of the convoy asked, "Why me? Why was I spared?"

Soldiers who survive physically intact while their comrades die may experience "survival guilt." Soldiers who witness death and mutilation frequently are also overwhelmed by survival guilt. Survival guilt does not only occur because they feel responsible for the death, but simply for having survived. It is important to recognize that survival guilt is a common reaction that should pass with time. If it does not, seek help for this painful symptom of trauma.

An Example of Survivor Guilt: Hero Ira Hayes

Ira Hayes was born on the Pima Indian Reservation in Sacaton, Arizona. The unnoticed son of a poor farming family, he struggled with the tough conditions of living in the desert, which worsened during WWII. In order to help his family have a better life, he joined the Marines and went to the Pacific theatre.

Only 23-years-old, Ira saw his life irrevocably changed in 1945 when as part of the American force that attacked the Japanese, he along with four other Marines and a sailor, struggled to raise the American flag at the battle of Iwo Jima. Just at that moment, an AP photographer snapped what became one of the most famous photos in history.

Of the six men in the photo, three died in battle shortly thereafter and two were wounded. Hayes did not see any of them die or get hurt, but his fate was sealed with theirs. President Roosevelt asked Hayes, the only unwounded member of the group, and the other two survivors, to help raise money for the war through a U.S. Government Bond Tour. They raised billions of dollars in war bonds. The photographic image was placed also on a postage stamp and became the biggest-selling stamp of all time.

Ira received many decorations and medals "for meritorious and efficient performance of duty [...] against the enemy." However, Ira never considered he was a hero and struggled with the recognition he received, preferring instead to call those who died during the battles "the real heroes."

By the end of the bond tour, Ira had become an alcoholic. Upon returning to the reservation, he received an endless stream of unwanted attention. He became a drifter, never married, and was often arrested for public drunkenness, never believing he was worthy of the fame he received. Ten weeks after the Iwo Jima Memorial dedication ceremony in Washington, D.C., Ira Hayes fell drunkenly into an irrigation ditch on his reservation and froze to death at the age of 33. The Pima people memorialized him as "a hero to everyone but himself."

WHY ME?

When people live through terrible tragedies, they often think that life is unfair. They feel singled out and abandoned by God.

After a tragedy, asking, "Why me?" is a normal question that has no apparent logical answer. As a spiritual leader once said "When dealing with misfortune, asking why is the wrong question. Any question that has no answer is a question that sets us up for confusion. Asking what we need to do to heal or what we can learn from the situation is more productive."

Although military personnel know they will face many more life and death situations than most civilians will, they will still ask "Why me?" when something happens to them. If they were injured, they wonder why they were injured when others were not. When they return home, they often question why they bore alone the burden of dangers confronting their country, and why so many at home do not even understand nor recognize the dangers they have faced.

HOW TO COPE WITH ANGER

In Chapter 5, we saw that chronically repressing or venting anger affects health and behavior. Biologically, the mechanism behind anger comes from a quicker and patterned activation of the fight-or-flight response, combined with a relatively weak parasympathetic calming response.

Furthermore, angry people drive others away with their hostility, thus failing to receive the support they could derive from social contact, depriving themselves of the health enhancing benefits and stress release of that support.

Military personnel are very aware of their anger and are often more worried about its potential destructiveness than about their injuries. They worry they may not be able to control the aggressive energy in their revved up nervous systems upon their return home. The fear of hurting others haunts them and magnifies their symptoms, taking a bigger toll on their recovery. Many obsessively attempt to manage their aggression by trying to control every aspect of their lives and environment. They judge themselves and others harshly and are beset by a poor self-image. Others simply re-enact the violence producing serious costs to themselves and society. Understanding these dangers ahead of time and knowing how to use the right tools to release and discharge traumatic activation—including and specially anger—can help returning soldiers regain self-control.

If you are carrying feelings of rage or murderous anger, you need to discharge these feelings with the help of a friend or a therapist. This will allow you to sense your anger as power a far more beneficial feeling to you and the people around you than denying anger, repressing it or chronically venting it.

Anger can be a transformational energy that allows you to understand yourself at a deeper level and that can move you toward needed change. Furthermore, discharging your nervous system from excessive anger will help you keep a healthy, centered anger, which can move you towards action for social change, if you so desire.

If you notice that you associate anger only with its negative expression, you must confront your stigma about it. Whether it is fear of anger, shame of anger, or fear of the feelings that anger masks, you must treat anger like any other emotion, in order to loosen its grip. You must discharge it by focusing on the sensations it creates in your body, and allow them to release, instead of acting out, or collapsing into fear and helplessness. Once you discharge its excess, you will feel the type of anger that keeps your nervous system stable instead of hyper-aroused; you will retain the knowledge that whatever made you angry is wrong and needs correction. You will be able to keep the lessons learned but without causing harm.

Releasing excessive anger allows us to connect with our healthy aggression, our capacity to be assertive and bold, and pursue energetically what we want. Healthy aggression can lead to vigorous, resolute, conscious action. Healthy anger quickens our mind and sharpens our understanding.

Without healthy aggression, we cannot bond well with people, because we would not have access to our instinctual energy. Without this energy, we cannot feel safe, and without safety, we are unable really to be present. Pleasure is connected with our ability to tap into our instincts—including our aggressive ones.

Working through Anger

"George" lost his hearing in the Gulf War due to the barrage of explosives used by the American Army during the assault on Baghdad.

He was hospitalized in the Ear, Nose, and Throat ward of a Veterans hospital. He constantly yelled at the staff, threatened the nurse with physical violence, and was so out of control emotionally that he almost got transferred to the psychiatric unit.

Under that threat, he agreed to enter therapy. The therapist helped George lower the agitation left over from his war experience and helped him deal with his chronic pain and medical treatment. In time, George regained his self-control and became one of the most helpful patients on the ward. After several sessions, he had discharged much of his nervous system's hyper-arousal.

He also received the help of his family when they came to visit him. They helped him assimilate his surgeon's information, which George had been too angry and activated to understand. He learned that he could get his hearing back and that the excruciating pain would eventually subside. Both the sessions and his family's support helped him see the medical staff as a crucial resource that could assist him in healing and getting out of his nightmare, instead of the focus of his anger.

THE IMPACT OF WAR TRAUMA ON RELATIONSHIPS

Too often, the lack of knowledge about trauma's symptoms contributes to a serious deterioration of relationships between veterans and their friends and families, especially spouses and children. Even when they know their loved ones are traumatized by the war, families of the traumatized don't have a full understanding of how trauma affects veterans' thoughts, feelings and behaviors, and how much they are run by their unconscious brain.

Family and friends need to know that their veterans are easily irritable and have a poor control over their reactions. Left with the burden of all the horrors they lived through and with a hyperaroused nervous system, their outlook on life has changed. They have become disillusioned, bitter, mistrustful, or cynical. Their thoughts, feelings and moods swings affect their psyche, impacting the small details of their everyday lives with others.

Family Trauma: A Veteran's Wife Speaks

"When I first met my husband, I did not know nor understood the meaning of "Post Traumatic Stress Disorder." I knew my husband had a very bad experience during the war and he suffered from nightmares. I did not fully understand what it all meant."

Triggers: Fear of Re-enactment

"I met him years after the war. At first, we had fun together; but when our child was born, my husband's behavior shifted completely. He stopped being playful with me and became angry and critical. He and his first wife abused drugs and their child was born with problems. Even though my pregnancy was unexpected and I initially had stated I did not want to have children, I decided to have my child and was totally committed to raise him. But I believe my husband worried that I could never keep my commitment and that our child would also be messed up.

"When I started helping my husband at work, he would often deride my financial skills, even though, when I met him, I had been financially independent for a long time. I never understood that it was all connected with his war trauma."

Fear of Optimism: Fear of Being Disappointed

"When good things happened to us, he did not view it in the same way. It seemed nothing was ever good enough. He dwelled on the negative side of every situation. I started shutting him out. I stopped listening to him and our intimacy suffered tremendously from this.

"As things got worse, I grew more fearful of him—fearful for our relationship and for a healthy future for our son. I refused to go out with him because it always ended with him screaming at me and telling me that I was naïve about life and that life was not a good thing."

Fear of Isolation

"He criticized everything, including my relationship with my family. Eventually, I avoided any real togetherness and intimate communication. It was too frustrating to feel I had to walk on eggshells whenever I was with him. I felt responsible for my family's behavior and always defended them without validating his perceptions and experience of them, and without recognizing how my devotion to my family left him isolated.

"Once, he attempted to do business with members of my family. They planned to share a booth in Las Vegas at a trade show, but my brother-in-law changed his mind at the last minute, leaving my husband with all the expenses. He kept mentioning this incident as if it were my fault, for the next 10 years. It felt there was nothing I could do to validate his anger, so I felt helpless and resentful at him for making me feel this way.

"I desperately tried to please my husband by trying to be the "perfect wife." All my efforts seemed to be invalidated and I just felt helpless. We tried couple's therapy for a couple of sessions, but not only did it not help, it made our communication worse. During these sessions, all he could do was scream and be angry. I hated going to therapy.

"Since he started trauma therapy, he is able to control his anger and desperation. He got a handle on his anger and actually is doing better than he realizes. He is not fighting authority and breaking rules like before. I see him enjoying life more and even wearing his seatbelt. However, my husband does not have friends. I now realize that he is afraid to have friends because he is afraid of losing them like he lost his friends that died in the war."

Violence Can Also Be Emotional, Not Only Physical

"I knew he would never hit me or hurt me, but I was afraid in my body. He has a strong will, and was scary in his anger, I was afraid of being influenced by his negative opinions about life and that one day I would not be strong enough to confront his negativity and would give in to it too.

"Now I understand that my own trauma was influencing my reactions. My fear of my husband had to do with the feelings I had at age six when my mom died and our house became chaotic. I was afraid of chaos and disorder; everything turned upside down. His mistrust and cynicism disorganized me.

"I now realize that blocking communication with my husband was hurtful to him. Now I know that more than needing me to be a "perfect wife" he wanted and needed emotional contact and support; he never understood the reason I stopped communicating with him. Every time we would argue, I felt I had to stay away for my own survival. I see now that the more I cut him off, the more he kept pounding at the relationship to feel heard.

"I felt he was trying to destroy my world, making me doubt my relationship with family and friends. I now understand his cynicism was a sort of protection for him, but for me it was depressing. I felt completely free only when I was without him and without my son.

"Now after our therapy, I understand he thought he was protecting me from a disappointing world, while I was convinced he just wanted to destroy my world. I really did not understand he needed a good relationship and someone committed to marriage with him. My husband left Israel right after the war and disconnected himself from his past. I am the one who brought his past and his identity back to him, hoping to help him heal.

"I wish my own issues didn't stop me from helping him heal. I believe that as we both continue with our healing, I can help him recover trust in life and in people, and maybe this will allow me to trust relationships."

Her husband initially reacted badly to what she wrote, feeling at blame for her fears at first. He attributed her fears to her own interpretations of events. As he became reassured that those fears came from traumas that occurred before she met him, he was better able to understand, have compassion, and look at ways he needed to change in order to help her feel safe.

SHAME, GUILT AND HUMILIATION

Feelings of shame, guilt, and humiliation are often natural companions of trauma even when they are irrational and not based in reality. These feelings are even stronger for military personnel because of military culture of encouraging stoic behavior.

Military culture, by necessity, emphasizes overcoming one's instincts, being strong and winning. However, in battle, there are many losses, failures, and uncompleted actions.

Shame and humiliation are facts of life on the battlefield that are rarely addressed, and more likely to be amplified by sanctions. These feelings haunt and torture young soldiers for years, when in fact, they can be processed, discharged, and integrated like any other feelings.

Even though shame and humiliation are powerful emotions, they must be treated like any other symptom. Focusing on the sensations they elicit in the body and allow them to move through using tools described in previous chapters.

RE-ENTRY AND CULTURAL SHOCK UPON RETURN

Re-entry issues come under all kind of guise and create many problems for returning soldiers.

The shock experienced upon return from battle in a foreign country with a very different culture can be very disorienting, as well as infuriating. Many veterans, who have developed another orientation towards life when living in conditions of scarcity during service, become very angry when they face the abundance of goods Western society takes for granted.

Having to deal with normal life interactions from a position of anonymity instead of the authority conveyed by the military uniform can also throw the veteran into a state of imbalance. Other problems of re-entry, such as dealing with normal life details like paying bills, fixing broken things around the house, running errands, dealing with landlords, maintenance personnel, banks, phones and computers may require a real reset of the soldier's expectations and military habits.

Additionally, military personnel have to contend with their addiction to the daily adrenaline rush that was very often part of their tour of duty.

Furthermore, the time veterans need to regain their self-control and rid themselves of their military experience is generally not a luxury long-awaiting families and spouses can afford. Veterans are not ready to be normal and engage in life as if they were not carrying the haunting images of the tragedies and atrocities of war. Their families, on the other hand, have been waiting for a long time for them to re-integrate their roles.

Furthermore, previously well defined roles in the family have been completely scrambled by the soldier's absence and much confusion takes place when attempting to reset the usual roles upon the veteran's return.

THE CHANGING MYTH OF THE WARRIOR

As noted in the introduction, the concept of the soldier as warrior and war as initiation into manhood has radically changed in modern times. The notion of war as a field of bravery, valor and heroism has been replaced by a view of war as a technological feat, precise and limited, of soldiers as paid professionals, and not as people sacrificing themselves for their countries.

Society—especially the media sector—have yet to differentiate between uncomfortable feelings about the justness of war, and the reception given to returning soldiers—who merely enact the nation's decisions. Especially in countries where serving in the military is voluntary, the old automatic empathy for and honoring of the soldier are withheld. This is even graver when the wars being fought are perceived as elective instead of survival wars; the misgivings about the war seem to cancel out the personal acts of courage and sacrifice that take place during war.

Finally, military personnel find their reputation at the mercy of a few traumatized soldiers, who act out their traumas and behave outside of the norms the military defined for itself and its members. The media reports it as a general military blunder or guilt and not as the result of the actions of a few.

HORROR OF DIFFERENT DIMENSIONS

It is also potentially traumatic for soldiers, who encounter on the battlefield behaviors which are crueler than the behavioral standards of their own culture. When working with a population who enact atrocities even against their own people, such military personnel becomes distrustful of these populations, and rightly paranoid. This is often true for ROE—driven troops fighting battles with fighters who do not abide by ROE.

Furthermore, in modern warfare, soldiers witness a growing number of civilian casualties, often many times higher than the number of military casualties. They also witness many more millions of civilians becoming refugees or displaced people, with the usual resulting poverty, famine, disease and squalor, in addition to mistreatment, degradation, human rights abuses, abductions, rapes and even killings. Sometimes, soldiers can connect these displacements with the result of their own actions. Furthermore, these situations can last for years before they are addressed, leaving soldiers to be exposed to a seemingly endless hopelessness and desolation.

THE COSTS OF HEALING

Sometimes, when very old traumas, that have left innumerous layers of pain and dysfunction are healed, you have to change or leave behind many habits and life conditions organized around the traumatic symptoms. This can include your relationship with your body, with your spouse, your family, and your friends; you may need to confront your sexual behavior and sometimes even your religious beliefs.

CHAPTER TEN

USING SE® ON THE BATTLEFIELD

W e were asked by a reserve officer to consider various traumatic situations that take place during military operations and indicate how we might help soldiers overcome them using SE®.

SITUATION 1: FREEZE RESPONSE IN THE FACE OF DEATH

D uring a battle, one soldier was killed and two others standing next to him went into shock. One of them froze completely and the other started shaking uncontrollably. What can be done to help them on the spot?

Discharging a Freeze Response on the Spot

Reactions to events of extreme stress depend on the state of each individual's autonomic nervous system at a particular moment in time, which also explains why the two soldiers have different reactions to the same situation. Freeze is how the autonomic nervous system responds to threat when an individual cannot fight or flee. Freeze may also result from an uncompleted or compromised fight or flight response due to previous unresolved trauma.

It is helpful to first normalize the freeze response as one of the survival responses (that can occur despite military training) and not as a character flaw, and to normalize the shaking and trembling as another response to shock.

This will help soldiers feel less of the shame inherent in the freeze reaction which needs to be discharged. The soldiers are helped to initiate the smallest movements in their bodies, helping them move out of the freeze.

To the soldier who froze, it is good to say: "You are O.K. You are in the freeze. This is a normal instinctive reaction. We are going to help you get out of the freeze. If your body could move right now, what would be the tiniest movement it would do? As you imagine this movement, notice where the impulse for the movement is in your body; allow your body to make this movement."

To the trembling soldier, it is good to say, "You are O.K. You are safe right now. Your body is discharging all the adrenaline from your system. Allow yourself to tremble and shake until your body stops.

After this intervention, watch the feelings that may come up, such as shame, anger, horror, fear, or rage—and help them titrate and discharge these feelings by asking them to focus on the sensations they triggered in their body. Ask them to "focus on one at a time and see what happens next." Help them track any sign of organic discharge that takes place—whether shaking, trembling, deep diaphragmatic breaths, gurgling in the stomach, etc. If a movement of fight or flight comes up, help them complete the movement and maybe process the grief of the loss (guilt for not being able to protect their comrade), by titrating and discharging the constricted sensations. Help them create healing rituals, whether within the unit or with their comrade's family and friends.

SITUATION 2: SHOOTING AT GHOSTS

An exhausted soldier on guard in the military camp, near the enemy border, heard noises at 3:00 a.m. He thought he saw something and just started shooting. Everyone in the camp woke up. When he realized that there was no dangerous target in sight, he froze, ashamed he had been caught feeling so frightened that he shot at nothing and woke the camp up.

Discharging a Fight Response Triggered by Exhaustion

Again, first normalize the fact that when someone is exhausted and serving in a dangerous zone at 3:00 am, the nervous system is more easily triggered. Sounds can find corresponding images in our minds triggering, like in this situation, an explanation for "seeing what is not there."

Help the frozen and alarmed soldier to discharge his freeze reaction, invite his body to make the smallest movement possible and help him titrate the discharge—such as shaking, trembling, sweating, etc. Ask him to focus on the sensations elicited in his body as he speaks of the shame and embarrassment he feels, then help him titrate and discharge the constructions it brings up. Check whether the feelings connect to other scary or shaming times in his life and help him discharge these feelings, too. Look for resources as they come up in his body or speech. Then have the soldier go over the shooting scene again in his mind's eye noticing and discharging any left over constriction. Imagine the possible teasing and shaming from his commander and comrades, feel the sensations elicited, titrate, resource and discharge, which will help build his resilience.

It is also important at the same time, to work with the other soldiers, normalize this type of incident (this can happen to anyone) assuring group cohesion and support.

SITUATION 3: SHOOTING A COMRADE BY ACCIDENT

At a remote checkpoint, a fatigued soldier shot his relief, mistaking him for the enemy. Although it was clearly an accident and his comrade only slightly injured, his officers sent him to jail. We will discuss two alternative scenarios—being incarcerated or not.

Discharging and Healing a Friendly-Fire Experience

Following the same principles above, discuss with the soldier about instinctive survival defense responses. Discuss how fatigue may supersede military training, giving him less control over his fear and leading to an impulsive reaction. Help him react from of proper vigilance instead of hypervigilance.

Also check whether previous unresolved fears may have left him more vulnerable, help him discharge the consequent activation, guilt, and shame in the same way: finding the sensory manifestations that were elicited by those feelings or thoughts, and discharging them one at a time to avoid overwhelming his system.

Have him put himself in his comrade's place. What would he feel? Help him talk to his comrade to have a realistic assessment of the situation, as his fear or shame may be exaggerating the damage done. Also explore his potential anger about being misunderstood and the jail sentence imposed as if he had purposefully fired on his comrade.

If this soldier is not helped to work through this regrettable accident, he may well remain stuck in his shame and anger for being incarcerated, become bitter, rebelling against the military and against society or become insecure and withdrawn.

In the second scenario—the soldier who was not incarcerated had his weapon confiscated, was cited for bad behavior, and confined to barracks. Overwhelmed by the guilt and humiliation of shooting his comrade and best friend and then going into a freeze, he began doubting his capacities and wanted to leave the military.

After helping him regain his self-control through tracking, titrating and discharging his feelings, ask him first to imagine meeting his friend and comrades then discharge any related activation. Then help him meet his friends in real time, validate his feelings of fear, humiliation, and shame then help him discharge them before he re-integrates his unit.

SITUATION 4: FEAR AND FLIGHT

In the midst of battle, a soldier was so frightened and confused by the shooting sounds around him that he left his position and ran away. He felt terribly ashamed because now everyone knew how frightened he was. He felt even more shamed when he was disciplined for his flight without any normalizing or validation of his fear.

Discharging Fear that led to Flight

The treatment in this case is a combination of all the cases above. Instead of shooting impulsively, the soldier in this case ran away, which likely made him feel even more shame and humiliation. Help him explore any previous unresolved threatening events that may have set the stage for this flight, and help him discharge the activation around it. Help him imagine a better scenario and help him ground it in his body/mind. Help him discharge the shame, loss of face, and guilt he may feel for having fled. Also help him process being with his comrades again.

SITUATION 5: FOLLOWING ORDERS, GUILT, AND CONSCIOUSNESS

A soldier received an order to capture terrorists hiding in a house. His precise orders were to send in troops only if the enemy fired at them first, because of the potential presence of civilians. He followed his orders and had his men fire back only when they were fired at from the house. However, a child who was inside that house, was severely injured. Although he had simply followed good and logical orders, the soldier felt terrible about what happened and could not live in peace with his decision to fire, despite the fact that his unit had warned the occupants to leave because of the imminent attack.

Responding to an Ethical Dilemma

In this scenario, the most important thing is to help this soldier work through the duality of war. Help him track and discharge his thoughts and feelings about what took place during his mission. Helping him resource, encourage him to focus on the sensory-motor manifestations of his troubling thoughts and feelings one at a time, and discharge the constricted sensations connected to his conflict of values. This will allow him to take action, which supports his values without self-recrimination. It will help him communicate with his superiors and bring other ideas for this kind of situation. It will help him accept the tragic dilemmas that war entails while also feeling and processing the grief of hurting a child.

The ability to discharge the activation over the situation will not change his value system, but will allow for empowered and balanced action in support of those values. He can also engage in other healing rituals, such as prayer or meditation.

Soldiers, who leave the Army over-activated and beset by moral issues and dilemmas, may turn against the Army and against their country. Some will dissent by going to the media, but against the military structure, and create more defensiveness in it instead of real change. A clear and open line of communication made available to soldiers who confront ethical issues, will help listen to the core issues they bring up. This open forum can help address these thorny issues and discharge the activation around them, avoiding much suffering for dissenting military personnel, negative media exposure to the Army, and loss of trust for enlisting personnel. Furthermore, being open to addressing these issues also helps the military to process and operate at ever higher ethical levels.

STORIES OF SPONTANEOUS HEALING VORTEX

Case 1

Overcoming Freeze

"Abe," a soldier serving in the IDF, described his experience as a paratrooper hiding behind the tanks. He had a grenade on his rifle when his unit entered the village. The order was to shoot at the window of a targeted building. With one hand, he fired his rifle at the building, while with the other hand he grabbed and hung on to the side of a tank. Two minutes later, a family of eight came out of the building to escape the grenade. Abe was in shock at the thought that he could have killed them and he could not move or do anything for 20 minutes. He was completely frozen. Soon after, his unit was in control of the village and Abe joined his comrades, looking for water and food. He felt himself come out of the freeze and felt he was doing fine. He was thankful for it, for he knew that some people could remain frozen for the rest of the battle.

Case 2

One Event—Two Different Experiences

"Fred" was commanding a troop carrier with his soldiers when they drove over a mine. Luckily, no one was hurt when the mine exploded, but the blast was enormous. Although shrapnel injured him slightly, Fred did not freeze and was not negatively impacted by the event. He was just relieved and thankful that he and his unit were not harmed. He recovered from the incident on his own.

Conversely, "David," the driver who was not originally from their unit, froze and could not move out of his seat. Although unhurt, he was in the locked carrier and yet unable to open the door. After the vehicle was unlocked and the team lifted him out, David remained frozen and was taken to the hospital. If the team members had been trained in trauma releasing tools, they would have been able to get him out of the freeze right on the spot by normalizing his reaction and inviting a tiny movement. The next time he was in a similar situation, he would have recovered on his own.

Healing Traumatic Symptoms

"Saul" is a well-educated and creative 51-year-old Israeli neurosurgeon, happily married with five children. In the 1980s, he was serving in the Israeli secret service when the Syrians took him prisoner and tortured him for three months. Later, he became part of a prisoner exchange between the Israelis and the Syrians. Remembering the horrors of his prison time, Saul again felt assaulted due to the suddenness and uncertainty of the prisoner exchange. The exchange, as well as the homecoming he received from his father, felt traumatic.

His multiple presenting symptoms were gastro-intestinal problems, migraines, and sleeplessness leading to sleep deprivation, heart palpitations, anxiousness, and what he called "being constantly in the Sympathetic. I knew my Sympathetic was always overworking."

When The Syrians freed Saul, he was terribly weak, exhausted, sleepless, and starved. He had lost 25 pounds, a significant and debilitating condition considering his slight frame. Immediately upon his return, his friends gave him a fancy party but he felt foggy, unable to concentrate, and very passive. When he went home that night, his father received him in his pajamas, shouting at him with an angry expression on his face.

"How bad can you be to come home so late without calling? Where were you? We worried like hell. You killed us when you were gone. You don't seem to understand that we had a harder time knowing that you were in prison than you had being in prison." His father's harsh and unsympathetic words were still ringing in Saul's ears years after his father's death.

In an SE® session, using a corrective experience where Saul would imagine his dad saying, "We are so worried about you. I love you. I did not know where you were, and I started worrying all over again," was unsuccessful. His father had always been abusive and it was too hard to imagine him speaking softly and lovingly.

After a few rounds of discharge, Saul was able to bring up as resources his children and the quality of his own parenting skills. Although he felt very good about his parenting it was a mixed resource because he harbored some doubts. He was measuring his capacity for good parenting against the level of arousal and activation he felt inwardly, instead of basing it on his amazing patience and capacity to be present with his children. He needed to judge his parenting skills based on his five intelligent, loving children.

The second session helped Saul to correct his erroneous definition of himself as a violent man, which was based on the on-going buzz of activation he felt in his body. He was also able to correct the unrealistic image he had of other people's anger as being more acceptable than what he called his "ugly and exaggerated anger." It was the first time he was able to feel his nervous system calm instead of buzzing.

SUMMARY: FACTS ABOUT THE HEALING VORTEX THE MILITARY NEEDS TO KNOW

The following is an at-a-glance summary of key facts related to healing trauma:

- Trauma is curable and preventable. As a member of the military you can develop resiliency to trauma before you go to battle.

- We have an inborn ability to heal ourselves. Our body/mind knows what it needs to heal. Some are more naturally resilient than others.

- Many do not seek counseling because "feeling bad feels right" in trauma. They do not know that their suffering can stop, because they fear the stigma of trauma.

- Our trauma history, childhood, family, and cultural histories, as well as our present level of stress, affect our response to traumatic events. The younger we are when trauma occurs, the fewer the resources, the more serious the damage.

- Resources help us self-regulate. We all have them. Some have more than others, depending on their trauma history and physical condition. We need to become conscious of whatever resources we have and access them at the level of sensation and also ground them in the body. Facing terror of trauma by using resources helps us lose the panic these feelings generate and prevents the development of traumatic symptoms.

- Discharging the energy triggered for threat and completing the instinctive flight, fight, freeze responses also help recover from traumatic events and prevent symptom development.

- Recognizing that a freeze response is an involuntary and valuable survival instinct, for which we do not need to feel shame, will help us overcome the bad feeling of our past inability to defend ourselves.

- Regaining the ability to connect to the body through the Felt Sense and giving the nervous system time to recover its capacity to self-regulate makes it easier to cope with overwhelming traumatic situations.

- Focusing on the sensations felt without judgment or criticism and allowing them to move through the body helps discharge traumatic activation.

- The breath acts as a bridge between body and mind. Merely by focusing attention on the breath and letting it come up on its own is one of the main tools used for self-regulation.

- Using "Corrective Fantasy" images when reliving a traumatic event may help elicit sensations of expansion in the body, the opposite of the constricted sensations, and facilitate the discharge of traumatic activation.

- Eliciting support and validation for your suffering from family, friends, clergy, and helping professionals will further contribute to healing.

- Survivor guilt is a normal reaction that can be released.

- Spirituality and a positive attitude are vital healing tools. Compassion for personal suffering and that of others will speed recovery.

- Resolving trauma at the level of the nervous system will help each individual process and correct the negative beliefs normally attached to the traumatic events.

- Trauma healing helps change negative beliefs.

Check whether the traumatic energy has been totally discharged by noticing the body's reactions when the traumatic event is recalled. Feeling over-activated and constricted is an alert for continued work. Calm sensations signal trauma resolution.

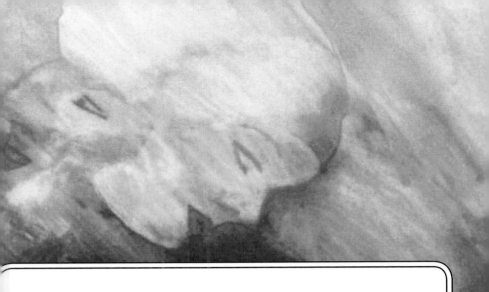

PART III
SECONDHAND TRAUMA
COLLECTIVE TRAUMA
THE MEDIA

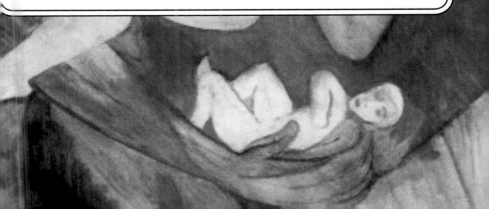

CHAPTER ELEVEN

SECONDHAND TRAUMA

Sensory Triggers of Secondhand Trauma

"Eli," a medic in the IDF says "I left my girlfriend after the Lebanon War. The smells, the perfumes and especially the sex life had become unbearable. I could not think about human flesh without becoming angry. The touch of skin made me remember only the burn victims I treated in Lebanon."

WHAT IS SECONDHAND TRAUMA?

Secondhand trauma refers to the traumatic impact individuals may suffer when exposed to other people's traumas, and can be as painful and symptomatic as firsthand trauma. Also called "vicarious traumatization," it arises from hearing about or living with the fear, pain, and suffering of traumatized people. Secondhand trauma victims feel many of the same emotions and after-effects as the traumatized. When they witness directly horrific tragedies, unimaginable cruelty or prejudice-driven-violence, they suffer from firsthand trauma.

War-generated secondhand trauma can affect soldiers, military personnel serving behind the frontlines, chaplains, medics, media personnel covering war, mental and physical health care professionals caring for the wounded, the families of traumatized veterans, and the public at home exposed to detailed and graphic war images through incessant media coverage.

Veterans speaking about the impact of traumatic events that happened to people they know have reported shattering stories, such as Leon in Tarawa (See Chapter 16). Soldiers have watched comrades exposed to extremely dangerous situations and shuddered at the thought that it could have been they. Others have witnessed the despair and horror of refugees fleeing their destroyed villages, and leaving murdered relatives behind.

Although more military personnel serve behind than at the front-lines, it is important to remember that one does not have to be in a combat position to be exposed to trauma; anyone is vulnerable, including military staff only involved in support services. Most combat support and non-combatant military personnel will not suffer from firsthand trauma. Those who may be at risk of developing secondhand trauma are:

- Personnel, who see soldiers returning from the frontline physically and/or psychologically wounded

- Non-combatants, who witness an inordinate level of accidental deaths from handling heavy military equipment or "friendly fire."

- Military personnel, who merely hear about kidnappings and explosions in non-combat situations, as well as stories of abuse and murder of soldiers.

- Military medics and chaplains exposed to the trauma of those they help.

They are also at risk, but many deny their own traumatic reactions. Having witnessed the horrors of traumatic wounds of fighting soldiers, these personnel are also at risk, but often deny their own traumatic reactions or PTSD, because others have it so much worse. Paramedics and chaplains focus only on the needs of wounded soldiers, unaware that the effect of witnessing horror is cumulative. Although focusing on their task is a salutary characteristic while on the job, they need to learn to discharge their activation once their work is finished. Non-combatants often strongly identify with those on the frontlines and feel inspired by them to carry out heroic acts themselves. Medical personnel may work extraordinary hours caring for the wounded or easing the last hours of the dying, and many volunteer to go out on dangerous missions.

In many of the present ongoing wars or armed struggles, suicide bombings have blurred the traditional notions of battle frontlines as today, any place may be a frontline. Combat support personnel exposed to traumatic events may be even more vulnerable to secondhand trauma than those who were trained for direct combat. SE® should be taught to all military medics, as part of emergency medical technician (EMT) trainings.

Secondhand Trauma

"Wanda" worked on a US Air Force base as a civilian employee in the contracts department. She was part of the negotiating team that purchased equipment and supplies for Iraqi forces in the air and on the ground. She took her job very seriously and was an expert in contract compliance. Because her offices were on base, she developed friendships with many military personnel, who subsequently were sent to serve in Iraq. When she heard reports of their injuries or deaths, she suffered from depression, despair and flashbacks of her last conversations with them, reacting as if they were family.

SIGNS OF BURNOUT AND SECONDHAND TRAUMA

People who witness the impact of traumatic events on other people without processing its effects on their own nervous system, run the risk of developing symptoms of cumulative stress-induced PTSD. Those behind the lines who have been exposed to secondhand trauma, must watch out for warning signs of burnout in themselves and in the personnel around them. Similar to many of the firsthand trauma symptoms, those signs include:

Physical

- Hyper-arousal and inability to focus
- Loss of appetite or overeating
- Loss of sexual desire
- Sleep disorders

Behavioral

- Turning to ineffective coping strategies such as alcohol or drugs
- Workaholism
- Engaging in dangerous behavior

Psychological

- Reluctance to recognize own pain because they are not the "real" victims
- Fixation on traumatic events to the exclusion of other aspects of life, looking at life through the narrow lenses of trauma, suffering from hyper-alertness, panic, dread, misplaced anger or indifference to violence
- Compartmentalization or dissociation from feelings in order to avoid overwhelm; maintaining an aloof distance
- Delayed reactions triggered by seemingly inconspicuous incidents or insignificant details
- Cynicism about humanity and loss of meaning from too much exposure to human cruelty: "the world is a bad place; humanity is hopeless"
- Loss of interest in hobbies and loss of creativity
- Denial of being affected for fear of stigma, and loss of face

There is still a stigma attached to being affected by first or second-hand trauma. As a society, it is important to keep pressing against this taboo; help people talk openly about trauma, and treat it as any other disorder. Because of this stigma, many people do not know where to go for help and are afraid to ask.

Military men in particular, fear that requesting support will be interpreted as a shameful weakness instead of wisdom. In general, people in positions of authority are reluctant to admit that they are vulnerable to any type of trauma.

HEALING INDIVIDUAL SECONDHAND TRAUMA

Part II and Part III covered the tools needed to keep the nervous system balanced. The same tools will help cope with secondhand trauma as well, develop resilience and become more effective in the task of serving in the military. Other measures that help stay healthy:

- Make sure to use time off to re-energize and heal. Rest and take time to balance and recuperate.

- Take good care of the body with proper diet and sleep; do not use drugs.

- Keep developing awareness of more resources on an on-going basis.

- Learn stress-relief techniques, including those related to breathing.

- Stay in touch with the body, honoring its signals and allowing it to feel what it feels without judgment. Practice the discharging techniques and the Felt Sense techniques described earlier in this book.

- Take the time to discharge, calm down, and relax for a few minutes after each stressful situation.

- Do not become isolated.

- Break traditional rules of silence and of "keeping a stiff upper lip." Acknowledging stress does not mean weakness or a lack of manliness. In fact, it is the opposite. There is more receptiveness today in the military to recognize and talk about traumatic stress. Use available on-base resources and talk to people, whether to fellow soldiers, commanders, human resources staff, chaplains, military psychologists, or outside mental health professionals.

- Keep an eye out for comrades who may show signs of trauma.

- Organize peer support meetings.

- Participate in an online support network. Veterans should reach out to existing groups that encourage the processing of difficult military experiences.

Use mental health professionals familiar with military scenarios and battle experiences. Many more people are now trained in the field of trauma and specialize in working with military personnel.

MEDIA-RELATED COLLECTIVE SECONDHAND TRAUMA

Our fascination with traumatic stories gives us the opportunity to overcome our fears and rehearse appropriate responses to tragic events. However, in the last few decades, we seem to have developed a sensory tolerance for the gruesome; e.g., tragedy and violence.

In observing and reporting tragedy, the media become unwittingly locked in a whirlpool of over-stimulation, and consequently the public is mesmerized and unable to stop watching the horrific.

This whirlpool fixates on collective traumatic wounds, feeding collective secondhand trauma and making us more fearful than need be. We begin to believe the world is more violent than our actual personal experience of it. This whirlpool may also emphasize political differences among people and nations, fueling paranoia and fear of "the other," and worsening violent responses.

Military personnel are exposed to media-related secondhand trauma just like the general public, in addition to military trauma. They may be even more at risk because the media is often negative about the military and make it carry the burden of political decisions gone awry. We cover the topic of the media and the military in Chapter 13.

Protecting the Troops against Secondhand Trauma

The military need to be aware of the impact of secondhand trauma on media professionals and their judgment for coverage. When covering victims of trauma in war zones, the media may be "pulled in" by the victims' trauma vortex becoming partial to their polarized beliefs and emotions. The media may innocently believe the distorted narratives, lose their impartiality, and more gravely, fail to double-check the information received. This becomes a real problem when biased coverage informs international policy or triggers mass riots.

The military must assess the various effects of the trauma vortex on the public and on its military personnel.

It can protect the morale of its troops from media-related secondhand trauma. Indeed, despite computers, I-pods and Blackberries, which at times make military personnel the greatest media contributors in the world, the military tries to protect its personnel from harmful exposure to media criticism.

One commander reported on his own commander's sage advice "It is highly recommended that military personnel that are between battles avoid the news. Those who followed this recommendation," he said, "thanked their commander later. He had also arranged for light films and comedies to be shown and for the soldiers to watch only one news report per day."

Military personnel can take specific steps to protect against media-related secondhand trauma:

- Be aware when you are exposed to disturbing media images; track your body for signs of activation, connect consciously with your internal and external resources, and discharge the constricted sensations.

- Avoid media's repetitive airing of traumatic images or criticism of the military. Shut off the TV or switch to another program. You may later return to the news to get the new information you want, but again, avoid the repetitive images.

- Let the media know that they affect you and your military performance with their coverage.

The following four chapters are written for command personnel, although interested military personnel may benefit from the information as well.

CHAPTER TWELVE

COLLECTIVE TRAUMA VORTEX

The concept of collective trauma is very important for the military because collective trauma causes and perpetuates violence and war. It also results from war.

DEFINITION OF COLLECTIVE TRAUMA AND COLLECTIVE TRAUMA VORTEX

Previously defined collective trauma is the impact of traumatic events that affect large numbers of people. Collective trauma can result from single collective events (tsunami and earthquakes) or chronic collective traumatic situations (long-lasting wars, on-going threat of terror, oppression or occupation). Collective trauma can be multi-generational, resulting in a legacy of cognitive and behavioral dysfunction at the group level through the generations.

Groups or nations suffering from collective trauma are caught in a "Collective Trauma Vortex," a whirlpool of traumatic fear, helplessness, humiliation and rage, experienced at the collective level, transmitted culturally, and magnified by the media. It activates aggressive defensive reactions and leads to murderous rage and revenge. Unresolved collective trauma can drive communities, nations and entire regions into violence, wars of aggression, and sometimes genocide.

REVENGE: VICTIMS BECOME VICTIMIZERS

> Victims who remain stuck in the
> trauma vortex may become victimizers

Trauma leaves people angry and with a strong need for justice. Coupled with helplessness, this anger becomes rage. However, for people with a nervous system altered by trauma, revenge seems the only way to get justice. When people seek revenge to get justice, anger and rage will dominate their reactions to tragedy and violence, keeping their traumatic energy fixated in their system where it becomes self-perpetuating. At the collective level, this takes on tragic proportions. Revenge perpetuates trauma and now victims become victimizers, adding to their problems and limiting their ability to reach peaceful and workable solutions to their conflicts.

The diplomatic service, the aid and humanitarian community, and the international community and media need to help groups or nations in turmoil. They can help them understand that seeking justice is different from seeking revenge, using defensive force is different from using retaliatory force, and expecting people to take responsibility for their actions is different from blame that leads to revenge. They need to be supported in the belief that they have the right to ask for justice and for validation of their suffering, and they can demand and receive help to seek both in constructive ways. Nations need help to understand that the difference between seeking revenge and seeking justice is a function of whether trauma is resolved or not; whether people are helped to release traumatic activation and regain control over their nervous system. With a balanced nervous system, people recuperate their ability to reason and base their actions on rational thought rather than fear or anger-driven impulsive reactions.

THE TRAUMA OF VICTIMIZERS

One of the most important and yet most difficult traumas to address is the trauma of victimizers (or perpetrators,) who are affected by trauma as much as their victims are. Most of the time, victimizers are also victims whose unresolved trauma and other circumstances turned into victimizers.

At the individual level, research showed that most hardcore criminals suffered from unresolved childhood trauma. At the collective level, an example from the second half of the 20th century is Rwanda's Hutus, who previously felt collectively victimized by the Tutsis under Belgian rule and committed genocide against them.

Collective victimizer trauma—the trauma of a group or nation of perpetrators of violence—leaves people's psyches even more traumatized and more vulnerable to re-enactment than 'collective victim trauma'. As an example, Germans in both World Wars have carried a double layer of trauma—the physical and emotional suffering of the initial unresolved trauma turned into violence, and the moral suffering of being the aggressor, which remains long after the trauma vortex passes.

Once the violence passes, the trauma of nations (or ethnic, religious and political groups) who have conducted belligerent acts must eventually be addressed and processed by those nations, as well as by the international community. International structures have been put into place to make people responsible for their past actions. However, when their traumatic emotional layers are not addressed, these groups remain vulnerable to trauma re-enactment; indicting them without healing only adds to this danger. They may not be able to resist the pull of their collective trauma vortex in times of crisis.

TRAUMATIC COLLECTIVE NARRATIVES

Trauma distorts group and national narratives

Nations (or groups) with unresolved trauma distort historical facts, focusing only on what was done to them and disregarding the part they played in the events. They blame and attribute to the "other" all evil motivations and design. Even when they significantly contributed to the conflict, they see themselves as righteous people, who have been wronged completely and with no responsibility to what happened to them. The conviction in their innocence blinds them to their own failings and makes them project all responsibility onto the "other." Passed on down the generations, traumatic narratives keep amplifying and exaggerating the suffering and the harm done to the group, acquiring mythical dimensions and rendering them more inflexible to reality-checks and to change.

The Pull of Traumatic Narratives

All militaries also need to become aware of the impact of traumatic narratives on their decisions. Military personnel need to be also aware, at the personal level, of the impact of trauma on their narratives and judgment during armed struggles or war.

Peacekeeping forces stationed in a foreign country must understand that they may easily be pulled in by the trauma vortex of the country where they are serving and align with its polarized beliefs and emotions. It is easy to be influenced by the trauma-distorted narratives of people we are helping resulting in the loss of objectivity and impartiality. There are several recent examples of peacekeeping forces abetting terrorist attacks.

NATIONAL TRAUMA VORTICES

There are many *collective trauma vortices* swirling around in the world today, seriously impacting several areas of the world. In the last two decades, many groups and a few nations have been triggered into a collective trauma vortex. They were confronted with a shared experience of gruesome and repetitive images of old traumas through the media or by present factors reminiscent of old traumas. Caught in their collective vortex, these groups and nations become easy prey to inflammatory slogans and primitive impulses. This results in calls for revenge, leading to striking-back behaviors, and mass violence, with some escalating to full genocide.

A mixture of currently unmet psychological and social needs added to previously unresolved trauma is fertile ground for a collective trauma vortex to gather strength. Tribal, ethnic, religious, political or economic struggles create high stress, keeping collective nervous systems in overdrive. They polarize and hijack emotional intelligence, push groups or nations to surrender to irrational and destructive behaviors. Previous victims become victimizers, perpetuating the cycle of victimization and pain.

The 9/11 attacks on New York City, Pennsylvania and Washington, DC in 2001, are an example of a single traumatic event that boomerangs into a world collective trauma. They are a perfect example of the multi-levels aspects of collective trauma. They have not only impacted the citizens of New York, Pennsylvania and Washington, DC directly, but also through the incessant media coverage, all of America and the entire world.

The unexpected success of the attacks further encouraged the trauma vortex of the attackers, deepening their conviction that their cause is God-ordained and validating the brutal means used. It also ignited the collective trauma of those groups and nations with a history of oppression or poverty, who felt vindicated by the attack on a nation that seemed invincible and previously impervious to collective pain. Furthermore, it activated the trauma vortex of the American people and eventually of the West, engaging them in the war against terror, and amplifying the "clash of civilizations" for Muslim fundamentalists.

At the international level, the world still lacks the awareness of the impact of collective trauma on the behavior and belief systems of all parties involved in a conflict and of the importance of misunderstood cross-cultural differences that ignite conflicts. Both of these lacunae may be partially responsible for the unexpected ramifications the war on terror took: an amplified response from the radical Islamic world; the tumult of the subsequent and still unresolved wars in Afghanistan and Iraq; Europe's response to Russia's renewed ambitions, and China's forays in Africa, the economic meltdown of Wall Street, etc. In addition, the play for oil and for economic interests among the different countries, the big powers, and the geographical blocs involved, further fueled the constant churning of all these collective vortices.

CONDITIONS PROPELLING A COLLECTIVE TRAUMA VORTEX

A collective trauma vortex takes time to develop, even when it appears to have erupted suddenly. Intervention is possible if we learn to recognize its initial signs.

Certain conditions help contribute to the unfolding of a collective vortex—such as difficult circumstances that frustrate people's ability to provide constructively for their basic needs and/or to fulfill their goals for self-improvement, meaning and progress. In addition, we can learn to identify and address several types of unresolved collective trauma—historical, cultural, religious and political—that, when re-awakened, contribute to collective dysfunction.

Circumstances Contributing to the Development of Collective Trauma

- Physical and emotional threat or economic stagnation
- Difficult life situations such as poverty and frustrated hopes; political and economic conditions that do not support growth and development
- Loss of cultural identity for native cultures exposed to a more dominant culture
- Retrigger of unresolved historical traumatic past, such as loss of land, political power, or empire; humiliation from defeat or from the rise of economic and technological superiority of a neighboring or competing nation
- Vulnerable and distorted societal self-concept derived from a poorly functioning society due to actual or past oppression, colonialism, racism, or slavery
- Particularly relevant to today's globalized world: fear of the loss of mores and of cultural fabric, loss of religious identity and mission, and threatened worldviews
- Major changes in the political system during the last ten years, creating instability and chaos

- Any change that endangers people's need for certainty and generates anxiety, such as disruption of group values, cultural traditions, and lifestyle due to rapid technological changes; amorphous threat to the group's established identity from cultural "soft" weapons such as music, films, and television programs selling tempting different life styles
- New learning that is happening too much, too fast, too soon, creating a sense of disintegration and/or destabilization
- Fear of annihilation linked to co-existence; threat to the group's identity, where its very existence and *raison d'être* seems inextricably associated to negating the other; and where the acknowledgment of the other is felt as an act of self-annihilation (specifically true in relation to religious, ideological, or land claims). The group's core identity (the essential, unchangeable self) is submerged by a constructed identity, derived from a negative comparison with others
- Feelings of shame and guilt over colonizer past
- Fear of conflict and of any violence, due to self-blame for recent violent past
- Having caused or having suffered from mass population transfers, burnings of towns and pogroms

Cultural Tendencies That Can Feed a Collective Trauma

- Strong cultural inclination and respect for authority
- A tradition of obedience to leaders
- History of violence where aggression is a time-honored, respected, and idealized way of handling conflict
- A historical mandate to enlarge the group's territory
- Culturally-embedded propensity to dictate one's religious, racial, ideological, or political values to others—recognizing the equality of the other and the validity of its experience brings into question the group's own interpretations of history, its ideology or its religious dogmas

- Embedded systematic discrimination against another group and its devaluation as separate and distinct from the collective identity, provoking a longing for "purity" and "cleansing"
- A low level of flexibility and adaptability in the culture
- Extreme relativism causing the loss and devaluation of one's own cultural or religious identity
- Too much flexibility and appeasement due to fear of perpetrator violence

The collective trauma vortex often turns inward in individualistic societies, where opposing parties within the culture adopt polarized positions against each other. They may also turn their anger towards their own culture as a whole. The reactions of their extremist factions, however, more closely parallel those in collective societies. The collective trauma vortex tends to turn outwards against other groups in collectivist societies as they value uniformity, stability of values, and most of all, social cohesiveness.

SIGNS OF A COLLECTIVE TRAUMA VORTEX

The following checklist of signs of collective trauma allows us to recognize (and potentially intervene) when a collective vortex is in action in groups or nations:

- Imposing the group's ethnicity, race, religion, or economic system over "the other"
- Creating closed systems, with a fiercely egocentric collective sense of self in relation to other groups
- Intolerance towards different or multiple worldviews and perspectives
- Adopting and surrendering to polarized thoughts and feelings, demanding isolation and disconnection from neighboring groups and groups in their midst
- Engaging in biased, prejudiced, and racist behavior

- Adopting a destructive collective pseudo-higher cause where individuals suspend their critical thinking and concern for their wellbeing
- Labeling and blaming "the others" for all their suffering and problems
- Distrusting anything originating from "the others"
- Manifesting xenophobia: forbidding, and destroying all religious, cultural, and artistic symbols of foreign influence
- Demonizing "the other;" portraying them as evil in literature, and in houses of worship
- Portraying them as incapable and unworthy of compassion
- Generalizing the actions of some to the whole group
- Dehumanizing "the other" through using visual and written media, song lyrics, caricatures, and propaganda to devalue their humanity
- Believing the destruction of "the other" will solve their problems
- Schooling children in hatred towards "the other"
- Adopting a belligerent language and inciting to violence
- Repeating , deepening and giving mythological characteristics to traumatic narratives
- Repressing free media: intimidating, threatening, imprisoning, exiling, or killing oppositional media professionals and intellectuals
- Promoting ethnic cleansing
- Using violence as a tool to recuperate a lost sense of control
- Encouraging and engaging killing, war, and genocide
- Victims act like victimizers

> **The trauma vortex is seductive and contagious**
>
> The collective trauma vortex is very seductive—blaming and finding scapegoats offers distressed people a psychological outlet. This focus on "the other" provides traumatized groups with the necessary glue to re-form groups that will provide connection and meaning and new social identity and world-view, even if done at the price of false hope.

COLLECTIVE BASIC NEEDS

Groups and nations, like individuals, have universal basic needs that must be met:

- Safety—physical, economic, emotional, and spiritual
- Autonomy
- Self-respect; positive self-image and identity; respect from others
- Validation of one's experience and reality
- Justice
- Competence, achievement, mastery, and empowerment
- Recognition, meaning, and a role in contributing to the world
- To be trusted and have trust in others

When people meet these psychological needs, they feel self-confident, capable, adequate, useful, and wanted in the world. When they cannot or do not meet these needs, they feel mediocre, inadequate, powerless and angry.

Traumatic events have also a much more devastating impact when these needs are not being met.

Trauma influences the way in which people meet their basic needs, distorting the priority and the intensity of those needs. Against a trauma background, frustrated needs acquire a more urgent and desperate quality, pushing people to try to fulfill them at any cost, meeting some of their needs to the exclusion of their other needs, and at the expense of other people's needs and in destructive ways.

Yet, there is a way out. Nations have served the healing vortex after war, such as with the American Marshall Plan after World War II. Nations have healed themselves, such as Germany and Japan, in response to the Marshall Plan.

In the next chapters, we explore how the military can contribute to helping people move out of the trauma vortex and the special dilemmas they encounter in this endeavor.

CHAPTER THIRTEEN

THE MEDIA'S ROLE

When referring to media, we mean traditional forms of media, i.e. newspapers, magazines, radio and T.V. broadcasts, both network and cable. They are still the only mass media concurrently accessed by millions of people. This is not to minimize the impact of all the new media outlets (Internet, blogs, websites, phone videos, personal satellites, etc.) but rather to address a specific media audience, professionals governed by a set of standards and following codes from professional organizations, as employees regulated by specific legalities, etc.

PREDOMINANT ROLE OF THE JOURNALIST

Journalists and their editors decide what to observe, where to go, what to report from what they observe, what questions to ask, not to ask, and how to describe what they are told. They decide the number of negative stories or positive stories they want to cover about a particular topic and event. They decide how much context to give and what words to use. What mood to evoke, what inferences to draw. The words they choose and the images they select subtly and not so subtly guide the reader or audience into a certain direction. It is the media that gives the content and perception about what's taking place.

Most media outlets, however, caught up in the continual vortex of reporting on tragedy and violence, are accused of amplifying and creating trauma with sensationalist coverage. They seem to inflict on the public a single-minded focus on violence. Nonetheless, accusing and blaming the media has not obtained and will not obtain the desired results. Asking the media to refrain from covering violence and tragedy is unlikely as well as undesirable; yet, it is still possible to develop a constructive dialogue with the media.

This is particularly important as the media plays now a special role during conflict and war. It has the power to change what happens in the arena of armed struggles. The language it uses can affect the public's reactions. Premature declarations of doom or catastrophic predictions such as, "They will be traumatized forever" deeply distress the public, and make it lose trust and hope. Seizing upon, or over-blowing politicians' premature declarations of victory or disastrous loss, can interfere with the successful conduct of war. The media's own premature assessments can affect the result of war. Military leaders, who take the time to engage in constructive dialogue with media professionals and help them cover both vortices, benefit the public and their military efforts in an important way.

Images of Carnage

Public pressure in the West has already convinced the media to develop guidelines regarding the depiction of details such as bodily remains or disposal of bodies, visual evidence of brutality and instruments of torture because of their disturbing effects on children and sensitive adults.

In the Middle East and other parts of the world, the media, however, continues to cover the gruesome details of war, mostly unaware of the generalized secondhand trauma they are inflicting on their viewers and creating further dangerous polarization that fuels conflict and war.

An Egyptian reporter in the US on a Daniel Pearl Foundation fellowship commented in a panel discussion that the Western and American media avoid covering the bloodiness of war and charred bodies. He stated the Middle Eastern media don't avoid such coverage and show it in full force. He was chiding members of the US media, completely unaware that the US decision not to show such details was deliberate, a result of understanding how it traumatizes the population. More importantly, he did not understand that one-sided coverage of war's atrocities without full context, polarizes audiences, keeping them in the trauma vortex, fueling anger and hatred, promoting more violence and maintaining the viewers in stuck conflict.

Indeed, the media has the power to heal or exacerbate trauma. A trauma-sensitive media can play a very important role in helping the public process the daily diet of tragedy and violence without surrendering hope. The media is in a unique position to facilitate widespread healing by informing the public about trauma's nature, characteristics and methods to heal it. For this, it must expand the scope of its mandate as reporters must balance coverage of tragedy and violence with news of coping, healing and helping gestures. This will add to the well-being of society, bringing calm and rationally-driven action.

MILITARY ENGAGEMENT OF THE MEDIA

Military innovations are indeed taking place over traditional reliance on firepower among conventional militaries and as we have seen earlier, psychologically oriented maneuvers such as learning the human terrain, becoming more cross-culturally aware, and co-opting the enemy are now employed. However, what still defines conventional militaries in the eyes of the public and of the media, is the strength of their fire power, and the number and sophistication of the weapons they possess. The images that represent them are tanks, uniforms, and soldiers marching in disciplined steps, impersonal and like automatons. These are the images that the military have to combat in the media wars taking place.

The American military has recently made inroads in engaging the media in constructive, responsible coverage by including embedded media and by humanizing its image.

Since the media has to focus inevitably on violence, it requires help from ROE-abiding militaries with information, direction and constructive guidelines to become a healing force and engage people's hope. It can do so by giving as much time to the healing vortex as to the trauma vortex; by giving as much coverage to heroism and caring for the wounded enemy as to the brutalities and humiliations of war.

The military must orient media to give as much coverage to heroism and caring for the wounded enemy as to the brutalities and humiliations of war, thus balancing the two vortices. The media can also show healing images when covering tragedy. It can show the many acts of kindness, compassion and service in times of collective tragedy. Reporting even small gestures of caring, doctors and nurses tending to the wounded enemy, soldiers carrying stranded people to safety or handing blankets to shivering victims can help communities reconnect with hope and overcome feelings of helplessness. Such reporting by the media can help build empathy and resilience in the public.

MEDIA PRESSURE ON THE MILITARY

The advent of televised global media has completely changed the nature of war. In most democratic nations, pervasive media scrutiny demands a new accountability and puts added pressure on both individual soldiers regarding their actions and the entire military regarding its decisions. While media scrutiny can keep in check the natural tendency in war to demonize the enemy, the conventional militaries find this scrutiny disconcerting, particularly when the media does not scrutinize their non-ROE-abiding adversaries. ROE-abiding militaries end up feeling that they often are not supported even by their own media.

Protecting Troops' Morale

In the eyes of the military, the media needs to understand how to protect the morale of the troops of conventional armies. It needs to understand the type of coverage that unwittingly promotes polarization and intolerance and turns a country against its own ROE-abiding military.

A ROE-abiding military can help the media avoid these results by enumerating, for example, its own efforts to diffuse its adversary's trauma vortex. It can report how it risks endangering its soldiers when it sends them into ground missions instead of aerial raids in order to minimize enemy collateral damage. It can demonstrate how it risks its troops to intervene against despotic leaders and protect civilian populations, such as in the Balkans.

The military can report efforts to protect an adversary population from its own internal trauma vortex, such as mediating between Shiites and Sunnis in Iraq, or mediating between fighting Christian sects during Easter in Old Jerusalem. This kind of coverage contributes to clearing misconceptions about the enemy, softening people's hatred and inflexibility.

It is also important for the military to emphasize the international guidelines it follows for prisoners when the media reveals exceptional cases of mistreatment and abuse. It must provide a contextual background to explain this abuse within the frame of the trauma vortex. This may avoid the exploitation of these abuses, where one event gets tagged and reported ad nauseum, distorting the actual events.

By advocating balanced coverage, military leaders protect their troops, develop public confidence in their actions and may actually contribute to a quicker resolution of the conflict.

THE MEDIA'S BENEFICIAL ROLE

The military has learned to co-opt some of the media. The military decision to allow embedded journalists cover the Iraq war helped educate the media on the perils of war with varying results. Embedded media ran the same risks as military personnel fighting terrorist warfare, thereby softening its approach to the military. This helped military personnel become more tolerant of media coverage.

Imbedded media such as Rick Atkinson, with then Major General David Petraeus' airborne division, opened up new vistas of the public's perception of media and the military. His book "*In the Company of Soldiers: a Chronicle of Combat,*" has proven beneficial in exploring the role of frontline reporting.

Alternatively, the media's investigative role was also a benefit for the military. The journalists' presence made military personnel avoid and resist behavior indicative of the trauma vortex. This scrutiny of the military puts pressure on them to fight according to ROE. In the current scenarios of usage of devastating weaponry and personnel's potentially traumatic impulsive reactions to terror and suicide attacks, the media can play a crucial role in helping the military to function ethically and minimize the abuses that traumatic stress may engender.

Media coverage, can indeed alert the military when they unwittingly slide towards the trauma vortex, such as in Abu Ghraib. The media also reports the military reality on the ground, which is sometimes different from the wishful thinking of governments, who through lack of accurate information, may endanger their troops unnecessarily.

Of course, media's sensationalism can also overdo the coverage and report out of context, hurting the military, its country and its just cause.

THE PULL OF VIOLENCE

The media has taken an unprecedented role in the present armed struggles and political power maneuvers. Most of these struggles are more value-driven than about physical survival (with certain exceptions). These armed struggles have invited more temptation for bias and advocacy from the media.

While media personnel are schooled to be objective observers and reporters of events, in reality they affect the outcome of events through their coverage, often merely through their presence.

By choosing to focus on violence as the most newsworthy event rather than the overall analysis of the situation, the media unwittingly helps create "media-directed warfare," i.e., violent actions directed specifically at the media's cameras to gain attention, spread inflammatory slogans, and create fear. Non-conventional groups are especially prone to using these tactics.

Giving these groups airtime gives them credibility and gives more power to their rallying calls to violence. This can directly affect a nation's military in its efforts to defend its population.

It also creates a schism between the media and the military, adding stress to military personnel. They see themselves as defending their countries against a merciless enemy, but unsupported and blamed by their own media. This kind of situation can be more psychologically devastating than the traumas they encounter on the battlefield as it seems to invalidate their sacrifices, as we will see later with the Vietnam experience.

They are at times also confronted by people who are politically-minded. The soldiers, often not as versed in geo-politics, may be unable to verbally defend themselves or their military for carrying out political orders. He may begin to doubt the nobility of his service and begin to suffer emotionally.

In today's era of ambiguous warfare, the media does not always succeed in its goal to be objective. It may be manipulated to turn battle outcomes into political issues, regardless of the reality of military actions on the ground. Indeed, there have been situations while ground battles are won, media wars are being lost, creating false realities and encouraging more violence. Today, events are happening so fast and perceptions formed so quickly, that media manipulation can lead it to report unsubstantiated facts and false sources as truth and change public perception in a negative way.

In addition to influencing events of collective proportion, the reporting of unsubstantiated claims and uncorroborated facts and numbers affects media credibility. While most of unsubstantiated claims and facts are eventually shown to be false, the irreparable damage they cause was done and the course of history altered.

Such an example is a 2002 report by the BBC that 800 civilians were massacred in Jenin by the Israelis. Further inflated reports of up to 3000 victims amplified the hatred against the Israelis around the world. The actual number of casualties was later verified to be in the 50s and almost all of them were combatants. The truth caused the British media to retreat from its "massacre" language and later neutrally reported that Palestinian authorities made unsubstantiated claims of a wide-scale massacre. This fact was not widely reported by the international media. Thus it did not correct people's perception. Moreover, it became the framework for the calculated spreading of more unsubstantiated facts in the 2006 Hezbollah/Israel war and other events, hugely reinforcing the Arab versus Israel collective trauma vortex, and weakening efforts for peace.

The warning of how the media can be misused does not seem to have sufficiently registered.

MEDIA AND MILITARY PROPORTIONALITY

Proportionality is another issue for the media. It is easy (and understandable) that when supplied with powerful emotional images by non-conventional combatants the media falls prey to such manipulation. When conventional armies use their full "shock and awe firepower they kill civilians in the process and cause much physical destruction. The images of destruction and the number of deaths are emotionally jarring even when the cause is just. On the other hand, insurgencies, by targeting civilians (especially women and children) create psychological terror but kill relatively small numbers compared to conventional armies, which allows these non-state, non-conventional combatants to successfully cultivate their underdog image.

As long as it is driven by the media, this psychological war will continue to work in favor of terror and insurgencies, further polarizing all trauma vortices involved. A concerted effort to understand how the media is being used must be made. Such an analysis is needed when the media is not reporting in the heat of action.

Just cause of war would normally be enough of a guideline to inform the issue of proportionality in the media. However, the value-driven nature of present armed struggles may require a more thorough analysis of the different collective trauma vortices affecting all involved (see Chapter 15).

Still, just cause of war can also be applied. For example, the declared and repeated intentions of each party must carry weight. Those which are threatening must be understood as coming from the trauma vortex, but must also be taken seriously. This awareness can help the media override the manipulation of facts and numbers or the use of emotional images in the immediacy of reporting on violence. For example, holding non-conventional groups (or states) responsible for prior provocative declarations or non-ROE abiding actions, which caused retaliation and resisting the psychological manipulation of images, can diminish the amplification of their trauma vortex.

At the same time, non conventional combatants need to be offered international forums where they can express political grievances and media representation that does not rely only on violence to report the messages of their unmet needs.

The media must learn to recognize when attempts to meet universal basic needs are trauma vortex-driven. This type of needs is expressed in destructive ways, and as inflexible demands. Their priority is also distorted, making people meet a few needs at the expense of their other needs and at the expense of other people's needs.

When inflexible expression of basic needs are identified as such and helped to process, this type of intervention can bring healing and resolution, contrary to the usual unconscious tendency of being pulled in by people's traumatic narratives and their destructive expression.

MEDIA'S SUPERVISORY ROLE

The devastating power of today's weaponry requires the moral restraint of its use. The traditional culture of war and the mystique of the soldier as hero have drastically changed. Sometimes, the image of the military as a brutalizing show of force (tanks, airplanes and spectacular explosions) seems to replace the historic notion of the hero soldier, with the less powerful enemy often portrayed as the underdog. At times, military technological might is portrayed by the media as evil, a portrayal that often overrides just cause of war, military use of defensive force or even the use of force to free people from oppression.

An example is the US intervention in the Balkans. Although the US intervened to save the lives of a Muslim population that was overwhelmed, they were still perceived as overbearing and belligerent because they used overwhelming force.

Benefits of Media Objectivity

In times of war or armed struggles, it is thus imperative to help the media maintain a resolute intention to serve objectively and be a helpful force. For example, it can help diminish the damage of war on the collective psyche by reporting, in addition to stories of abuse, military humanitarian efforts. This is especially true in times of ambiguous wars, where conventional armies are fighting against non-conventional, non-state combatants operating among a population itself not at war. Reporting humanitarian efforts gives hope and reassurance, diminishing the manipulation of virulent feelings against the foreign troops instead of inflaming an already aroused collective nervous system.

GAGING THE DEPTH OF THE TRAUMA VORTEX

It is sometimes hard for anyone—media or military—to imagine that a group completely entrenched in a violent trauma vortex can access its own healing vortex. In those times, the only way to stop such a vortex seems to be the use of strong defensive force. However, it is crucial for both military and media to hold onto the possibility of healing, even while the military is engaged in war. Holding this possibility for the groups caught in the trauma vortex with deeds and words (for example, avoiding using demonizing, polarizing words and retaliatory threats) can help speed the process of getting them out of it.

We have seen many groups and nations eventually step out of their trauma vortex, e.g., Japan and Germany after World War II. Some vortices do remain dormant to be reawakened decades or centuries later and some have been stopped only by formidable and compelling force.

The Media's Influence

In war, truth is the first casualty.
—Aeschylus, Greek tragic dramatist
(525 BC–456 BC)

DANGER DURING WARTIME

The media must follow specific guidelines to be able to report events factually.

- Pose the tough and difficult questions
- Test people's logic and action at every point
- Remain objective, and retain your skepticism
- Explore and cover gaps of credibility
- Denounce and aggressively oppose intimidation of news organization and threats against them
- Resist temptations of giving sympathetic coverage in return for exclusive interviews   and to discount sources, who are less likely to deliver in the future in favor of sources that deliver regular updates
- Resist out of context, repetitive, and obsessive coverage
- Take the time to substantiate claims of facts and numbers. Learn from previous deceptions

Specific obstacles for media objectivity include:

- When war or conflict is taking place in their own country, they may become part of the trauma vortex they are covering. They cannot and should not be expected to harm the military endeavors of their country unless these endeavors are hurting their own population, e.g., using their own civilians and children as shields

- When they and their audience are sympathetic to one side of the conflict

- When they and their audience are prejudiced against one side of the conflict

Manipulation, Bias and Advocacy

Non-conventional insurgencies and combatants are fighting asymmetrical battles and thus understand that they have to use different tactics. Besides the psychological terror of unexpected suicide-bombings targeting civilians and IEDs used against military and diplomatic personnel, they have perfected the use of the media in support of their causes. They understand in a way that conventional armies with powerful weapons have yet to come to grip with, the fact that a major portion of the battle is taking place through the media, and not by the number of inflicted casualties or captured territories. Media images have become paramount, and wars are being fought in the minds of the people, through public perception and not on the battlefields, giving an unprecedented role to the media.

However, over the last few years, media bias, media advocacy and media manipulations in war have become such a standard fare, that special organizations were created to monitor the truth of media accounts. Organizations have been also been created under the guise of media watch to continue misrepresentation and discrediting process. Furthermore, non-western media finds it natural not to differentiate between advocacy and fact-finding.

Adding to this are all the new media outlets that spread more disinformation, such as populist blogs, one-sided advocacy radio programs, satellite dishes, videophones, laptops, partisan bloggers and websites with polarizing rhetoric. They use little fact-based information, spreading unsubstantiated numbers of casualties and false innuendos.

By the time this misinformation gets cleared up, it has already permeated and brainwashed the collective memory and fuelled the trauma vortex of large populations.

The analysis of media manipulation, bias and advocacy in politics and war is just being advocated by cutting-edge media organizations. Yet, little has been noted about non-state organizations which use sophisticated media manipulation and not enough analysis has been made about it by most media and human rights organizations. Militaries aware of the media's vulnerable areas can be more efficient in addressing them with media organizations, as well as creating counter interventions.

Examples of Media Manipulation

The media is sometimes given press tours by non-state groups of non-conventional combatants of bombed sites in their area, where they go through a "dog-and-pony show," according to some reporters. This term expresses careful staging, misrepresenting destroyed areas out of context of the general area being left intact, and strict control over when and with whom reporters could have interviews. Many reporters acquiesce to this kind of interviews, because they catch an "inside look" into this secretive group. They stage funerals and even fights for the camera's benefit, disseminating staged or manipulated images and videos; even well-intended reporters are susceptible to the manipulation and unwittingly fuel the collective trauma vortex on all sides.

In addition, some of these groups use blatant censorship, threats to the media, and intimidation by using videos of beheadings of media members.

Journalistic ethics and independent verification may also be circumvented by a phenomenon described as the "halo effect," wherein journalists simply reprint NGO reports without question or verification. By foregoing skepticism and fact-finding steps, journalists tend to ignore the bias from these NGOs and repeat the statements as fact, unwittingly fuelling all trauma vortices involved. While they may question an unreliable person, they often fail to question an unreliable organization.

Examples of Media Bias

Doctored videos of events have been created and broadcasted all over the world by advocacy journalists to misinform, polarize and inflame passions. Even when some people, with much hard and diligent work proved the videos to have been doctored, the media refused to take those errors on and repair them. The damage has been done anyway; collective trauma vortices have been fuelled, triggering youth riots, prejudice, violence and killings.

Another example is the use of doctored photographs. Reuters withdrew almost a thousand photographs by Lebanese freelance photographer Anan Hajj, after it was discovered that he digitally added and darkened smoke spirals in his photographs of an Israeli attack on Beirut. Pictures were published of the same woman, mourning in two different pictures by two different photographers two weeks apart. Military counter intervention would include satellite filming to disproof doctored media material.

Examples of Media Advocacy

Another important potential pitfall for the media is a moral manipulation of the principle of the 'equivalency syndrome,' whereby it ends up equating defensive with aggressive use of force, giving airtime and validity to aggressive intentions and inflammatory slogans as if they were just normal.

Another issue is media consistency in reporting. Journalists sometimes are faced with having to balance their role as objective journalists with their role of loyal citizens of their countries. They have to take personal, national, and patriotic considerations into account. Free national media will support the war efforts and government goals of its country if it seems that the war is justified. Indeed, journalists have reported feeling they were required to postpone criticism and moreover did not have to apologize or feel abashed about their patriotism.

However, if their countries seem to be loosing the war or things do not seem to be going well, media criticism emerges despite the potential harm it poses to military objectives. This is especially true when the tone of the coverage creates polemics, polarization, and demoralization, at a time when the military personnel and the public need all strengthening.

Coverage that seems to be for the sake of coverage is harmful for the public. Journalistic criticism can be done in a helpful manner. Constructive criticism as opposed to "expository criticism" may be the answer. By pointing to topics of importance or relevance in a constructive way rather than in an adversarial and confrontational manner, the media creates objective yet patriotic reporting.

While media professionals worry they may be too uncritical of their government, most often, soldiers and veterans believe that the media is actually uncritical of itself.

Examples of Media's Impact

Uncensored and overly negative coverage turns the public against the war and the military. An example of media's influence on war is the coverage of the Vietnam War. Public perception about the progress of the war was shaped by the media. Many veterans believe that television news dramatically changed its framework for reporting the war after the Tết Offensive which dramatically impacted public and political opinion.

For them, reports of the Tết Offensive were a major turning point in the war, and a political and media disaster for the US. Coverage of the US led-massacre at My Lai, without reporting the context or referring to the Bui massacre (an entire village massacred by the Viet Cong), damaged the image of the US Army. The failure to report the enemy's policy of committing atrocities, and their exponentially higher number (1:1000) blamed the military, turned public political opinion against the war, causing America to withdraw, and leaving a taste of failure. Whether it was the result of a lack of resolve of the country or the portrayal of the enemy as victims of American brutality, veterans were outraged.

They also believe that sometimes, journalists conveyed negativity in a deliberate way. They felt much damage was done to them, as they were portrayed as baby-killers and psychopaths with their flashbacks when they returned home. Many veterans still report being haunted by the image of Jane Fonda mounting an anti-aircraft gun in 1972, and broadcasting anti-American propaganda over Radio Hanoi. Many claimed that Fonda's anti-war activities were "tantamount to being wounded." The Vietnam polemic has still not been resolved and seems to be part of the American collective trauma vortex, with on-going consequences.

MONITORING MEDIA BIAS

The military can monitor whether the media has a bias towards the trauma or the healing vortexes using the following questions as a guideline:

- Is there a balance in the coverage of the trauma vortex and the healing vortex?

- Is coverage of the military harming their efficiency or safety? Is it blaming them for misguided governmental decisions?

- Is the media coverage eliciting military defensiveness or ethical pursuit?

- Is coverage encouraging copycat phenomenon?

Once aware of the pull of the trauma vortex on media personnel, the military can insist that the media continue to inform the public of military humanitarian efforts on the frontline, showing how personnel acts to minimize destruction through the use of precise targeting and house-to-house searches instead of indiscriminate carpet bombing. They can request that the media avoid the repetition of the same disturbing images. Repetition drives the image deep into the psyche and puts people at risk for flashbacks, obsessive thoughts, feelings of dread and exaggerated fears. It is better to show the public a variety of images and better still to see healing images juxtaposed to traumatic ones.

The military can also suggest that the media resist the pull of horror and sensationalism, and refrain from distorting the bigger picture when it gives disproportionate coverage to certain events. The media can balance the airtime given to terror by additionally covering all failed attempts, or by describing the cost of the terror on non-conventional groups' own people.

Moreover, the media can speculate on other means to reach one's goals without terror and violence, and the way they make such goals illegitimate, just by asking questions that "seed the field" with the healing vortex.

THE MEDIA AND COLLECTIVE TRAUMA VORTEX

When covering a collective trauma vortex, do media professionals objectively report it? Do professionals from opposite sides of the political spectrum check and abide by the facts they report? Many errors can occur when the media covers war and other politically charged conflicts. Taking the following steps can help you react more responsibly to their errors:

- Realize that the observer of any event affects the event itself. The media influences stories just by its presence, by the act of observing and reporting. The military can help the media and the public redefine media objectivity.

- Be wary of media speculation about political conflicts. Errors are almost inevitable, as journalists must report events before all the information is available. In an age where the media is often used as political and psychological weapons and where media speculation can have lethal consequences, the accuracy of military information plays a crucial role in minimizing these errors.

- Call attention to media reporting that instinctively idealizes the underdog against images of overwhelming military power, notwithstanding the justness of a military action.

- Stay open to coverage of political and military conflicts that humanizes both sides because it will diminish everyone's trauma vortex and help people reconnect with each other's humanity—the loss of which is the first immediate by-product of war. Humanizing both sides means showing pain and suffering and describing the life, goals, wants and unfulfilled needs of each side. However, it is understandably an almost impossible task to ask from soldiers subjected to the war asymmetries cited above.

- Keep an objective eye on the beliefs, ideologies, and worldviews of your country and of the enemy, even if the media shows a biased view. Collective trauma engages entire populations in viewing the "other" either as uniformly dangerous or not seriously dangerous even when they are indeed dangerous. By resisting blind attraction for one ideology, we encourage groups to face and move through their own suffering instead of acting it out.

- Resist media coverage slanted with emotionally evocative words and avoid accepting journalists' opinions or views as facts, even when they are on your side. Watch out for propaganda. Get thorough information on the issues. Help the media gather the facts to differentiate between protective and defensive forces versus aggressive or imperialistic ones.

- Help the media become aware of misleading temptations for moral equivalency. Try to read coverage that reflects the views of all sides involved. This requires everyone to overcome prejudices and intolerance.

THE MEDIA'S NEW ROLE

Rules of engagement are an important factor in the media battle. Conventional nation-state democracies, still reeling from the bloody wars of the 20th century, have held themselves to high standards of behavior on the battlefield. Non-conventional non-state groups of combatants and autocratic nation-states are using these standards to hamstring these democracies' ability to defend them; the international media must learn how to hold non-ROE-abiding combatants to the same standards as those who do abide by ROE.

There is more awareness in the media field about the changes that have taken place and about the unprecedented connection between the press, politics, and public policy, albeit it is far from being a generalized effort yet. The challenge for journalists, who take their responsibility seriously about covering asymmetrical warfare, especially in this age of the Internet, is new, overwhelming and frightening. The challenges go beyond admitting to, identifying and resolving issues of media manipulation, bias and advocacy that interfere with the objective reporting of the truth. Most of all, the media must become fully cognizant of its power to feed or to help heal collective trauma. Media personnel must fully embrace a role they were not prepared for—that they become a more active and conscious tool for healing.

CHAPTER FOURTEEN

THE DILEMMA OF ROE

We have used the terms Rules of Engagement (ROE) as a general term to illustrate the combination of concepts addressing the ethics of war—Rules of Warfare, Military Ethics, Purity of Arms, the International Law of Land Warfare, the Law of Nations (the international norms which apply to all states), the Law between Peoples (treaties and agreements among sovereign nations), and the international humanitarian law. They refer, in general, to the sets of laws that regulate the conduct of armed hostilities in order to mitigate the effect of violent conflicts, and protect civilians, prisoners of war and the wounded or sick. They constitute the restrained use of weapons and force while carrying out missions only to the extent required for accomplishing them, without undue harm to others and to self.

For our stated purpose, "conventional militaries" or "conventional armies" refer to those who subscribe to ROE and "unconventional forces," or "unconventional combatants," refer to those who do not respect ROE.

It is beyond the scope of this book to address the many factors that influence the decision-making process in regard to the setting of ROE. This chapter attempts to address the complexity of the Ethics of Warfare only as it applies to the emotional well-being of military personnel obligated to follow ROE while fighting against an enemy who does not.

The following sentence illustrates the core issue of the problems we are addressing and that are at the heart of many emotional reactions in military personnel.

"Which is more correct? To suffer the killings of the best of our fighters to prevent the slaughter of enemy villagers and be the most moral army in the world, or to wipe out the villages that serve as hideouts for terrorists to save the blood of our sons and be considered less moral? . . ."

Rafi Ginat, editor of the daily Yediot Aharonot, July 28 (The Jerusalem Report, 9-4-2006).

ROE: THE NEW FACE OF WAR

Designed to protect civilians during wartime, all these codes condemn indiscriminately unleashed deadly force, which causes considerable collateral damage against non-combatant civilians.

The quote from *Military Ethics*, by Kasher, summarizes the spirit of ROE: "Soldiers will use their weapons and force to the extent necessary for subduing the enemy and will exercise restraint in order to avoid causing undue harm to human life, person, dignity, and property, especially helpless dependants, during war and everyday security operation in armistice and peacetime."

Today's modern warfare poses enormous ethical problems and often impossible choices about ROE. Instituted to make conflict less brutal, ROE sometimes create situations where war becomes a tangle of strategic, legal, and moral issues that impact the psychological well being of soldiers.

ROE-abiding conventional militaries are often confronted in armed struggles by non-state enemies, who do not respect ROE. These non-conventional combatants are fighting asymmetrical battles and are using different tactics. Besides the psychological terror of unexpected suicide-bombings targeting civilians and IEDs used against military and diplomatic personnel, they have perfected the use of the media in support of their causes. They understand in a way that conventional armies focused on augmenting and perfecting powerful weapons have yet to grasp, that a major portion of the battle is taking place through the media, not by the number of inflicted casualties or captured territories. Media images have become paramount and wars are being fought in the minds of the people, through public perception and not on the battlefields.

These insurgencies use their disrespect for ROE as part of their strategy to shackle conventional ROE-abiding armies and flaunt their disregard for humanitarian guidelines even towards their own people. They pose a real dilemma to ROE-abiding militaries when they claim it to be religiously sanctioned to not only sacrifice their own lives, but to also endanger their own civilians purposefully to exploit the ethical rules of conventional militaries to demoralize and defeat them.

In the words of Navy Seal "J.K.," who fought in Iraq: "The toughest enemy to fight is the one who truly believes that God is on his side, as he is ready to cut with a knife the same hand which just helped save him from certain death."

ROE-abiding soldiers are also restricted from causing unnecessary harm or offense when dealing with local enemy populations at roadblocks or in house searches. This often frustrates their ability to seize objectives, makes them lose their fighting edge when their adversaries hide behind civilians, and puts them at more risk, pulling them in the trauma vortex.

PRINCIPLES OF JUST WAR

The international community has accepted a series of principles related to the moral discussion of war, some of which we will explore briefly in the context of the stress they place on soldiers.

We will concern ourselves only with those principles that impact soldiers' emotional well being and affect their actions. There are eight principles of just war, such as legitimate authority (the authority to declare a war) just cause, last resort (everything else has been attempted to resolve the problem), right intention (for self-defense and not for revenge), chances of success, macro-proportionality (refers to the question of whether the positive effects on one front morally justify the negative effects on another, in the overall decision to take military action, micro-proportionality (the same principle as above, applied to specific military actions), and distinctions (between military and nonmilitary targets).

The issue of distinction may be the more potentially traumatic one for soldiers. In terms of international law, when they are in uniform, concerns for their own safety come last, including after enemy civilian population; and they are held accountable. Often what is lost in the media's understanding is that these rules also require soldiers to act to save human life, including their own, and endanger themselves or others only in support of their military mission.

In today's warfare, however, conventional militaries find themselves having to choose between using what others may consider as indiscriminate firepower to save their soldiers and risk more civilian "collateral damage," or risk their soldiers' lives to avoid civilian casualties.

The morale of conventional military personnel strictly held to ROE is deeply affected by the asymmetry of non-conventional guerilla type warfare fought without ROE. When comrades die due to the added risks of ROE related restrictions, soldiers become more vulnerable to the pull of the trauma vortex, feeling defeated, angry, mistrusting and betrayed, besides feeling shackled from accomplishing their goals.

Beyond the dilemma of following international law, ROE-abiding personnel face the even more poignant dilemma: following their own moral compass. What do you do in the face of combatants purposefully exposing their own civilians to your enemy attacks, in order to exploit the images of destruction to polarize their population and mobilize the media, when these deaths weigh heavily on you?

Eyal Ben-Reuven, 2006

Deputy to OC Northern Command Maj.-Gen. Udi Adam was quoted speaking about the collateral damage in the war against Hezbollah in the *International Jerusalem Post* (6-12 July 2007) article, "Escaping the quagmire:" "I am still bothered by my decision to O.K. heavy artillery fire in a village from which Hezbollah fired *Katyushas* on our civilian population." At first, Adam held off the heavy artillery fire, but having lost some of his soldiers in a previous village encounter, he changed his strategy and called for an aerial attack prior to entering the village. "My conscience bothers me. But once again, if you ask me whether I would do it again, the answer is yes."

A NEED FOR DIALOGUE

It may be that these issues need to be addressed collectively, involving all the parties interested in assuring the protection of civilians on all sides, diminishing military trauma and facilitating conflict resolution. It may mean think tanks composed of military personnel, media organizations, diplomats and NGOs, as well as international forums—those sectors that have the power to fuel or diminish collective trauma vortices.

A dialogue between these distinct bodies must be focused on stopping the manipulation through the media of ROE against ROE-abiding militaries, that helps non conventional groups to gain traction in the psychological war of terror being waged. This dialogue may produce solutions outside of the box, diminishing the psychological war of terror and better assuring the protection of civilian populations.

In media wars, tactical victories do not matter significantly. While many ROE-abiding commanders have warned enemy civilian populations of their eminent attacks, in order to minimize civilian losses, their efforts were not covered by the media, thus forfeiting a perfect opportunity to engage the collective healing vortex.

These commanders believe that collective clarity, supported by the media, of the right to defend one's people against focused aggression may disarm a trauma vortex-driven use of purposefully orchestrated "collateral damage," ultimately protecting civilians on all sides. When this clarity is obscured by biased reporting, the civilian populations are held hostage to the collective trauma vortex. By holding nations bound to ROE to impossibly high standards when they are fighting unconventional combatants, the media risks turning ROE into a self-defeating measure and fail all children and civilian populations ROE is meant to protect.

Thus, holding non-conventional combatants responsible for the destruction wrought upon their population (they use their civilian sites—including schools and hospitals—as launching sites for attacks, storage for weapons and as shields) is one way of diffusing a collective trauma vortex. This stance denies them the psychological weapon of using images of dead children and women as proof of enemy brutality and presenting themselves as the underdog. Besides helping soldiers feel that their efforts and sacrifice are valued, this will ultimately protect enemy civilian populations from planned harm.

On another note, war atrocities—going outside the accepted standards of war—happen in all armed struggles and must be addressed by the military. However, the media's approach in terms of engaging the collective healing vortex or at least not amplifying the collective trauma vortex, must cover stories of abuse within the context of quantity, intention, and accountability within the specific armed forces. Media coverage must avoid lashing unto these incidents as if it were the entire military or military policy, thus fueling the collective vortices involved.

Other military rules are being exploited. Military absolute commitment to the safety and rescue of its personnel helps soldiers feel safe and valued. The policy of "leave no wounded or dead behind" reassures soldiers the military will do every thing in its power to care for them and helps them stay self-regulated. These expectations within conventional army ranks are today used to kidnap soldiers and blackmail their governments. Again, the manipulative use of military culture by the enemy creates another area of threat and of psychological stress in soldiers, which they need to be able to navigate well.

For example, the capture of the Israeli Sgt. Gilad Shalit in a cross-border raid by Hamas launched from Gaza and the inability of the government to secure him three years later, have received persistent media coverage. Presented as a lack of dedication by Israeli authorities to its soldiers' safety, it has impacted some young people now unwilling to join the military.

In summary, understanding what amplifies the trauma vortex will give better tools to help diffuse it. This is a cutting-edge role for the media (See for more details the *Guide for the Media*) as well as for international organizations *(Guide for Diplomats and NGOs)*.

BENEFITS OF ROE

Rules of engagement have become stricter under the media's live scrutiny of battlegrounds, creating more stress for personnel. Following ROE, which requires discipline, unit pride, and professionalism, can, on the other hand, mitigate war's impact after service and guide personnel towards their healing vortex.

The successful application of ROE can be enhanced with SE®. The ability to access or recover self-regulation—by discharging powerful emotions instead of acting them out—is the way to assure the capacity to follow ROE.

Furthermore, ROE can guide on-going efforts of conventional militaries to perfect self—defense tactics while minimizing the use of aggressive force.

Path for a Clear Conscience

Many returning war veterans feel guilt and shame over having killed and/or having enjoyed killing. War is a dirty business. It is often a source of uncontrollable feelings, spurring action driven by fear, adrenaline, and intoxicating power. Combatants are prey to an incredible array of feelings that civilians cannot possibly comprehend.

Somatic Experiencing® helps veterans move out of this haunting trauma vortex, and differentiate between feelings and acting out.

ROE, along with the help of a self-regulated nervous system is part of the answer for not acting out.

As American Army captain Tim Wright serving in Baghdad wrote in an article in *Infantry Magazine:* "The new ways of war may well offer possibilities for soldiers to make the effort of not being debased or degraded by war." Yet, the challenge to lead a moral war under these new conditions is truly great. Wright further writes: "That's the tough thing about this job, if you f*** up, sometimes people will die. And people will die on both sides."

In many current armed struggles, military personnel confront the inherent contradiction of going to war against the enemy while having to understand and empathize with it at the same time. To be culturally sensitive and understanding of one's enemy puts an added psychological burden on military personnel, as they may still have to kill this enemy in war. But the ability to self-regulate on an ongoing basis with SE® gives them the tools to handle this type of stress. Furthermore, with more control over their feelings of anger, they can open up to meeting civilians and understanding and enjoying the culture from closer, and in turn be more accepted by them.

ROE are also a better guarantee for soldiers' well being after the war. The challenge of having to eventually reconcile with an enemy after a war is over remains. Military personnel, who fought a war with a neighboring country, will have to deal with living side-by-side after the impact of losses on both sides. Those who fought far from their country will go back to a far away home, but with their minds and psyches also imprisoned by the ghosts they left behind. ROE accompanied with self-regulation seems the path for soldiers' well being. Chapter 15 further explores the possibility of going beyond ROE and contains guidelines to engage the collective healing vortex.

CHAPTER FIFTEEN

•

THE MODERN MILITARY: HEALING COLLECTIVE TRAUMA

"War is just the extension of politics by other means.
You call in the military when diplomacy fails."
—Air Force Commander

This long-held reality is changing. The military's role seems to be encompassing many diverse and new aspects. Including the concepts of collective trauma vortex and healing vortex may make a significant difference in military success.

Collective trauma vortices have become potentially so destructive that conventional militaries now understand that they cannot engage in war anymore without an assessment of all emotional, psychological and cultural factors involved, and of how military interventions strengthen or diminish the enemy's trauma vortex. This chapter explores the different issues to consider and the combinations of skills—strength, ethics, diplomacy and psychological and cultural understanding—that will enable conventional armies to diffuse collective trauma vortices and engage their healing.

There are two parts to this chapter: The work that militaries have to do regarding the pull of the trauma vortex on their own military personnel and the work they have to do regarding the pull of the trauma vortex on their adversaries.

PULL OF THE TRAUMA VORTEX

The military sector is particularly vulnerable to being pulled into its adversary's collective trauma vortex. The degradation and humiliation of Iraqi prisoners at Abu Ghraib in Iraq by some American soldiers is a good example of the collective trauma vortex in action. The American soldiers' behavior is understandable from the point of view of the trauma vortex. They were enraged by the actions of terror-based warfare and unpredictable bombings. Such feelings may have driven some of the soldiers to demonize and dehumanize their enemy, sacrificing ROE and their own Army's goals and reputation.

Indeed, the broad media dissemination of the debasement of Abu Ghraib's Iraqi prisoners further fueled the collective trauma of the Muslim worlds and the worldwide media criticism against America. This trauma vortex weakened the American military image at home and abroad, and sidestepped its successes. In Chapter 13 we address more specifically media-related issues.

Shock and Awe

Conversely, the use of overpowering military might may contribute in amplifying collective trauma. "Shock and awe" seems to trigger a pervasive sense of fear and helplessness in others—allies and adversaries alike—pushing them to use all possible means to bring disarray to their superior adversary (or ally) even at their own expense. It becomes a psychological war with deadly consequences.

Pulverizing Force

In a documentary on Al Jazeera television, a moderate Yemini journalist, who deeply disliked Saddam Hussein, watched the images of the first few days of the 2003 Iraq War in disbelief and dismay.

"My God, what happened to the strongest Arab Army? It was wiped out in just a few days" he said as he looked in disbelief and dismay. He did not care for Saddam but he did care that a military force pulverized the most powerful Arab Army in just a few days.

The First Gulf War in 1991 left the Arab world in shock, from which they had not yet recovered. These unresolved feelings deeply affected the Iraq War. Again, a foreign power destroyed an Arab Army in a matter of a few days. During the First Gulf War, the military action was in the defense, and at the request of another Arab state. The next time, the invading forces were targeting a tyrant whom many Arabs feared and disliked. Nevertheless, the appalling symbolism of a foreign power overwhelming a member of the Umma was not lost on radical Muslim Arab fundamentalists, who used these 1991 unresolved issues as a tool to recruit and mobilize more fighters to their Jihad.

While modern weapons create feelings of overwhelming powerlessness in the enemy, paradoxically the same feeling of powerlessness can be felt by military personnel using it, as well as by the populations subjected to it. Handling and utilizing overwhelming force engenders traumatic reactions in some soldiers. Addressing feelings of powerlessness and their related issues during military training and strategy sessions builds personnel resiliency, leading to a better safeguard of soldiers and populations alike.

Processing these feelings/issues works on another level. While war inevitably creates or amplifies individual and collective trauma, military personnel with healthy self-regulation are better equipped to stop its amplification. The military can keep the humanity of the enemy in mind, thus avoiding fuelling collective trauma or committing atrocities. In addition, self-regulation allows for better understanding of the other, a capacity which may lead to transformative attitudes on the other side, turning collective war trauma vortices into seeds for future peace and cooperation.

Indeed, awareness of the others' collective trauma vortex and of the existence of its healing vortex makes it easier to follow ROE, and commit not to harm unnecessarily lives, bodies, dignity and property. It promotes attention to the adversaries' dignity, religious symbols and the honor of their women. It seems that more experience with this new type of warfare will yield more creative ways of engaging the enemy's healing vortex in the future.

Today, ignoring the characteristics of the adversaries' trauma vortex -and their capacity to be in the healing vortex—will backfire and create more violence. Even the use of justifiable defensive force, if it unwittingly disrespects or humiliates opponents, automatically amplifies the trauma vortex, fueling hatred and increasing resistance.

An increased number of polarized groups are gaining worldwide attention. Many of these groups garner the Internet and global media in order to mobilize dispirited youth. A nation's security goals and efforts for peace can be helped through the combination of military strategies, diplomatic interventions, and incentives founded on cross-cultural understanding that engage the adversaries' healing vortex.

There are also times when groups are so deeply caught in the trauma vortex that they have become too mistrustful, paranoid, inflexible and hateful to let anyone engage their healing vortex. They can only be stopped by force. In such cases, relying on the healing vortex and not fighting for a definitive victory can be too costly.

HEALING VORTEX-INSPIRED STRATEGIES

Modern conventional armies are currently engaged in conflicts whose resolution is not in the foreseeable future, and which involve forces other than these armies and their non conventional combatants. Many of these conflicts are fought against the backdrop of religious and political claims of hegemony rather than the need for physical survival, corresponding to universal basic needs for autonomy, secure identity, positive self-image, and meaning. These claims are simultaneously interacting with varying degrees of backlash against a destabilizing globalization and political secularization; the tumults of global information, uneven economic development and the power of oil revenues, all can provoke a collective trauma vortex. This vortex must be diffused.

In principle, military decision-making can diminish a collective trauma vortex and assure better success if it does the following:

1. Avoid interventions which deepen the enemy's trauma, such as in the story about Lt. Col. Chris Hughes.

2. Base interventions on fulfilling unmet needs, such as in the story about co-opting the enemy.

3. Change from hard power to soft power, shifting their way of operating.

4. Base interventions on cross-cultural understanding

5. Work on the Enemy Collective Vortex, at the individual and collective level.

6. Engage domestic and international media, such as working with embedded media (Chapter 14).

7. Include in strategic thinking the decision to engage only in battles where victory is assured militarily (purity of war) and diplomatically.

Many officers with battlefield experience understand now that military might, alone, cannot overcome these types of insurgencies; and that extraordinary force creates much more damage than just destroying military targets.

Some Examples in the Field

Carefulness:

The following story is an example of avoiding interventions which can deepen the trauma vortex of adversaries. It describes a wartime healing vortex and provides an illustration of what is possible.

Fulfilling Unmet Needs

American commanders in Iraq have understood the importance of fulfilling the unmet needs of insurgents in order to disarm them. The story below illustrates such a strategy.

Creating a Healing Vortex in the Midst of War

Dan Baum reported in the January 17, 2005 issue of *The New Yorker* in his article "Annals of War: Battle

Lesson," on an event in Najaf that he had witnessed on an Iraqi TV station on April 3, 2004.

"A group of Iraqis were shrieking and screaming, frantic with rage. From the way the lens was lurching, the camera-man seemed as frightened as the (American) soldiers facing the Iraqis. This is it, I thought. A shot will come from somewhere, the Americans will open fire, and the world will witness the My Lai massacre of the Iraq war."

Baum writes that at that moment he noticed an American officer, Lt. Col. Chris Hughes, step forward holding his rifle very high over his head pointing the barrel down towards the ground. "It was a striking gesture—almost Biblical, against the backdrop of the enraged crowd," wrote Baum.

"Take a knee, and point your weapon towards the ground," Baum heard the officer order his soldiers in a calm voice. The soldiers looked at the officer as if he were out of his mind. Still one after the other they also knelt in front of the angry crowd and pointed their guns downward.

It was the Iraqis turn to be astonished. They fell silent and their anger dropped rather quickly as the officer withdrew with his men, diffusing the situation. This non-verbal sign of respect and appeasement engaged their calm (or the Iraqis' healing vortex) at least for the moment, in the middle of a potentially explosive situation.

The reporter, curious about what enabled the officer to take such an action, asked Lt. Col Hughes for an interview. The officer told Baum the gesture of respect, which elicited the Iraqis' healing vortex, was not part of his training. He just followed his instincts, which told him that a sign of humility perceived as respect would diffuse the tension. It was his own resources, which inspired him to be ingenious and creative on the spot.

Rightly or wrongly, Baum speculated in his article that because the "Generation X" officers came of age during chaotic and complicated peacekeeping missions in Serbia, Kosovo, Bosnia, Hait and Somalia, they are particularly unimpressed by rank or status. Because they grew up either with working parents, or in single parent homes, they had to learn at an early age how to think for themselves. Lt. Col Hughes grew up with two busy working parents and was forced to learn to think for himself on a daily basis. Baum also believes that because Hughes' was an Internet generation, they may have been discussing online ways to handle unanticipated problems in frontline situations.

However, military history is full of examples of heroic and creative initiatives by military personnel of all echelons throughout the ages.

These military leaders understand the importance of cross-cultural concerns for the benefit of military operations. Men like General Petraeus, the commander previously in charge of the U.S. Army in Iraq, and Lt. Col. Chris Hughes, brought the healing vortex into their strategies in order to diffuse anger and the possible amplification of violence. In the current conflicts, they calculated the best ways to save lives and to shorten or stop war. They committed to paying attention to cultural issues, to understand the psychological attributes of their adversary, conduct careful observations and base their strategies on these observations.

They understand they must be impeccable when fighting just wars and must have a steely determination to win, while also keeping their minds open to dialogue and to the possibility of the enemy's healing vortex. They work to find ways of diffusing conflicts with diplomacy, softening the enemy's will, and lessening the potential for unnecessary damage. It is this combination of strength, ethics, diplomacy, psychological and cultural understanding that will enable conventional armies to diminish violence.

THE TRANSFORMATION OF THE MILITARY

The above examples show that modern war does indeed have a new face. In many present conflicts, conventional militaries, whose blazing-gun tactics can bomb whole cities into rubble in a few hours, are being thrown off by guerilla-type insurgencies using suicide bombings and IEDs. Operating as small groups they can easily go into hiding or mix with civilians. Most disturbing of all, they use their own civilians as shields. Conventional militaries are facing insurgencies that keep moving, adjusting and learning new and more efficient ways of fighting and that enter ever-shifting alliances.

In the face of such an adversary, the use of overwhelming force and/or technology has slowly given way to strategies such as learning to "understand the human terrain," "co-opting the enemy," and using money for winning over allies. A creative military leadership also involves the domestic and international media, adopts healing vortex-inspired strategies, that engage the positive side of the enemy and makes better decisions about military and diplomatic victories.

"Scions of the Surge," an article in *Newsweek* on March 24, 2008, reported how American officers are being transformed by this new kind of war. They painfully are learning to change their tactics. Their soldiers have witnessed their comrades lose arms and legs when roadside bombs hit their vehicles. They have witnessed enemy snipers shoot their comrades in the head while they are in conversation with them, witnessed decapitations of comrades and others, with bodies dragged through town. They swell with rage and hatred with these evidences of barbaric cruelty and want to seek revenge on those who have perpetrated these acts. Yet, those are the same people they must now co-opt.

General Petraeus and his officers understood this new face of war to be a great challenge for their soldiers. Still, they coaxed them to "act as mayors, mediators, cops and civil engineers." They had to convince them to "reach out and ally themselves to men who have tried to kill their soldiers," when these men may in fact still change their minds and try to kill them again in the future.

This new scene flies against warrior norms in which personnel were taught clear concepts of right and wrong—black and white, with no ambiguity. Now, they have to learn to hold opposites—fight enemies while attempting to understand their needs; fight them while also reaching out to them. They have to accept to take risks whose wisdom only the future can corroborate. These are situations that generate their own type of stress.

Understanding the Human Terrain

Even when military forces deliver them from tyranny, targeted populations feel humiliated as this might sharply contrast their helplessness with the foreign military's extraordinary power. Besides exacerbating their sense of inferiority and shame it also triggers their cultural mistrust of foreigners, mobilizing their fear that this military might could be used against them too.

Newly-aware officers understand the importance of not making a show of force, not using shock and awe, not rounding up prisoners by the hundreds and not raiding homes. They understand the power of building trust to win a war. They know they must learn to understand the human terrain even better than the geographical one. In SE® language this means understanding what triggers the enemy's trauma vortex, what can engage its healing vortex, and how to help it meet its needs in constructive ways. Although the knowledge of SE® theory and language should first permeate the political and diplomatic echelons, some creative military leaders are at the forefront. These leaders are committed to spare military lives yet still protect their country, its interests and ways of life. They are at the vanguard of learning it first and being able to implement it on the frontlines.

General Petraeus drafted a "guidance" book on counterinsurgency for his soldiers: "walk… stop by, don't drive by. The objective is to win the people over, not to storm a place or take a hill." He advised his soldiers to move out of their secure "mega-bases," live among the people to earn their trust, form small outposts and venture deep inside alien, hostile territory, despite the apparent risk.

Understanding Cross-Cultural Issues

Part of the human terrain is also a new-found awareness of the importance of cross-cultural understanding which is quickly gaining traction in military quarters. Military leaders understand now that their personnel must learn the complexities and limitations of the enemy cultures.

Because understanding how cross-cultural matters impinge on collective traumas can make a big difference in conflict resolution, our model has identified the different cultural aspects of the foreign population to pay attention to: the power dynamics at work, their channels of authority, the operating family, social and religious hierarchies, their core values and the priority of their universal basic needs.

We include the following list of cross-cultural issues:

- Level of trust towards foreigners; the cultures' past history in relationship to the government you represent; and in relationship to being occupied
- Level of corruption of their own governmental organizations
- Role of family members, clans and social class
- Relationship to leaders
- Role of helpers in the culture—whether familial, medical or religious
- Role fate plays in the culture's belief system, in relationship to disasters and to healing
- Responsibility towards the collective in disasters and wars
- Importance of religion, or lack of: an essential understanding in today's climate, to orient towards diminishing the trauma vortex

- Respect for religious symbols; belief in the supremacy of their faith over others, and belief in religious prophecies
- Sense of time emphasizing "history and tradition" versus the "here and now" or the future
- Type of activity—how much "doing" is valued over "being" and vice-versa
- Relationship of man towards man: authoritarian vs. equality
- Relationship of man to nature—being harmonious and submissive to nature versus conquering and subjugating nature

Application of Cross-Cultural Understanding

Understanding the cultural components of the adversary's trauma, as well as of one's own civilian populations' will further assist in achieving military goals.

While all people have the same universal basic needs, different cultures prioritize different needs and express them in different ways. The inability to prioritize those distinctions, for example, can make one side judge the "other" as barbaric and give up on dialogue, or one side judge the other as weak, and become more aggressive, leading to tremendously costly misunderstandings on both sides. We present a few examples of the importance of understanding culture in conflicts.

In cultures where honor is highly valued, further polarization can be avoided by searching for the right words and actions that make it possible for a defeated enemy to save face and not lose their dignity. They will thus be less likely to seek revenge.

Furthermore, an enemy civilian population which feels respected and is not humiliated, will be less likely to be manipulated and used by non-conventional insurgents. In addition, when faced with the inevitable death and trauma of military interventions, humanitarian actions (such as tending to the wounded enemy or allowing food and medical transport into besieged areas) lessen collective trauma, anger and resentment.

On the other hand, one's own civilian populations who are told the truth and helped to process tragedy within the bigger context will support the efforts of their militaries, despite the costs.

Another important distinction to note is that the lack of democratic process in many cultures leaves their populations with only two choices: they either adopt a passive, fearful stance (a freeze response) or assert their needs and opinions violently (a fight response).

Religion, a Crucial Cross-Cultural Matter

Religions, for example, are powerful symbols of the healing vortex. Religion is an identity symbol, a distinctive element that sets groups apart from each other and acts as a source of centuries-old dignity and important self image. Combined with ethnic identity and traditional mores, it forms a group of tightly knit identity symbols that is often hard for foreigners to understand. Yet, the understanding of this collection of symbols will be essential to help these groups negotiate traditional social structures with modernity.

> Personnel who do not understand or neglected the importance of respect for religion, religious symbols, and religious leaders for certain cultures have inflamed these cultures' collective trauma vortex more than any other issue, including deaths in their populations.
>
> U.S. military officials suspended a Marine in 2008 for distributing coins quoting the Gospel to Sunni Muslims, an incident that enraged Iraqis who viewed it as the latest example of American disrespect for Islam.
>
> "We demand the Americans leave us alone and stop creating religious controversies. First, they used the Koran for target practice and now they come to proselytize."
>
> Desecrating sacred books, attacking places of worship, criticizing or spoofing prophets, calling people names that are religiously debasing, or making them eat food contrary to

their dietary laws, etc. deeply offends people, excites their passionate rage and mobilizes them to join the violence.

Humiliating instances at Abu Ghraib prison were symptomatic of personnel disrespecting the culture and religion of the enemy. Photographing the male prisoners in the nude and in sexually demeaning poses in the presence of women revealed the insensitivity of the American military for its adversary.

DEFENDING AGAINST THE COLLECTIVE TRAUMA VORTEX

The paradigm of the trauma and healing vortex metaphors can also guide efforts to cope with two types of collective trauma vortices: our own *individual collective enemy vortex*, as well as the *collective enemy vortex of the enemy*.

It is generally difficult for anyone directly involved in conflict to maintain any sort of objectivity; however, well-informed and well-intentioned military personnel, grounded in the healing vortex and with regulated nervous systems can better remain in control when facing populations with strong emotions and help guide them towards more constructive behavior.

Today, the military finds itself intervening in local conflicts and/or helping traumatized peoples such as the Iraqis or Afghanis while conflict is still ongoing. How can the military best accomplish these complex tasks? Understanding collective trauma dynamics at all levels can add much in this important endeavor.

At the collective level, the capacity to get out of the trauma vortex translates into learning to differentiate between the need for sustained alertness to secure safety, and hyper-vigilant activation, which keeps the collective ANS hyperaroused. The latter bears the imprint of a collective trauma vortex, which keeps a population in fear, unable to function positively, and results in costly short-term solutions in order to lower unbearable activation, even during periods of relative safety. Hyper-vigilance, like all trauma symptoms, is a normal reaction to conditions of chronic threat. Problems of violence arise when situations warrant varied and nuanced responses rather than operating from a fixed pattern of fight, flight or freeze as the only response available.

Finally, the safety and security of a nation are among the major responsibilities of the military. Distinguishing which responses lead to safety and which lead unwittingly to escalation of warfare can be a most helpful goal in military strategic planning.

Exploring Inner and External Collective Enemy Trauma Vortices

Learning to identify and discharge one's own negative beliefs, prejudices, and fears in relation to particular groups makes it easier to control negative impulsive reactions. Being in charge of your process will allow you more likely to be guided by reason and ethics as well as decreasing the likelihood of fueling your opponents' trauma vortex. Each soldier can benefit from exploring and discharging his/her collective enemy vortex at the personal level.

It is also helpful to be aware of those groups who see you as their own collective enemy trauma vortex. You need to understand the tenor of their negative beliefs, prejudices and fears towards you. This understanding can help you find ways to diffuse their negative vortex.

This work also needs to be done at the collective level. Military leaders may need to address during trainings the tendency to demonize the enemy in order to overcome the natural repulsion to kill. Although this tendency is understandable, it can be driven too far with some personnel experiencing some autonomic nervous system deregulation. It can eventually throw off a soldier's sense of self because the vortex of violence can be contagious. When this vortex leads soldiers to commit unnecessary excesses, they become haunted by them for the rest of their lives. The controlled and justified killing they must do to defend their countries need not do damage to their sense of self. The findings of Wilfred Bion address this issue.

An Old-Time Military Collective Healing Vortex

Wilfred Bion was a British psychoanalyst who pioneered the field of group relations. He served as a frontline combat veteran in World War I, which affected him profoundly. During WWII, he served again on the frontlines, this time as a psychiatrist. He was able to use his experience in understanding the effects of combat and the need to extricate soldiers stuck in immobility and dependency into activity and responsibility again.

At the Tavistock Institute for Applied Social Sciences in London, Bion's experience helped him formulate one of the most profound theories about the nature of human relations. He developed basic principles of group relations, projection, and demonization. He described how scapegoating and the fight-flight response occur not only in individuals, but also in groups and organizations. This body of knowledge about group relations has gained international acceptance and has become a fertile field of study.

During his war experiences, Bion realized that English and German soldiers on the front often developed a profound respect for each other, whereas the military brass could more readily demonize the enemy, as they operated far away from the frontlines, without a first hand knowledge of "the other."

Frontline soldiers on each side were horrified when they realized the opposing forces were just like them—normal people determined to win, feeling the same terror and rage about the war. The capacity to feel horror when recognizing the enemy in oneself is an essential part of the capacity to recognize oneself in the other, and that we share a common humanity.

Vietnam War veterans with direct experience of the enemy often expressed these same points of view about the Viet Cong soldiers.

The Somatic Experiencing® self-regulation work, advocated earlier in the book to help individual military personnel identify the consequences of traumatic stress, prevent and cure it, can be applied to the collective vortex as well. This therapeutic technique allows people to move from being at the mercy of intense and uncontrollable emotions and impulsive actions, even if momentarily, to recovering the capacity to contain difficult emotions and making decisions based on rational thinking. Other tools are added and combined to diffuse collective enemy vortices, such as understanding our own unmet needs and the unmet needs of our adversaries.

STRATEGIES TO DIMINISH THE TRAUMA VORTEX

Identifying Collective Activation

It is helpful to understand that inhumane actions result simply from misguided attempts to meet basic needs in desperate ways, as world views are distorted and the nervous system deregulated by trauma. However, the capacity to get out of the trauma vortex is always present (as proven by people's capacity to live in peace after years of war) and needs to be harnessed, even while force is being used, to stop the uncontrolled violence.

Military personnel can learn to identify the specific signs of a collective trauma vortex, recognize and deal with traumatic collective narratives and media wars. Are the groups or states they are fighting exhibiting any of the following signs of collective trauma?

- Their collective traumatic narratives see their group as the only victims, at the expense of historical truths.

- They hold beliefs, ideologies, and worldviews that see the "other side" as dangerous, overly powerful, and pervasively evil.

- Their media lacks objectivity; using pictures of civilians victims to exploit the population antagonism towards the enemy.

- They use intimidation and manipulation of the international media with misrepresentation and fabrication of facts and numbers, and controlling what is seen and how it is seen.

- They use propaganda to revive past traumas, amplify a present collective trauma vortex and perpetuate their traumatic narrative. They use powerful media images of their civilian victims to garner world sympathy. They make sure to keep the passions of their "street" perpetually inflamed.

- They school their children in hatred and use them as child soldiers or as suicide bombers.

- Their responses to difficult events are automatically destructive, risking their population's safety, autonomy and control.

- Initial signs of their collective trauma vortex manifest as using demeaning language against their adversaries (cockroaches, pigs, dogs and evil), a stream of stereotyped media depictions; and generalizing from a small group to the whole population, calls to violence; later signs as destroying property, and vandalizing sacred sites or cemeteries.

- Their full vortex manifests in the unrelenting use of media propaganda demonizing, dehumanizing the "other" manipulating events during armed struggles; active violence.

- Breaking all international rules of engagement, including using their own civilian sites as launching pads and shields, purposefully endangering or sacrificing their children's and women's lives in the name of the cause.

- Telling signs are the inflexible demands they make, where there are no possible solutions to the conflict, and the needs of "the other" cannot be met at all.

- Another telling sign is framing the conflict in emotional terms and not according to territory or number of victims. It is set up in such a way that their ability to attack and disrupt the enemy already means victory, irrelevant of the costs to their own people. Any enemy response other than their own total destruction proves the enemy's weakness, a sign of their own fierceness and a victory and boost to their cause—a very effective remedy for restoring pride and meaning to an otherwise humiliated and disempowered population.

Responding to the violence generated from a collective trauma vortex may well require the use of force to stop its immediate destruction. However, because there are so many trauma layers, each of them needs to be addressed.

Correcting Traumatic Collective Narratives

World leaders and nations interested in diminishing insurgencies, or non-state non-conventional combatants (such as Hamas, Hizbullah, Al Queda, etc.) must understand the texture of the traumatic narrative: what facts were distorted, what reasons were behind the need for distortion; and to understand single-minded and obsessive focus of the narrative. They need to empathize without accepting the distortions in the narrative. They must help create a counter-narrative by offering correct information supported by validation of the emotions; acknowledging responsibility where it is due showing a cross-cultural understanding of constructive values and meaning and generating hope by offering the benefits of peace.

Against Demonization

Conventional militaries confronting insurgencies take into account that when a collective trauma vortex has been in existence for a while, it has already generated years of misinformation and demonization against the adversary group or state, making the possibility of peace dim. This kind of long-term vortex presents an upward battle to attempt to correct its traumatic and polarized narratives. These narratives have to be counteracted by clear explanatory campaigns, that must be delivered on a consistent basis, not only in times of crisis. The explanatory campaigns must emphasize their good intentions to the population with leaders in the trauma vortex and they must persist until they break through, never loosing sight of the potential of the healing vortex for the other.

Recognizing Unmet Universal Basic Needs

It is necessary to explore and assess the groups basic unmet universal needs. When unfulfilled, these needs create populations craving stability, moral authority and credibility, making people vulnerable to groups who exploit their needs and provide sympathetic platforms. The unmet needs behind most present insurgencies seem to be the need for autonomy, safety of spiritual identity, positive self-image, meaning and a role to play in the world. The swirl of intense negative emotions, thoughts and resolutions also fuel them. The most significant are:

- Traumatically-driven mixture of fear, terror and hatred of "the other," from bestowing a mythical power to the enemy, due to its reputation for invincibility, its shock and awe firepower, and often its economic superiority

- Devastating sense of humiliation with a deep sense of being the underdog, that can be alleviated only by actions that prove any kind of power and control, irrelevant of the price to be paid

- Rage and humiliation for economic disparity

- Paranoia and complete mistrust of the other and wild conspiracy theories

- Disconnection from the other's humanity

- Generalizing to all the enemy population, thus incapable of differentiating between civilians and military personnel, or extreme and moderate voices

- A pervasive sense of competing victimization leading to a
- Decision not to take responsibility for the problem's resolution

Conditions for Engaging the Healing Vortex

Recognizing a collective trauma vortex in its initial phase makes it easier to diffuse it. The following needs are important:

- To be objective; to differentiate in speeches between protective/defensive use of force and aggressive use of force.
- To cultivate cross-cultural sensitivity to better address cultural issues such as:
  › Taking into account the impact of collective humiliation and/or humiliation of leaders, and the loss of honor on the belief system and behavior of cultures.
  › Addressing such cultural differences as the expression of anger. Misunderstood or mishandled collective anger can quickly gain momentum and become contagious, setting the stage for violence.
  › Understanding the different cultural expressions of violence—verbal threats and labeling more easily provoke the trauma vortex of honor-based cultures, making them sacrifice life for honor; while realistic measures of self-protection tend to be interpreted as firm boundaries and encourage reasonable behavior. In contrast, modern individualistic cultures tend to take threats literally and value life over the issue of honor.
- To cultivate emotional intelligence and factor in other elements, which reinforce the trauma vortex and make it contagion—fear, shame, humiliation, inequality, hopelessness and helplessness.
- To remain aware of the extraordinary complexity of any given situation; of trauma's impact on political processes and its con-

nection to violence; and to recognize the recurrence of historical and political cycles.

- To help allies and intermediaries validate the suffering of the enemy and help create a sense of safety and support.

- To make sure to differentiate between validating suffering and condoning destructive behavior.

- To encourage the development of a sense of empowerment instead of power over.

- To recognize the signs indicating that people are using destructive means to fulfill universal basic needs.

- To recognize what unmet basic needs are behind the adversary's symptoms. Whenever possible, providing practical help to help people fulfill their unmet needs constructively (e.g., the example of co-opting Iraqi insurgents fighting to make a living to serve in the police or Army) helps them move out of their trauma vortices and engage in healing.

Conventional militaries interested in diminishing the impact of the adversary collective trauma vortex assess its different signs and methodically counteract them one by one. Every propaganda tool coming out of the trauma vortex needs a quick response, delivered relentlessly and impeccably, coming from the healing vortex—that means always keeping in mind its potential in the enemy population. When caught in the trauma vortex, people's intelligence and drive are put at the service at its service. Redirected, this same intelligence will serve the healing vortex.

Conventional armies responding to the violence of insurgencies can break through the deadlock by reversing the traumatically-driven actions:

- Not generalizing to the whole population; listening carefully to the moderate voices on the other side (addressing the enemy population through pamphlets and radio and T.V. shows with proofs against the erroneous claims of wrong doing (for example, after a specially hard hitting armed encounter in which civilians died, distributing pamphlets with pictures proving the passage of humanitarian trucks and the offer for medical aid, etc. during and after the war, in order to correct the insurgencies media's traumatic narrative of "evil" enemy intentions.

- Keeping in mind the humanity of the enemy (following ROE) and searching for their healing capacity (using the respect and dignity policy).

- Refuting paranoid statements in the on-going campaign one by one; not letting slide any misconception; reiterating simple messages of self defense and of having no desire to control others (populations who live under autocratic control do not believe that it is possible for powers to give up a control they have); seeking the help of acceptable intermediaries and motivate them to be impartial.

- Lowering the rage by carefully choosing non-inflammatory and non-polarizing words, concepts and slogans, avoiding catching haphazardly the wind of the trauma vortex (such as the word "Crusade" inadvertently used by President Bush, which unwittingly lit up the collective Muslim collective vortex). This also includes the name of military operations (they must sound firmly defensive, not aggressive nor punitive).

- Avoid triggering more humiliation and powerlessness by steering clear of shock and awe use of firepower as much as possible, all while showing determination to succeed in the military goals established; not claiming grandiose goals nor absolute victories; helping or facilitating economic development to help the population gain a sense of competence and a positive self-image.

- Respect for the religion and the meaning it gives them.

- Using and affirming the capacity to use defensive force, without retaliatory tones; avoiding the humiliation of the enemy; at the same time, imagining war without the use of extraordinary firepower, and adopting flexibility, speed, and innovation.

With time and consistency, and a continuous focus on the healing vortex, the civilian populations living among non-conventional combatants will be better able to ascertain when their leaders are in the throes of the trauma vortex, as well as they will be better able to access the consequences of their traumatic narrative. Those desirous of leading a normal life -and sparing their children' lives—may learn to detach themselves from the trauma vortex and to cooperate with the healing.

This is an example of using the understanding of the nature of a trauma vortex in order to diffuse it (albeit by negative forces).

In Lebanon: An Example of Diffusing a Collective Vortex

Hezbollah showed an astute sense of addressing the collective trauma vortex it unleashed on the Israeli Arab population during the 2006 war with Israel. It recognized immediately that it had alienated part of the Israeli Arab population when its *Katyushas* destroyed their homes, killed their children, and made them feel confused about their Arab identity. Hezbollah has a keen understanding of how to track and sway the emotional states of the Arabs. It understands how to fuel their trauma vortices against the Israelis and how to disarm it when it is directed against them.

Once their intelligence is directed towards the healing vortex, members of Hezbollah can greatly contribute to the development of their Arab brethren. Right now, as it happens, it is directed to serve fully the trauma vortex.

Hezbollah understood the unmet needs of the Israeli-Arabs. They understood that they needed to address them directly if they wanted to diffuse the developing trauma vortex against them, which already overlapped the blame against them from the Lebanese population. Their main spokesperson addressed the Israeli-Arabs and validated their terrifying experience, diffusing their anger and mistrust. He openly apologized for having subjected them to be unwitting victims of Hezbollah assault on Israel and offered to help them rebuild their homes, meeting their need for self-respect.

Validating their experience and apologizing to them helped the Israeli-Arabs assuage their confusion of identity. Despite the destruction and deaths caused in their community, this acknowledgment allowed the Israeli-Arabs to feel they fully belonged to the Arab world and to identify with the Lebanese instead of the Israeli victims. Hezbollah's attention and apology validated their sense of victimhood and cleared the confusion and isolation they felt. They let go of their anger against Hezbollah, became further polarized against the Israelis, and supported more openly Hezbollah's politics against their own immediate interests.

CHAPTER SIXTEEN

MILITARY VOICES

90-day Wonder, Darkness Remembered; Difficult Questions

"Why am I here? What am I doing here? Why is this happening to me?" Those questions haunted "Leon," an 88-year-old U.S. Naval officer and veteran of World War II, during his service in the Navy.

"I served in an elite group in the Navy as a deck officer. I took part in six major battles as a landing craft officer, landing on beaches with assault troops to fight the Japanese. I often questioned the wisdom of our strategy during the Pacific War of landing on airstrips such as Tarawa, 6500 miles from Tokyo.

"I wrote about my skepticism in the wisdom of our island-hopping to approach Tokyo in my books, *90-Day Wonder, Darkness Remembered*, and *The War in the Pacific—A Retrospective*.

"We were called 90-day wonders because we got our commission after 90 days of training instead of the usual four years. I was a two-stripe officer, Lieutenant. I achieved this status because I had simply survived, not because of any meritorious conduct or bravery. One of my best friends was killed; but I saw so many guys get killed that by the time I learned about my best friend's death, the sadness of the news was softened.

"I don't like to talk about killing any Japanese. It makes me feel sick in the stomach. My hatred toward Germans and towards what they did has still not softened.

RETURN TO TARAWA
"I am still plagued with the memories of the Battle of Tarawa. Its demons still haunt me 65 years later.

The beaches of "Bloody Tarawa," as they are known are today as a big garbage dump, littered with the remains of the 'Western diet' left there by the locals. They throw garbage on the beach, just like they have done for centuries. However, now, they use non-biodegradable food containers, and their garbage does not get naturally recycled. Now it is made of potato chip bags and Coca-Cola cans.

My friend Tony kept telling me, 'You keep complaining about the garbage at the battle site. Go do something about it.' I went there but I hardly survived the visit. I visited Red Beach, where I landed assault troops during my several trips and kept wondering: would the killing ever stop? I kept thinking of each landing, and watching men being cut to pieces by Japanese gunfire. During three days of the slaughter, more than 6000 men were killed, 4000 Japanese, 1000 Korean laborers, an unknown number of Korean 'comfort women,' and 1034 U.S. Marines.

"There is nothing honoring the memory of those who died and I am not at rest because of it.

When I was in the service, I could excuse my moments of rage. I thought it was natural to be angry. Over the years, with my children and my loving wife, I became more conscious, more mature. I no longer have the flashbacks or the terrible dreams that haunted my nights, but I have trouble sleeping because they persist in my head. I had to make sure that at the end of the day nothing would upset me so that I could sleep. I used many self-therapies.

"I am still very sensitive to loud and sudden noises. I feel my bones rattling. Noise jolts me and impairs my concentration. I connect this with the loud gun we used in the Navy.

"I read the material about trauma and it is very good. I recognize many of my reactions. I do have a real issue with anger, certainly not as bad as in the past, but it is still alive and real, and I would like to get rid of it. The two sessions we had have been very helpful."

Cooper is a feisty 88-year-old man who will not give up until he realizes his mission. He came back from Tarawa, giving dozens of radio interviews, intent on getting all the help he needs to implement his "Action Program for Tarawa." He believes the two "beaches should be cleaned up and restored to their pristine condition" so they can become a permanent memorial. He has petitioned the US and Kiribati governments to establish monitored garbage control centers in a number of locations He has many projects he wants to accomplish including moving the monument for the Marines 2nd Division from a parking lot to Red Beach. In April 2009 his documentary, "Return to Tarawa" aired on The Discovery Network's new Military Channel. Narrated by actor Ed Harris, the program is a synopsis of all the projects Cooper has under development for reclaiming Red Beach from its current garbage dump status, erecting a proper memorial to those who died there in WWII, reclaiming the bodies of those killed in action, and gives a status update of all of Cooper's lobbying efforts with the governments of both nations.

Cooper summed up his position with a quote from the 19th century British Prime Minister William Gladstone, "One can judge the conscience of a nation by the recognition it gives to those who died for it."

USING HEALING TOOLS IN THE FIELD

Helping Soldiers Function

"Benjamin" was a soldier who left Israel right after his compulsory service, afraid he would be called to the reserve Army. He returned to Israel only for a few days at a time to avoid the call to serve.

He had seen two of his best friends killed during the first Lebanon war when the enemy badly ambushed his unit across the border. He suffered from survival guilt. He was also convinced that he would die in service. He was terrified at the thought that they could ask him again to cross the border into Lebanon, where this terrible tragedies occurred.

He avoided the Army for eight years, feeling guilty about it and missing his country. He finally decided to work on his traumatic issues in therapy. After several sessions with a therapist who used cutting-edge trauma healing techniques, including EMDR and SE®, he finally was able to release his fears and re-enlist as a reserve officer in a fighting unit and return to the Israel-Lebanon border.

Treating Soldiers Using Somatic Experiencing®

"Avi" is a 45-year-old veteran of the first Lebanon war. He was on a troop transport truck heading out of Lebanon for a break when an explosive hit the truck and he suffered light facial burns. He participated in the chase after the attackers and after the incident, he and his comrades continued their seven-hour journey together to Jerusalem. After that event, there were two additional upsetting ones, one in the refugee camps and one during his reserve service.

Avi remembered the image of the huge flash of the explosion and his commanding officers laughing about him turning into a "black" man. No one referred to the detonation and all acted as if nothing happened. A month after the event, Avi began to suffer from outbursts of rage and refused to board any truck of the type involved in the explosion even if it meant not going home on leave from Lebanon. Fortunately, his veteran soldier status allowed him to choose a different job from the newly enlisted soldiers and he became an operations sergeant.

After Avi completed his reserve service, he immediately flew to the United States, lived there two years, and then returned to his country.

Each recall to reserve duty caused him great stress. His wife hid the letters from the Army and secretly asked the Army to release from military service. After five years of avoiding reserve service, he was released from the Army.

Avi finally sought therapy when the Army called his eldest son to serve. His symptoms had worsened considerably. He suffered from recurring nightmares, various physical pains and numerous outbursts of rage. At his first therapy session, his presenting complaint was his son's eminent mobilization.

Avi responded very well to therapy. He realized that his PTSD manifested in avoidance, his primary coping mechanism. While discussing this issue, Avi suddenly reported unusual pain in his midriff area. When asked to focus on the exact location of the pain and to notice if there were images that came up, and to remember the resources previously discussed, Avi reported that the pain was very pointed, and that he was having trouble hearing the therapist. Avi focused on several resources in his body, and then on the pain and the images it evoked and suddenly said the word *harrow* (a very rare word in Hebrew, describing an instrument used to break up clumps of earth before sowing seeds).

Asked to focus on that word for a bit and report what he felt, Avi said he was feeling some discomfort but also was suddenly able to hear again. He recalled the explosion, smelled gunpowder and remembered that *harrow* was the name of his unit in the Army. Avi was impressed that "his body remembered" and regarded this moment as a breakthrough in his therapy. He had a newly found appreciation of the power of his sensory-motor experiences and he made rapid progress in therapy.

———

Benefits of Early Detection

A reserve Army regiment was in a "municipal" area on a week's exercise learning to fight in an urban environment. During their military exercises, soldiers were required to enter a *Kasbah*—a densely populated area with houses close to each other built for the military trainings.

"Glenn," one of the medics, entered the *Kasbah* and immediately experienced a flash back to the *Kasbah* in Nablus where he served as a medic when many soldiers had been wounded. He asked his medic commander to excuse him from the exercise and even to release him from reserve service completely.

The regiment's medics had completed a six-hour workshop led by an SE® practitioner on post-trauma symptoms and very basic SE® principles "Nahum," the commanding medic, fresh from the SE® course, recognized Glenn was having a flashback and wanted to help him release it. Nahum asked Glenn to leave the *Kasbah* and go 50 meters away from it and there, to concentrate on his resources.

Glenn did as told. He focused on several of the resources he had listed in the workshop—his girlfriend, the beauty, of the area where he lives and the sea. Nahum asked Glen to go back near the *Kasbah,* feel his resources and notice what other sensations come up. Glenn did so and felt calmer coming near the *Kasbah.* Nahum asked him then to resource again and to go this time inside the *Kasbah* and track his sensations. Glenn did what Nahum told him, and discharged with deep breaths and some trembling in his legs. Within a few minutes, he was able to re-enter the *Kasbah* area without feeling activated. His flashbacks were gone, and he did no longer asked to be relieved of his duties.

Guilt over a 30-Year-Old Flight Response

"David," a 65-year-old veteran who fought in the 1967 war (*Yom Hakipurim*) as a tank commander, came for therapy. Until age 54 (30 years after the war), he had never given much thought to the effect the war had on him. Only after the break-up of his latest romantic relationship had he found himself overcome by very intense flashbacks from the war and survivor guilt.

During the war, he was taken away from his original crew at the last minute and placed with an unfamiliar tank crew. A short time later, he realized that his tank radio was broken and he was cut off from the rest of his unit. Their lone tank was confronted by an enormous force of Egyptian tanks. Additionally, he realized that there was also a mechanical problem in directing his tank fire towards the targets.

As they were trying to escape, they were hit by Egyptian fire. David jumped from the tank, without taking the time to see if any of the crew members were wounded, not noticing that he was wounded in his arm. He started running away "like an animal," as he described it in therapy, trying to save his life, not looking backwards nor taking care of any of his crew members. After hiding behind a boulder for a few hours, surrounded by the sound of Egyptian soldiers around him, he managed to escape and rejoin the Israeli forces.

After they took care of his wounded arm in the Army hospital, they told him that all three soldiers in his tank were killed.

David's war trauma had been complicated by a very deep developmental trauma he had suffered as a child. He did not have many resources as a child and it took him a while to agree to let his therapist use SE® with him. The therapy consisted of resourcing and discharging the very intense guilt feeling he had regarding his abandonment of his soldiers.

For the first time in a very long time, David is looking forward to the future with hope. He does not obsess about his guilt feelings—quite a big change for him—is not depressed and finds himself smiling more often and feeling more optimistic.

His flashbacks do not overpower him anymore. Although David's therapy needs to go on longer because of the trauma he suffered as a child, his war trauma symptoms have subsided significantly.

Raz: Discharging Summer Triggers

"Raz," a 35-year-old married engineer and father of two young boys, was called for *miluim* (reserve service) during the second Lebanon War where he served as part of a tank crew. A few days into the war, a barrage of cannonballs (*katyushot*) fell close to his unit and wounded several of his unit comrades. During the barrage he felt he could manage, but when the shouting of the injured soldiers and the harried activities of the medics started, he felt terrified, lost all control and could not stop shouting and crying. He felt completely helpless and wanted to run away, but he didn't. His friend could calm him only a bit.

Since the war, Raz has not been able to recuperate his pre-war level of function. He did go back to work, but felt very little motivation. Most of the time, he felt tired, bored and depressed. He could not engage in any of the sports that kept him healthy and gave him time with his friends. He was particularly distraught because he was unable to spend quality time with his children and his boys were complaining. He also suffered from many body aches and had many unsuccessful doctor visits seeking an organic reason for his pain and the correct treatment. He finally sought psychological help, with much reluctance.

For months, he could not make the connection between his symptoms and his war experience, despite his war flash-backs every time he thought of that period of *miluim* service. He was triggered by seasonal changes, especially when the first bright sun and summer heat began. His symptoms flared up when he heard or read stories of soldiers on the news or heard talk about the Syrian, Iranian, Hamas, or Hezbollah threats. Other triggers such as the smell of mosquito bite medicine kept arousing his symptoms.

Initial attempts to resource Raz were not very successful. His resistance to resourcing was a sign of the depth of his depression and the pull of the trauma vortex on him.

Gradually, after he understood that trauma's nature is to cut us off from our resources and after he experienced the polarity principle at work, he engaged more actively in his healing. Directed by his therapist, he pendulated back and forth between the sensations of constriction and of expansion until the tightness in his chest released.

After a few sessions, Raz started discharging the energy stuck in his body by focusing, one at a time, on the sensations triggered by his flashbacks. He was amazed every time that one of his horrifying 'pictures' or sensations of pain that these feelings was discharged.

Convinced for months that he had a medical problem, Raz was stunned to see many of his physical symptoms disappear and understood they were connected to the war images that haunted him.

Raz has been in therapy for six months. Many of his symptoms subsided. Although he has not yet returned to his pre-war energy level, he now wakes up in the morning ready for his day and does not need his middle of the day naps. His body aches have subsided and he stopped his weekly doctor's appointments. His flashbacks have significantly subsided; and are much less intense and rarer. In his last session, Raz told his therapist he felt "light like a feather" and felt very fortunate to have his wife, children and other resources, something completely absent at the beginning of his therapy.

Andrew's Story

"Andrew" was a sergeant in the Special Forces Unit in Iraq who retired after 10 years service. He witnessed a particularly gruesome death of an Iraqi who he was hit by a powerful weapon. His experience was further exacerbated by the effects of an anti-malaria drug, which compromised his senses, triggering auditory and visual hallucinations.

"It was a breakthrough for me to go forward from cognitive behavioral talk therapy.

"Cognitive behavioral therapy allowed me to step back and look at my experiences and have someone to talk with about them. But after a while, it did not do anything for me. The effects had reached a plateau. My physical symptoms of deregulation were still there. Then I did EMDR which was also good, but the effects of that therapy reached a plateau. I continued to have a startle reflex, nightmares and bad dreams with intrusive images. My mind raced continuously. I had problems sleeping and was dealing with depression.

"While my symptoms had lessened, many were still present. Sensory triggers such as diesel fumes smells, or auditory and visuals cues reminded me of the trauma and I still couldn't cope with them. I was still deregulated. Eventually, I developed more serious syndromes, such as Irritable Bowel Syndrome and acid reflux. I had developed lower back problems and always felt fatigued. I gained weight and generally was not well.

"In my quest to get well, I finally got to SE®. By then, I knew about the impact of trauma on the body, how it lingers and how it compromises the physiology

"I did 16-20 sessions of SE® and all my symptoms disappeared. The therapy helped me regulate again. Most importantly, I learned tools of EFA, like working with the breath and discharging. While all my symptoms had disappeared, they could come back to a small degree whenever I was stressed. However, now I have the tools, and when intrusive thoughts are triggered by strong events (such as when two people I know committed suicide), it is a temporary deregulation that gets quickly regulated.

———————————

CHAPTER SEVENTEEN

THE INTERNATIONAL
TRAUMA-HEALING INSTITUTE

THE ROSS MODEL: "HEALING THE COLLECTIVE NERVOUS SYSTEM"

> Healing trauma at mass levels is necessary to world peace.

Learning to heal trauma at collective levels may be key to diminish violence and support a peaceful environment. Several social sectors, given the right information, can ease the effects of "collective trauma" by designing interventions that promote healing and avoid those interventions that amplify trauma.

The International Trauma-Healing Institute (ITI) sponsors a series of books to introduce a universal and apolitical language to make sense of conflicts and facilitate their resolution. The books address the impact of individual and collective trauma on conflicts between people. They also introduce coping tools to the various sectors interfacing with trauma. These tools can be institutionalized within the structure of each sector. We hope that this information contributes to solutions for the seemingly intractable conflicts that beset us.

We have developed workshops and written materials for the social sectors cited below. Once informed about trauma, its effects and healing, these sectors help the general public deal with the issue of trauma:

- The military, its commanders, soldiers, doctors, psychologists, chaplains, medics and corpsmen
- Health professionals—doctors, surgeons, anesthesiologists, nurses, Ministries of Health and Surgeon Generals, emergency medical technicians (EMT)
- Paramedics, firemen, policemen, and emergency personnel
- Frontline responders, rescue teams
- Mental health professionals: psychiatrists, psychologists, body/mind workers, and social workers
- Educations systems—schools, teachers, parents associations, school counselors, psychologists and Ministries of education

- Clergy—pastors, rabbis, priests, nuns, imams, lamas, gurus and all spiritual and lay leaders
- The justice system—judges, divorce lawyers, family law attorneys, family courts, juvenile systems, child protective agencies
- Diplomats and Non-governmental organizations (NGOs)—the Red Cross, Doctors Without Borders, the World Health Organization; UN personnel and international support teams; Local and international political leaders and think-tanks
- The Public

TRAININGS FOR THE MILITARY

Our custom-designed trainings for the military provide the skills to cope with war-related trauma, with exercises that help identify personal and collective traumas that affecting performance and safety.

It is also important to factor collective trauma vortices before, during, and after engaging in armed conflicts and wars in order to avoid amplifying the existing vortices. The trainings are intended to help the military face these difficulties with efficacy.

Military participants in the ITI's trainings learn about the devastating consequences of traumatic events when they deregulate our nervous system and how the nervous system can be brought back into balance. They explore the "collective military trauma vortex" and its impact on the conduct of war. They learn how to avoid responding in a dysfunctional and unproductive way (too fast, too slow, too strong, too weak, or by withdrawing at the wrong moment based on unresolved past experiences hurting military goals).

Touched by the commonality of suffering, trainees from diverse ethnic, religious, and economic backgrounds learn to overcome their differences, reaching out to bond with each other. Learning about trauma helps smooth internal racial and ethnic differences.

Participants become aware of media-related trauma. They learn skills to protect themselves from the incessant coverage of tragedy and violence and from coverage critical of the military, that affects morale and makes soldiers feel disconnected from their country.

The trainings provide:

- State-of-the-art information on the nature and impact of trauma, how it deregulates the nervous system, and tools to cope, develop resilience, and heal from personal trauma
- Information on the nature and impact of collective trauma, how it deregulates the collective nervous system of a group or a nation, and tools to diffuse it
- Empowerment to attend ethically to one's needs

The custom-designed, one or two-day workshops are experiential and didactic, with a two-pronged goal.

In the one-day workshops, participants benefit personally from SE® Emotional First Aids tools, and learn to enhance their work with their traumatized constituents. They learn to recognize signs of activation in themselves and others, to release traumatic activation, and learn resilience-building tools.

The two-day workshops provide SE® Emotional First Aid tools the first day and tools for healing collective trauma. Participants learn to address the powerful emotional layers of trauma that underlie conflict. They learn to recognize signs of collective trauma and unmet universal basic needs behind the negative actions of their group or the adversary group seeing how it contributes to conflict, and release the negative charge of their own collective trauma using defensive force without being pulled by the magnetism of the enemy's trauma vortex or responding with destructive revenge.

The trainings also teach how to identify the signs of collective trauma in other groups the power of words or the type of interventions that feed a group's collective trauma vortex, and those that engage a group's collective healing vortex.

PART IV
APPENDICES AND RESOURCES

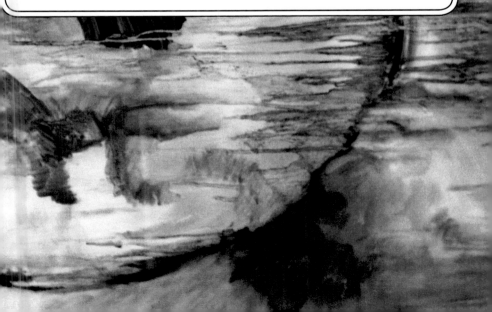

APPENDIX A

OTHER TRAUMA TREATMENTS

Researchers are actively unraveling the impact of traumatic stress in the aftermath of war and terrorism. This chapter is an introduction to cutting-edge trauma-healing techniques other than SE®. These techniques have proven quick, easy, and effective with wide applicability in the range of the trauma they can heal, in the prevention of trauma, and in the development of resiliency.

COGNITIVE BEHAVIORAL TREATMENTS AND EXPOSURE THERAPY

Cognitive Behavioral Therapy is a focused, problem-solving approach developed by Dr. Aaron T. Beck in the 1970s. It is direct and potent, and its efficacy has been empirically validated for the treatment of PTSD. It identifies thoughts (automatic or unconscious thoughts, assumptions, and core beliefs) that produce negative or painful feelings as well as maladaptive behaviors. It relies on changing the thinking, which then changes the emotions and behavior. Behavioral techniques are also used, such as relaxation techniques, anger management, assertiveness training, and gradual exposure to the feared situations. The treatment is usually brief. Many qualified therapists practice CBT in the U.S. and around the world.

Schema-Focused Cognitive Therapy: Jeffrey E. Young, a protégé of Dr. Beck, developed Schema-Focused Cognitive Therapy, an offshoot of CBT. This technique is useful with people who have longstanding self-defeating patterns, themes, or schemas in thinking and feeling. It combines CBT, experiential, interpersonal, and psychoanalytic therapies into a unified model of treatment.

Exposure Therapy is the invention of Dr. Edna B. Foa, professor of clinical psychology and psychiatry at the University of Pennsylvania. She is one of the leading experts in the area of PTSD, and her program for rape victims is considered to be an effective therapy for trauma. Foa believes that if the person is encouraged to think of the traumatic images while in the presence of a therapist for as long as is needed, no matter how difficult this seems, the fear of these images will disappear.

MEDICATION

Medication is available for reducing overwhelming symptoms of arousal (sleep disturbances and exaggerated startle reflex, intrusive thoughts, avoidance, depression, and panic) and for improving impulse control and behavioral problems. Presently, drug companies are attempting to develop medication that may be stress-protective. It is strongly suggested that medication be accompanied by therapy. Please note that many medications for trauma have mild to significant side effects.

INNOVATIVE TECHNIQUES

Although cognitive behavioral therapies have been the more recognized techniques for healing trauma, a new wave of body-centered therapies has appeared in the last fifteen years and now permeates the clinical field. These cutting-edge techniques have begun to integrate the body into the field of trauma. They each use the technique of exposure with varying gentleness.

We now know that trauma lives in the body, not only in the mind. Neuroscience discoveries are providing a scientific foundation for somatic psychotherapy and body-based treatment of trauma and dissociation. Understanding how neural networks function allows us to understand the relationship between mind and body, why traumatic stress can be healed through the body, and how psychological change can occur.

Over the last two decades, several innovative treatment methods have emerged that provide particularly effective treatment against the ravages of trauma. Most of these methods can be applied to a broad range of symptoms including grief and loss, panic, anxiety, phobias, depression, pain, and addiction. These tools can offer dramatic results, sometimes within a few sessions. They draw upon our own resources and inherent capacity to heal. Both external and internal resources are extremely important in such work, and time is devoted to helping people identify them.

Some of these tools work well in the hands of dedicated lay people, especially those in the addiction field. Some can be self-applied, and some can even be taught via the media in emergency collective situations. There is an ever-growing field of such therapies, but most still need to be supported by research. Only a handful of these techniques are covered in this chapter. We believe SE® to have the broadest mass application. SE® can be added to most methods and is one of the few techniques which is culturally transportable. It includes both an elaborate and detailed theory of trauma, as well as a method for coping with and healing trauma.

EYE MOVEMENT DESENSITIZATION AND REPROCESSING (EMDR)

Eye Movement Desensitization and Reprocessing (EMDR), a healing method developed by psychologist Francine Shapiro, Ph.D., involves visual, auditory, and kinesthetic bilateral stimulation while the traumatized individual processes and reintegrates traumatic material. The person thinks about the traumatic memory and the negative beliefs associated with it (e.g., "It was my fault that I got raped") while visually tracking the rapid back-and-forth movements the therapist makes with two fingers or a wand in the line of vision. Alternately, physical taps or sound may be used. Like the eye movements, taps or sounds are alternated left and right. The bilateral stimulation seems to be an essential element of the treatment. It has been speculated that this stimulation creates a synapse connecting the stuck material with the innate capacity of the individual to heal.

Recent work on the developmental process of creating neural networks that mediate various functions and traumatic memory may provide a plausible mechanism to explain the efficacy of EMDR and other therapeutic approaches, which use repetitive, rhythmic sensory stimulation with cognitive recall to treat trauma.

Not only were more EMDR patients cured than those in standard care, but they also recovered twice as quickly. On average, they were symptom-free after just six sessions, as compared to twelve for standard care. Psychological tests also showed that eye-movement therapy did a better job of easing depression and anxiety, with most EMDR patients testing in the normal range after therapy. EMDR is also an excellent tool for processing negative self-beliefs.

Neuro-imaging researcher Bessel Van der Kolk recently investigated the efficacy of EMDR treatment effects. He found that the flashbacks with which several Vietnam veterans had been plagued for over twenty years remitted in a few sessions. After three sessions exactly, their symptoms were greatly relieved.

TRAUMATIC INCIDENT REDUCTION (TIR)

TIR is a highly focused and repetitive desensitization and cognitive imagery approach that was refined in the mid-1980s by California psychiatrist Dr. Frank Gerbode. It is a directive and control-based tool, addressing thoughts, feelings, emotions, and sensations. The process works well with adults and children. In a single session, the client is directed to review a traumatic incident, first silently, then aloud, repeatedly, until arriving at an internal resolution. The client is enabled to reach his own insights and resolve his difficulties. The therapist's role is to keep the client's attention tightly focused on the incident. TIR can be applied informally, even though it is structured. Therapists from many different theoretical backgrounds can use it cross-culturally. The technique can also be taught to lay people. The limitations are that one needs to take as long a time as it takes to process a traumatic event in one sitting. Going through the retelling of a traumatic experience repeatedly can also be very painful.

VISUAL KINESTHETIC DISSOCIATION (VKD)

VKD, demonstrated by Florida therapists Maryanne and Edward Reese, is related to Neuro-Linguistic Programming (NLP), developed in the early 1970s by Richard Bandler and John Grinder. It is an approach based on close observation of verbal, behavioral, and sensory patterns. In VDK's application of NLP to trauma incidents, clients are led through a step-by-step program of purposeful dissociation from the trauma, watching a "movie" of themselves reliving the traumatic event and being instructed to imagine communicating with and reassuring their younger, traumatized selves. The entire experience is thereby integrated into their present lives.

THOUGHT FIELD THERAPY (TFT)

TFT, created by Roger Callahan during the early 1980s, requires only that the client think briefly about the traumatic event while specific acupuncture meridian points (believed to stimulate the body's bio-energy system) are tapped or rubbed. The technique allows traumatic events to loosen their hold on victims. It works to rid clients of their flashbacks, upset emotions, and obsessive thoughts.

EMOTIONAL FREEDOM TECHNIQUE (EFT)

Emotional Freedom Technique (EFT) is an offshoot of TFT. Gary Craig, a student of Callahan, simplified TFT by creating an all-inclusive sequence that tapped all seven body meridian points. This allowed people to bypass the need for detailed diagnosis. EFT, like TFT, is based on the idea that emotional problems are directly linked to disturbances or blockages in the acupuncture meridian system. Clients who have had successful experiences with it feel transformed and relieved of their pain.

Craig maintains an active list on the Internet of methods based on his approach. He is determined to make EFT available to as many people as possible. Videos and tapes are sold at cost. Treatment is aimed at neutralizing, balancing, or in other ways clearing blockages, often by tapping on or holding acupuncture points while keeping the problem in mind. In my private practice, I have found that children, in particular, have taken very well to the tapping and do it at home, by themselves. Some children have also taught their friends to use it, feeling very happy and proud of themselves, that they could be of any help.

THE WAVE OF THE FUTURE

The current economics of managed care demand shorter therapies, making brief, affordable, and effective treatments attractive. No two people experience PTSD the same way, and there is no quick fix that works for every person. The variety of new tools available allows for more flexibility and more customized therapy. These new approaches are techniques and tools that stand on their own, or it can be integrated in traditional therapies. They all rely on the innate ability of the client to heal.

APPENDIX **B**

---●---

HEALING RESOURCES ONLINE

SOMATIC EXPERIENCING® FOUNDATION FOR HUMAN ENRICHMENT

6685 Gunpark Drive, Suite 102
Boulder, CO 80301
Phone: (303) 652-4035
Fax: (303) 652-4039
http://www.traumahealing.com

EMOTIONAL FREEDOM TECHNIQUES (EFT)

36808 Greencroft Close
The Sea Ranch, CA 95497
www.emofree.com

ASSOCIATION FOR COMPREHENSIVE ENERGY PSYCHOLOGY (ACEP)
P.O. BOX 61838
SANTA BARBARA, CA 93160
PHONE: (619) 861-ACEP (2237)
FAX: (805) 683-2141

Email: admin@energypsych.org
www.energypsych.org

CHILEL QIGONG

For health, longevity, creativity, and
mental clarity
P.O. Box 2097, Rocklin, CA 95677
Phone: 888-864-0588 or
916-772-0868
www.chilel.com

EYE MOVEMENT DESENSITIZATION AND REPROCESSING (EMDR)

P.O. Box 750
Watsonville, CA 95077
Phone: (831) 761-1040
Fax: (831) 761-1204
Email: inst@emdr.com
http://www.emdr.com

TRAUMATIC INCIDENT REDUCTION ASSOCIATION (TIRA)

5145 Pontiac Trail
Ann Arbor, MI 48105
Phone: (800) 499-2751
(Toll-free USA, Puerto Rico,
Virgin Islands, and Canada)
or 734 761 6268 (Elsewhere)
FAX: +1 (734) 663-6861
Email: info@tir.org (For fastest
response, use email)
Phone: (800) 499-2751 (U.S. and
Canada) / (816) 468-4945
Fax: (816) 468-6656
Email: tira@tir.org
http://www.tir.org
http://www.healing-arts.org/tir

COGNITIVE BEHAVIORAL THERAPY

New York Institute of Cognitive
Behavioral Therapies
2424 Avenue R
Brooklyn, NY 11229
Phone: (646) 267-7630
Email: info@nyicbt.org
www.nyicbt.org
http://www.cognitivetherapy.com

SCHEMA-FOCUSED COGNITIVE THERAPY

Schema Therapy Institute
36 West 44th Street, Suite 1007
New York, NY 10036
Phone: (212) 221-0700 (Monday-
Friday, 9am-4pm, EST)
Fax: (212) 221-1818
Email: institute@schematherapy
.com
http://www.schematherapy.com

DEFENSE CENTERS OF EXCELLENCE

Sponsors multiple programs for veterans' psychological health
http://www.dcoe.health.mil/default.aspx
1401 Wilson Blvd, Suite 400
Rosslyn, VA 22209
877-291-3263
Resources@DCoEOutreach.Org

IRAQ WAR VETERANS ORGANIZATION, INC.

For Iraqi Operation Freedom veterans
www.iraqwarveterans.org
Long War Veterans Organization, Inc.
PO Box 571, Yucaipa, CA. 92399

IAVA - IRAQ AND AFGHANISTAN VETERANS OF AMERICA

www.iava.org
292 Madison Avenue, 10th Floor
New York, NY 10017
community@iava.org

NEW DIRECTIONS, INC.

Clean and sober living for veterans
11303 Wilshire Blvd.,
VA Bldg 116
Los Angeles, CA 90073
Ph (310) 914-4045

REAL WARRIORS

A program to promote the processes of building resilience, facilitating recovery and supporting reintegration of returning service members, veterans and their families.
http://realwarriors.net
a program of the DCoE

THE SOLDIERS PROJECT

www.thesoldiersproject.org
Free psychological counseling for soldiers and their families
info@thesoldiersproject.org
Toll free: 877-576-5343

TRAGEDY ASSISTANCE PROGRAM FOR SURVIVORS

www.taps.org
National Headquarters
1777 F Street, NW, 6th Floor
Washington, DC 20006

800-959-TAPS (8277) U.S. DEPARTMENT OF DEFENSE

Outreach Center
For Psychological Health and Traumatic Brain Injury Information and Resources
866 966 1020
http://www.defenselink.mil/

US DEPARTMENT OF VETERANS AFFAIRS

http://www.va.gov/
VA Benefits: 1-800-827-1000

VETERANS ADMINISTRATION SUICIDE HOTLINE

1 800 278-3TALK (8255)

APPENDIX C

---•---

REFERENCES

1. American Psychiatric Association: Diagnostic and Statistical Manual of Mental Disorders, Fourth Edition, DSM-IV, American Psychiatric Association, Washington, DC 1994, pp 424-229.

2. Atkinson, Rick. In the Company of Soldiers: A Chronicle of Combat.

3. Bennett, Lance. "The perfect storm? The American media and Iraq". Open Democracy, http://www.opendemocracy.net/media-journalismwar/article_1457.jsp1 August 2009.

4. Blake, John. "A POW's Tears in the Darkness." CNN, 15 July 2009. http://www.cnn.com.

5. Boulder, Colorado, 2005.

6. Brant, Martha. "The Fallout: The Things They Carry." *Newsweek*. August 21, 2005.

7. Carey, Benedict. "Mental Stress Training is Planned for U.S. Soldiers," New York Times, 18 August 2009, www.nytimes.com.

8. Center for Media Literacy beyond Blame: Challenging Violence in the Media, October 29, 2008, http://www.medialit.org/beyond_blame.html.

9. CNN Newsroom, July 1, 2009, 13:00 ET, Kyra Phillips, http://transcripts.cnn.com/TRANSCRIPTS/0907/01/CNR.05.HTML, accessed 7/7/2009.

10. CNN Newsroom, July2, 2009, 13:00 ET, Kyra Phillips, http://transcripts.cnn.com/TRANSCRIPTS/0907/02/CNR.05.HTML, accessed 7/29/09.

11. Cooper, Leon. *90-Day Wonder: Darkness Remembered*. First Books Library, CITY 2003.

12. Cote, William, and Roger Simpson. *Covering Violence: A Guide to Ethical Reporting About Victims and Trauma*. Columbia University Press, 2006.

13. Dehghanpisheh, B, and Thomas E: "Scions of the Surge." *Newsweek*. March 24, 2008, pp. 28-34.

14. DeYoung, Mary. "Collective Trauma: Insights From a Research Errand." American Academy of Experts in Traumatic Stress. http://www.aaets.org/article55.htm. 12 June 2007.

15. Figley, CR and Nash, WP. Combat Stress Injury: Theory Research and Management. Routledge Taylor and Francis Group, Florence, Kentucky. 2009.

16. Foa EB, Tolin. DF: Comparison of the PTSD Symptom Scale-Interview Version and the Clinician Administered PTSD Scale. Journal of Traumatic Stress, 2000;13:181-191.

17. Fox News. "Sanchez: Media's Reporting of Iraq War Endangered Soldiers' Lives." 15 October 2007. http://fox news.com.

18. Frankel, Rafael D. "Check (point) it out." *The International Jerusalem Post*. February 24-March 2, 2006.

19. Gendlin, Eugene. *Focusing*. Bantam, 1982.

20. Greenberg, Hanan. "Anti-pullout solider goes directly to jail." *Israeli News*. June 6, 2005.

21. Hamad, Taj and Swartx, FA. "Code of Ethics and Conduct for NGOs," v.5, WANGO, New York, NY, 2005.

22. Hart, A.B. "An Operators Manual for Combat PTSD: Essays for Coping." iUniverse.com. Lincoln, Nebraska, 2000.

23. Hazan, Jenny. "Home on the (firing) range." *The International Jerusalem Post*. February 24-March 2, 2006.

24. Hedges, C. *War is a Force That Gives Us Meaning*. Anchor Books. New York, 2002.

25. Heller, Diane and Heller, Laurence. *Crash Course: A Self-Healing Guide to Auto Accident Trauma and Recovery*. North Atlantic Books. Berkeley, California, 2001.

26. Herman, J: *Trauma and Recovery*, Basic Books, New York, NY 1992.

27. Hight, Joe. *Tragedies and Journalists: A guide for more effective coverage*. DART Center for Journalism and Trauma. 2002.

28. insert all the CNN references in the statistics portion

29. Ironson, GI, Freund, B, Strauss, JL, and Williams, J: Comparison of two treatments for traumatic stress: A community-based study of EMDR and prolonged exposure. Journal of Clinical Psychology, 58,113-128.

30. Jaffe, Greg. "The Aftermath: For Nate Self, Battlefield Hero, Trauma Takes a Toll." *Wall Street Journal*. October 6, 2005.

31. Joint Services Conference on Professional Ethics, Panel on "Commander Self-Care." National Defense University. Washington, D.C. 1997. http://www.usafa.af.mil/jscope/. *See also* Parameters: U.S. Army War College Quarterly 28 (2): 93-105, Summer 1998.

32. Kalb, Marvin. "The Israeli-Hezbollah War of 2006: The Media as a Weapon in Asymmetrical Conflict." Joan Shorenstein Center, Research Paper Series, February 2007.

33. Kasher, Asa. "Operation Cast Lead and the Ethics of Just war." Azure, 37: Summer 5769/2009.

34. Kessler, RC et al: Posttraumatic stress disorder in the National Comorbidity Survey, Arch. Gen. Psych, vol 52: 12, December 1995. Institute for Social Research, University of Michigan, Ann Arbor, USA.

35. Kilcullen, David. *The Accidental Guerrilla: Fighting Small Wars in the Midst of a Big One.* Oxford University Press, New York, NY. 2009

36. Kleber, Rolf J., Charles R Figley, et. al. *Beyond Trauma: Cultural and Societal Dynamics.* Springer Series on Stress and Coping. Springer. New York, NY 2001.

37. Lahad, Mooli. "The Integrative Model of Coping and Resiliency." ISTSS Conference. Chicago, October 2005.

38. Leitch, ML: Somatic Experiencing® Treatment with Tsunami Survivors in Thailand: Broadening the Scope of Early Intervention. Traumatology, 2007; 13; 1.

39. Levine, P and Heller, D: SE® Theory and Training. Foundation for Human Enrichment, Boulder, Colorado, 2005.

40. Levine, P: Manual for Somatic Experiencing® Trainings, Advanced and Intermediate Years in SE®, Foundation for Human Enrichment, Boulder, Colorado, 2005.

41. Levine, P: Manual for Somatic Experiencing® Trainings, Beginning I Year in SE®, Foundation for Human Enrichment,

42. Levine, Peter A.—*Nature's Lessons in Healing Trauma, We Are All Neighbors, Understanding Childhood Trauma, the Vortex of Violence, the Body as a Healer,* and *Memory, Trauma and Healing.* Article Packet. Foundation for Human Enrichment. Boulder, Colorado, 2005.

43. Levine, Peter. *Waking the Tiger: Healing Trauma.* North Atlantic Books. Berkeley, California , 1997.

44. Losi, M., S. Reisner, et. al. "Psychosocial and Trauma Response in War-Torn Societies." International Organization for Migration. Geneva, 2002.

45. Makovsky, D and White, J: "Lessons and Implications of the Israel-Hizballah War." The Washington Institute for Near East Policy, October 2006. http://www.washingtoninstitute.org/templateC04.php?CID=251, 5 August 2009.

46. McLaughlin, Erin. "Television Coverage of the Vietnam War and the Vietnam Veteran." http://www.warbirdforum.com/media.htm. 5 August 2009.

47. McNally, Richard. "Revulsion to War Isn't a Mental Disorder." Editorial and Commentary. *Los Angeles Times.* July 8, 2004.

48. Meir-Levi, David. "Big Lies: Demolishing the myths of the Propaganda war against Israel." David Horowitz Freedom Center, Los Angeles, California. 2006

49. Moore, KL: *Essential Clinical Anatomy, Third Ed.* Lippincott Williams and Wilkins. Philadelphia, PA, 2007.

50. Mount, Mike. "Army: Suicide rate among soldiers continues on record pace." http://www.cnn.com, 11 June 2009.

51. National Geographic, "Polar Bear Alert," National Geographic Videos, 1997.

52. National Library of Medicine, National Institutes of Health Website: http://www.nlm.nih.gov/medlineplus/posttraumaticstressdisorder.html, February, 2007.

53. Netter, FH: *Atlas of Human Anatomy, Fourth Ed.* Saunders Elsevier. Philadelphia, PA, 2003.

54. Ogden, P, Minton, K, Pain, C: *Trauma and the Body: A Sensation Approach to Psychotherapy.* W.W. Norton & Company, Inc., New York, NY, 2006.

55. Parker, C, Doctor, RM, and Selvam, R: Somatic Therapy Treatment Effects with Tsunami Survivors, Traumatology, vol. 14, no. 3, September 2008.

56. Parker, L.A., and R. Selvam. "Somatic Experiencing: A Note on Working with Anger in the Context of an SE session." unpublished.

57. Paulson, DS and Kripppner, S. Haunted by Combat: Understanding PTSD in War Veterans Including Women, Reservists, and Thos Coming Back From Iraq. Praeger Security International. Westport, Connecticut. 2007

58. Pearlman, Laurie, and Ervin Staub. "The 2002 Training Healing and Reconciliation: A Seminar for Community Leaders." Trauma Training for Journalists Workshop. Foundation for Human Enrichment. Boulder, Colorado, 2002.

59. Petersen, Melody. "U.S. military: Heavily armed and medicated." Men's Health. Mayt 2009: 17 June 2009 http://www.msnbc.msn.com/id/30748260/.

60. Press release, "Innovative Family Camp Targets Iraq/Afghanistan and Other Veterans with Traumatic Brain Injury," Casa Colina, Chino, CA, www.casacolina.org, 2 August 2009.

61. Rifkin, Ira. "How Media Coverage Favored Hezbollah." The Jewish Week, April 25, 2007: http://frontpagemag.com/Printable.aspx?ArtId=26298, 5 August 2009.

62. Rosenberg, Marshall. *Non-violent Communication: A Language of Life: Create Your Life, Your Relationships, and Your World in Harmony with Your Values.* Puddledancer Press. Encinitas, CA 2003.

63. Ross, G: Beyond the Trauma Vortex into the Healing Vortex: A Guide for You, International Trauma-Healing Institute, Los Angeles, CA 2008.

64. Ross, G: "Trauma Training for Doctors Workshop," International Trauma-Healing Institute, Hadassah Medical Center, Jerusalem, Israel, 2004.

65. Ross, G: "Trauma Training for Journalists Workshop," Education for Life and the International Trauma-Healing Institute, Jerusalem, Israel, 2005.

66. Ross, Gina. *Beyond the Trauma Vortex Into the Healing Vortex: A Guide for You.* International Trauma-Healing Institute, Los Angeles, CA 2008.

67. Ross, Gina. *Beyond the Trauma Vortex Into the Healing Vortex: A Guide Psychology & Education.* International Trauma-Healing Institute, Los Angeles, CA 2009.

68. Ross, Gina. *Beyond the Trauma Vortex Into the Healing Vortex: A Guide for Diplomats and NGOs.* International Trauma-Healing Institute, Los Angeles, CA 2009.

69. Ross, Gina. *Beyond the Trauma Vortex Into the Healing Vortex: A Guide for the Medical Field.* International Trauma-Healing Institute, Los Angeles, CA 2009.

70. Ross, Gina. *Beyond the Trauma Vortex: The Media's Role in Healing Fear, Terror & Violence*, North Atlantic Books. Berkeley, California 2003.

71. Ross, Gina. *Beyond the Trauma Vortex: The Media's Role in Healing Fear, Terror & Violence: Guidelines from Trauma to Healing.* International Trauma-Healing Institute. Los Angeles, 2003.

72. Ross, Gina. "Trauma Training for Journalists." Workshop organized by Education for Life and the International Trauma-Healing Institute. Israel, 2005.

73. Scaer, R C: The Trauma Spectrum: Hidden Wounds and Human Resiliency, W.W. Norton & Company, Inc., New York, NY, 2005.

74. Scaer, RC: *The Body Bears the Burden: Trauma, Dissociation, and Disease*, Haworth Medical Press, New York, NY, 2001.

75. Schore, AN: Affect Dysregulation and Disorders of the Self; Affect Regulation and the Repair of the Self, W.W. Norton & Company, Inc., New York, NY, 2003.

76. Schore, AN: Affect Regulation and the Origin of the Self: The Neurobiology of Emotional Development. W.W. Norton & Company, Inc., New York, NY, 2003.

77. Schrader, Esther. "These Unseen Wounds Cut Deep." *Los Angeles Times*. November 14, 2004.

78. Shane, Scott. "A flood of troubled soldiers is in the offing, experts predict." *New York Times*. December 16, 2004.

79. Shay, Jonathan. *Odysseus in America: Combat Trauma and the Trials of Homecoming*. Scribner and Sons. New York, 2003.

80. herer, Richard. "Statistics Show Large Number of Vets with Psychiatric Diagnoses." *Psychiatric Times*. May 01, 2007. www.psychiatrictimes.com.

81. Siegel, DJ: The Developing Mind: How Relationships and the Brain Interact to Shape Who We Are, Guilford Press, New York, NY, 2001.

82. Siegel, DJ: The Mindful Brain: Reflection and Attunement in the Cultivation of Well-Being, W.W. Norton & Company, Inc., New York, NY, 2007.

83. Sites, K. *In the Hot Zone: One Man, One Year, Twenty Wars*. Harper Perennial. New York, 2007.

84. Soldiers' Creed, http://www.army.mil/soldierscreed/flash_version/index.html, 26 August 2009.

85. Stamm, B: Traumatic Stress and Secondary Traumatic Stress, Comparison, Fatigue and Vicarious Traumatization, University of Illinois, October 28, 2008, www.isu.edu/-bhstamm/ts.htm.

86. Staub, E, Pearlman, L.: "Healing and Reconciliation-A Seminar for Community Leaders," June, 2002, Gitarama, Rwanda.

87. Staub, Ervin. *The Roots of Evil: The Origins of Genocide and Other Group Violence.* Cambridge University Press. 1992.

88. Stone, D., Conant, E. Barry, J: "Love is a Battlefield." Newsweek 15 June 2009:36.

89. Sykes, MW: Going for the Cure. Family Therapy Networker. July/Aug. 1996.

90. Tick, Edward. *War and the Soul: Healing Our Nation's Veterans from Post-traumatic Stress Disorder.* Quest Books. Wheaton, Illinois, 2005.

91. University of Illinois Cooperative, Extension Service, October 31, 2008, http://www.web.extension.uiuc.edu/disaster/facts/emotion.html.

92. Van der Kolk, BA, McFarlane, AC, Weisaeth, L: Traumatic Stress: The Effects of Overwhelming Experience on Mind, Body and Society. Guilford Press, New York, NY, 1996.

93. Van Der Kolk, BA: Psychological Trauma, American Psychiatric Publishing, Arlington, VA, 1987.

94. Volkan, Vamik. *Blood Lines: From Ethnic Pride to Ethnic Cleansing.* Farrar, Straus & Giroux. New York, 2007.

95. Wagner, Matthew. "Escaping the Quagmire." The Jerusalem Post, 31 May 2007, http://www.jpost.com 5 August 2009.

96. Yehuda, R: Psychological Trauma, American Psychiatric Publishing, Arlington, VA, 1998.

BEYOND THE TRAUMA VORTEX INTO THE HEALING VORTEX: GUIDE FOR THE MILITARY is sponsored by the International Trauma-Healing Institute (ITI), a non-profit educational organization whose goals are to educate and inform the public on the issue of trauma and to further trauma's healing at the community, national, and international levels.

Author's Note: The names in the book have been changed to protect the identity of those who so kindly shared their stories.

This book is available through ITI, the Foundation for Human Enrichment, and Amazom.com. For further information call (323) 954-1400 or visit our website at www.traumainstitute.org

Substantial discounts on bulk quantities are available to corporations, professional associations, and other organizations. For details and discount information please call (323) 954-1400

About the Sponsor

Founded by Gina Ross, the mission of the International Trauma-Healing Institute is to bring awareness to the issue of trauma and its impact on conflicts and violence between nations at a global level; in addition, the institute develops resources and collaborates with organizations to further the healing of trauma at a large-scale level.

ITI accomplishes its mission by creating programs and activities to:

- promote global awareness of trauma's costs and its link to violence;
- promote awareness of existing resources and techniques for coping with and healing trauma, and for facilitating their availability to the community at large; and
- develop new models, programs, and delivery systems for healing collective trauma.

Contributions

We thank you for your contribution to the International Trauma-Healing Institute (ITI Israel), as all proceeds from the sale of this book go directly to support the goal of ITI of helping heal trauma.

We invite your continued participation. Together we can promote and encourage healing around the world. For more information on the activities of ITI and to learn about the various ways you can help, visit us at www.traumainstitute.org. All financial contributions are tax-deductible and can be made to the "International Trauma Healing Institute" at: International Trauma-Healing Institute

269 South Lorraine Boulevard, Los Angeles, CA 90004 USA
Tel: (323) 954-1400
On the website: www.traumainstitute.org
By email: info@traumainstitute.org

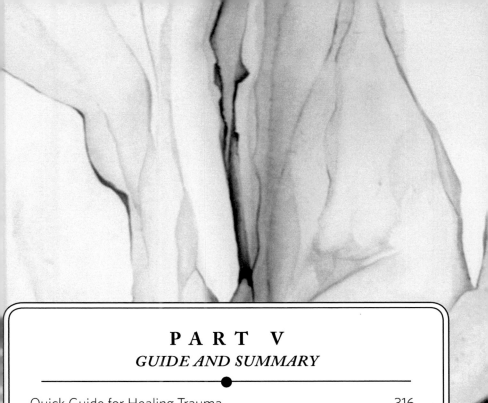

PART V
GUIDE AND SUMMARY

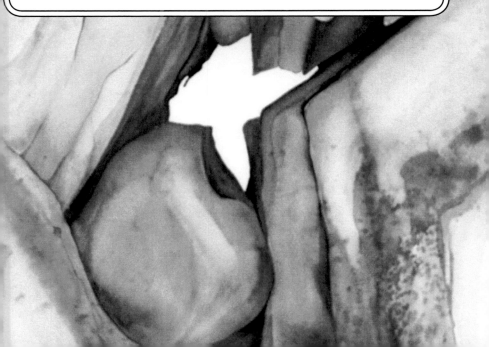

QUICK GUIDE FOR HEALING TRAUMA

PHYSIOLOGICAL RESPONSE TO TRAUMA: SIGNS OF ACTIVATION

After (or even during) a traumatic event, it is helpful to recognize signs of activation, without worrying or panicking about them or misinterpreting them—fast heartbeat, difficulty breathing, elevated blood pressure, stomach, chest and throat tightness, muscle tremors, muscle tension in neck, shoulders or limbs, cold skin, dry mouth, racing thoughts or speech. These reactions will quickly dissipate if you just notice them, don't fight them, and give them time to release. If you do not release them, you may later experience difficulty sleeping or eating; crave salty or sweet foods, and/or drink excessive alcohol or take drugs. Be aware of those impulses, accept that you are deeply upset, and allow yourself to experience your feelings a bit at a time in order to discharge them.

WHAT TO DO

Once you recognize your nervous system is hyper-aroused, it is easier to regain your balance. Simply focus on one sensation of activation in the body at a time and this sensation will release.

PHYSIOLOGICAL RESPONSE TO RECOVERY: SIGNS OF DISCHARGE

These are the signs of discharge, which you may notice when releasing tightness and constriction: slight shaking, trembling, vibrations, flow, warm sweat, waves of heat, stomach gurgles, deep diaphragmatic breaths, yawning, goose pimples, and spontaneous crying or laughing. Observe the shift in sensations without judgment or explanation, relying on your body's innate ability to regain its balance and give it the time to do what it wants to do.

The symbol of infinity on the next page is a summary of the essence of the healing process in SE®. It illustrates the natural pendulation, or oscillation you can count on in your psyche, to move through sensations of tightness and constriction triggered by traumatic arousal.

Quick Guide for Healing Trauma   **317**

If we practice staying present to our difficult traumatic or stressful experiences without trying to escape them and without labeling, stopping, judging, or criticizing what we feel, we have the opportunity to release and heal from the negative impact of our experiences.

While it seems counterintuitive, focusing for a short period of time, one sensation at a time, on the uncomfortable sensations generated by a traumatic experience in fact relaxes these constricted sensations rather than amplifying them, allowing the body to shift, change, and re-establish its natural balance, which is the foundation for our well-being. This symbol of infinity represents the principle of the innate pendulation at work or the back-and-forth movement of the organism between constriction and expansion, between tightness and openness, between trauma and healing. It is this natural oscillatory process that can bring movement to the stuckness and fixity of trauma.

SUMMARY OF EXERCISES

Here is the series of exercises from the text, summarized here for your convenience

1. FELT SENSE AND THE LANGUAGE OF SENSATIONS

Exercise 1: Getting Acquainted with Your Felt Sense

Feel your feet on the ground and feel the way your body makes contact with the chair. Feel your body in as many details as possible; feel how the chair is supporting your back. Sense the way your clothes feel on your skin and how the collar of your shirt touches your neck. Feel where your pants or skirt touch your legs and where your hair touches the nape of your neck.

Now, sense the sensations inside the walls of your body. What sensations do you feel when you sense underneath your skin? Take all the time you need to notice the subtle (and not so subtle) sensations. Notice your breath, your heartbeat, and the feelings in your chest, stomach, and limbs. Notice your jaw, your face, and your head. Notice if your body feels comfortable. Allow your body to move until it feels comfortable.

How did you know that you felt comfortable or uncomfortable? How did you know your body wanted to move? Which sensations contributed to your feelings of comfort? Did your sensations get more or less intense when you focused your attention on them? Did you feel more or less comfortable? Did your sensations eventually change? What part of you noticed the sensations?

The Felt Sense is the ability to focus inward and get a quick appraisal of how we feel about our environment and how we want to respond. Focusing on our internal sensations with our Felt Sense allows us to assess our comfort or discomfort levels, giving us a measure of our experience.

Exercise 2: Practicing the Felt Sense

It is possible to exercise and practice the Felt Sense like we exercise a muscle.

Take one minute only to look around you, making a mental note of every single detail in your external environment. Notice all the details you may not have noticed before.

Then take another minute, close your eyes, and notice every sensation inside of your body. Notice your breath and heartbeat, and notice the muscle tone of your arms and legs. Notice your jaw, your face, and your throat. Notice if there are any sensations in your stomach. Notice if and where there is flow or tension in your body. Just take a mental note without doing anything about it. Do this exercise two times a day for two weeks, and you will have your Felt Sense at your beck and call.

Exercise 3: Tracking and Interviewing Sensation

When you notice a sensation inside your body, "interview" it: notice where it is in your body; notice if it has a shape, color or temperature. Notice if it is solid or hollow, and if it has a texture. Use the list above to describe four sensations you are feeling right now, giving two or three characteristics to each one. Try to choose sensations of tension and of comfort. Example: my breath is calm, deep and flowing; my jaw is tense, tight and achy. I feel a pleasant tingling and warmth in my chest; or tightness and butterflies in the stomach.

TIME FOR SENSATIONS AND MOVEMENTS
Time is an important element when releasing traumatic energy. We are usually not focused on our felt sense and we don't listen to our instincts. It takes some time—though just a couple of minutes—to tune into our internal landscape. It takes time to become aware of what our body/mind needs, and time to practice speaking the slower language of sensations and imagery.

It takes time to feel sensations and release excess energy; time to complete interrupted defensive movements engaged in response to threat, time to notice the details that escaped us during the traumatic event, and to respond now in ways that were unavailable then.

Exercise 4: Experience of Constriction, Expansion, and Pendulation

This exercise will help you understand and feel what sensations of constriction, expansion and discharge are and how to pendulate.

CONTACTING YOUR FELT SENSE AGAIN

As in the Felt Sense Exercise #2 above, sit comfortably in a chair, close your eyes, and scan your body. Scan your face, head, breath, heartbeat, back, neck, shoulders, arms and legs. It is easier to focus inward with your eyes closed. Notice how your clothes feel on your skin and sense how the chair holds your back. Notice where you feel most supported physically; where it feels most comfortable in your body. Take the time to just sit and feel for a few minutes. Take inventory of your sensations without judging, analyzing or interpreting what you notice and without trying to change anything.

CONTACTING A CONSTRICTION

As you are checking your inner landscape, see if you notice sensations of tension or constriction in your body and "interview" them. Focus on one of these sensations and identify its size, shape, texture, color and temperature. Just notice the tension without doing anything about it yet.

If you do not notice any tension, think of a mildly unpleasant occurrence that happened to you and see if this thought elicits constricted sensations in your body.

DISCHARGING: MOVING FROM CONSTRICTION INTO EXPANSION

As you focus your attention on this one constriction (always take only one constriction at a time) notice what happens next. Notice when it releases. Notice what happens when it releases. Does a deep breath come up; do you feel a gentle shaking, trembling or vibrating in your hands and feet, or down your arms and legs? Maybe you noticed a heat wave cross your chest or your back. Did you feel a warm sweat in your hands, face, or chest? Did you hear the gurgling sounds in your stomach, or started yawning? Notice what discharge feels like for you and allow it to happen, giving it all the time it needs. You may feel different signs of discharge at different times.

CONTACTING AND DEEPENING EXPANSION
Notice the signs of expansion in your body as you discharge. Does your breath feel deeper and calmer? Does your chest feel expanded and more open? Do your shoulders feel released? Do you feel a pleasant sense of flowing in your body?

CONTACTING CALMNESS IN YOUR BODY AND PENDULATING
If the tension you focused on does not release and you feel no signs of discharge, focus your attention on a part of your body that feels most comfortable. Notice if it feels calm, stable, or grounded and whether there is a sense of flow. If you can't identify a calm place, imagine a pleasant experience and notice the sensations that the image brings up in your body. Now take your attention back and forth between the sensation of constriction and the sensation of calm and expansion, back and forth several times until you feel the discharge. Do you now notice that you are taking deeper breaths, or feeling heat waves, or warm sweat? Do you hear your stomach gurgle? Notice then the sensations of expansion in your body, a sense of more openness and integration.

Sometimes, sensations of constriction release and keep coming back. Often, there are thoughts, beliefs, emotions or images connected with them, which need to be addressed. In Exercise 5 we show you how to work with these thoughts, emotions and images and release them.

2. THE SIBAM

Exercise 5: Transforming the SIBAM Elements into Sensations

I order to quickly release traumatic stress it is useful to learn to identify signs of stress in our senses, emotions, and thoughts; and to transform them into sensations, which allows us to discharge them swiftly.

TRANSFORMING IMAGE INTO SENSATION

Imagine an unpleasant sound, smell, taste, touch, or image, connected to a traumatic event. Notice what sensations come up, focus on one at a time and allow it to discharge. If the constricted sensory experience keeps hold of you, you can go to the opposite sensory experience by asking yourself: what do I feel in my body when I imagine the opposite image, smell touch, taste or sound? Then track the sensations that the question elicits in your body, pendulate between the two and notice the discharge.

TRANSFORMING BEHAVIOR INTO SENSATION

As you start paying attention to the involuntary movements of your body, such as your arm stiffening, your leg moving incessantly (restless leg) or your hand tapping on the table, what do you notice happening in your body? These movements may be related to an uncompleted survival response that wants to come through or it may be that your body is giving you more information on what happened during the event. In the first case, you focus your attention on noticing whether an organic movement wants to complete and allow it to happen slowly and then see how it feels in your body. In the second case, you may ask yourself: "what does this part of my body want to do?" If you could put words on that movement, what would it say? Do you notice anything else happening in your body? Keep tracking the sensations that arise, and discharge the constrictions that come up.

TRANSFORMING EMOTIONS INTO SENSATION

If you have any recurring intense negative feeling, such as fear, rage, despair, sadness, or shame t, just notice where you feel this fear, anger, rage or shame in your body. What kind of sensations do you experience? You may feel cold; your breath may get shallow or you feel you stopped breathing. You may feel paralyzed, frozen or constricted. Notice the sensations underlying the emotion and focus your awareness on one sensation at a time until the constriction dissipates.

Focus on a negative or obsessive thought (about yourself or the world) that bothers you, such as "I can't do anything right." "You cannot trust anyone," "Nothing ever works for me," etc. Notice what sensations of constriction come up, whether tightness in your belly or a collapse in your chest, etc. Again, focus on one sensation at a time, until it discharges or call on the opposite thought—"I am efficient," or "Some people are trustworthy, some are not." Or simply recall a time when your life seemed to flow and focus on how that mempry registers in your body. You may then feel a sense of grounding and stability in your legs, strength in your back, warmth in your belly or expansion in your chest. Then pendulate between the two sensations until the constricted one releases.

Exercise 6: Preventive Emotional First Aid after Injury

If you are injured and you are being taken to a hospital in an ambulance still conscious, if you were in a car accident or just suffered a bad fall, there are things you can do for yourself that will help you get better faster and help others take care of you. Remember all you now know about the nervous system, SE, and emotional first aid. Focus on helping your body discharge the energy triggered by the threat of being seriously hurt.

Give your body the space, time, and stillness it needs to regain its balance. Focus inward and scan your body, noticing sensations of activation such as a rush of adrenaline, quickened breath, faster heart beat, tensed muscles, feeling hot or cold, or general numbness. Stay present to your sensations, choosing to focus on one sensation at a time. Allow each sensation to move through you, keeping your awareness on it until it discharges and releases the shock.

You can use any of the tools and resources available to you to help your body return to normal. Simply experience what is happening without interpreting or trying to make sense of what you are feeling and sensing. Observe the memories, emotions, or thoughts that may come up without lingering on the meaning attached to them.

The best information for stabilizing the nervous system comes from sensations rather than thoughts, pictures, or insights. Move through your Felt Sense as you would move through a stream.

At the same time, you may notice several signs of discharge: shaking and trembling, feeling a wave of heat, taking one or a series of deep breaths or hearing your stomach gurgle. *While you track the discharge, take all the time you need to allow the shaking and trembling to subside.* You may notice a slow and progressive release of muscle tension. The adrenaline dissipates, your breath will return to normal, your hands and feet will become warm again, and you will feel a general sense of relief. Once your nervous system has settled and returned to its normal rhythm, you can then give your attention to the people trying to help you. If you have released the traumatic energies that otherwise would result in symptoms long after the incident, you will have more strength to focus on recovering from the injury.

If the people around you are unfamiliar with the tools you are using, just tell them you need some time to relax your body, which is full of tension and fear, and reassure them that you are aware and conscious. Ask for all the time you need to bring your nervous system back to normal and allow your body to re-adjust. You can explain, "I am discharging the arousal of the event, trying to catch my breath," so that they do not worry or attempt to rush you. Remember, it is important to encourage your mind not to interpret or explain. This is not a thinking matter; it is not for the neo-cortex.

After discharging the energy from your nervous system, you may focus on the meaning that the memories, emotions, or thoughts evoke and finish processing them by integrating them in your sensory-motor experience. Concentrate on the emotions aroused— whether it is fear you may have been seriously injured, or feeling rage at the injury and at what was done to you. Take each emotion into sensations in the body and attend to it one sensation at a time. Focusing on thoughts and emotions that come up before you have fully discharged the traumatic energy may only add to your activation and feeling of trauma. However, once your nervous system is balanced, allow yourself to make connections that help you recognize patterns of thinking, emotional reactions, or behavior.

Even if you are able to do all of this, sometimes a traumatic incident leaves such a profound impact that you cannot fully discharge its energy on your own. If you are too activated and cannot bring your system down—the event may have re-triggered deep old traumas—ground yourself immediately (see exercise below). Look around the ambulance or the hospital room and count 10 to 20 different textures or the primary colors in the room, bringing yourself into the "here and now." Ask a nearby friend or relative to help you come back to the present by talking to you. If your symptoms persist, seek professional help. Our hope is that in a near future, all medical personnel will be aware and trained to help trauma sufferers lower this kind of hyper-arousal.

Exercise 7: Grounding yourself when you feel too agitated

If you start feeling more and more constriction, without being able to get out of it, you can "ground" yourself immediately and bring yourself into the "here and now" by feeling your feet on the floor and pressing them softly against the floor. If you are sitting, feel how the chair is holding your back. Look around the room, and notice 10 different textures in your environment, or 6 same color objects. If you still feel agitated, look around the room and count how many different colors there are. Slowly, you will feel yourself calm down and regain control over your body. You cannot be in the "here and now" and be in the trauma vortex at the same time. Notice how your breath gets deeper and calmer. You may want to go outdoors and find a peaceful place to sit on the grass. As you sit on the grass, feel how your bottom is being held and supported by the ground.

After you ground yourself, you can re-engage in the exercises. If, however, you are still agitated, call a family member or a friend, and ask them to talk to you until you calm down. Try again, and if you feel drawn into the trauma vortex every time, seek the help of a professional.

3. FLIGHT, FIGHT, FREEZE RESPONSES
Exercise 8: Recuperating the Instinctive Flight Response

Think of something or someone that makes you feel threatened, and provokes fear, terror, anger or hurt in you. What sensations does the situation bring up in you body? What do you feel?

Now move your attention back to the spot that feels good. *The going back and forth between the sensation of activation and that of resource helps discharge the activation.* We call it looping. You can repeat it as many times as it takes for the pain to clear, at first only touching into the edge of the pain.

You notice that it is possible to run away to escape the threat. What are the different sensations in your body as you notice that you can run away? What are the movements that your body wants to do? What parts of your body would start moving first, when you run?

We don't try to relax the pain by directly focusing on the tight spot because it may create more tension. We break the pain into the smallest components of sensation, focus on one component at a time, and pendulate between this sensation and a relaxed area until it subsides.

Imagine yourself running. What would be the first part of your body to move? Imagine allowing your body to move as it wants. Imagine running and getting to a safe destination. What do you notice now? Do you feel your body vibrant and energized, or fatigued in a good way, with a sense of calmness and safety? Keep imagining escaping the situation until your body feels calm and capable of defending itself.

RECUPERATING THE INSTINCTIVE FIGHT RESPONSE
Maybe you notice that there is nowhere to run to, but you can fight your way out of danger. As you imagine yourself fighting, what parts of your body want to move? Which one wants to move first? As you imagine yourself moving your body to fight, what sensations does the image of fighting elicit in your body? Where do you feel the strength, the flow of energy?

As you imagine again the scene that frightened you or angered you initially, what do you notice now in your body, after you imagined fighting your way out of the situation?

OVERCOMING FREEZE, THE OBSTACLE TO A SUCCESSFUL FLIGHT RESPONSE
The first part is the same as the exercise above. You are confronting a situation, with events, people, animals, thoughts, images, dreams, etc., that really upset you, frighten you or disgust you. You want to get away from the upsetting experience. Feel the sensations that come up in your body. How do you feel in your body? What do you notice?

When you concentrate on the sensations that come up in your body, this time you notice that you want to run, but you can't. You feel frozen. What's the inner force that prevents you from running away, or avoiding the situation?

Notice the thoughts of more fear, shame, or guilt or even fear of hurting someone, or loosing their love, that may come up and which stop you from defending yourself by running away. Focus on the paralyzing thought or emotion that came up, and notice the sensations this thought or emotion brings up in your body. Focus on one sensation at a time, and notice the discharge signs that come right after. Is it a breath, a trembling, a warm sweat? Allow the discharge to take place. Give it all the time it needs. Then go back to the previous negative thought or emotion. What do you feel now in your body? Can you run away from the difficult, fearful or hurtful situation?

4. RESOURCES

Exercise 9: Grounding a Resource in the Body

Think of a resource—a time, place, situation or being with a person—when you felt relaxed and safe. Notice the details of that image: what are the sounds, smells, colors, and temperature associated with it?

What do you notice happens in your body when you think of that time, place, situation or person?

When you think of the safety and calmness it makes you feel, where do you feel the relaxation in your body? What are these sensations like? Does it feel like an opening, an expansion, or a stream flowing down your limbs? Does your breath get deeper? Do your muscles relax? Is there a sensation of warmth around you? Is there a gentle flow down your arms?

Each person will feel these sensations of safety and relaxation in different ways. Allow yourself to connect with and enjoy the sensations that this memory elicits in you.

Exercise 10: Making a Resource Inventory

Choose from the list below and make a list of:

- At least 10 external resources (hobbies, travel, pets, family members, etc.)
- Ten internal resources (sense of humor, imagination, determination, etc.)
- five missing resources (not having people, money, friends, or love as a support system)
- Make sure to add to your resource list every day. It is useful to include resources that can be available daily (such as flowers, pictures, textures, smells, sounds or food you like, meditation, etc.), weekly (time of rest or the Sabbath), monthly (rituals for the new moon), or yearly (vacations).
- List items from each time category.

Resources can be small and fleeting or major and long-term—from a flower that just bloomed to being in a life-long supportive relationship.

Exercise 11: Using Pendulation to Diminish Pain

Go into the Felt Sense—your capacity to tune into your inner experience. Sit and feel both of your feet on the floor and focus your awareness on your internal sensations.

The first sensation that grabs your attention may be the place that feels painful in your body. Notice the pain, but also find some place in you that feels comfortable and relaxed. Focus on where you have pleasant feelings in your body, even if your attention still goes to the painful spot. Keep your awareness there; notice the size of the area that feels pleasant; notice it spread.

After you spend time getting acquainted with the relaxed spot, take a moment to focus your awareness back on your pain. Working to stay at the edge or periphery of the pain is an important concept to help release pain.

Now move your attention back to the spot that feels good. The going back and forth between the sensation of activation and the sensation of resource helps discharge the activation. We call it looping. You can repeat it as many times as it takes for the pain to clear, at first only touching into the edge of the pain.

We don't try to relax the pain by directly focusing on the tight spot because it may create more tension. We break the pain into the smallest components of sensation, focus on one at a time, and pendulate between this sensation and a relaxed area until it subsides.

Exercise 12: Inviting Corrective Experiences

Think of a past situation in your life that still feels painful and unresolved.

- As you imagine the situation, ask yourself: if anything were to be possible, what would have helped me in this situation? What would I have liked to see happen?

S SENSATIONS:	**I** IMAGES:	**B** BEHAVIOR:
External Resources TIME MOVIES EXERCISES WITH BREATH AND BALANCE	**External Resources** COLORS NATURE PATTERNS BEAUTY GOOD SMELLS MUSIC - SOUNDS ART OBJECTS TOUCH	**External Resources** DANCING, READING, ARTS, SPORTS, PLAY SCHOOL SUCCESS TRAVEL HEALTHY SEXUALITY TALENTS
Internal Resources BEING GROUNDED BEING CENTERED SENSE OF BALANCE PHYSICAL STRENGTH HEALTHY BODY HAVING A SENSE OF BOUNDARIES ABILITY TO FEEL SENSATIONS, AND CONTINUOUS FELT SENSE INTUITION SENSE OF CONTROL PHYSICAL BEAUTY BREATH	**Internal Resources** PLEASURE IN USING THE 5 SENSES SEEING, SMELLING, TOUCHING, TASTING, HEARING AND OTHERWISE SENSING CAPACITY TO IMAGINE CAPACITY TO DAYDREAM	**Internal Resources** ABILITY TO MAKE THINGS HAPPEN ABILITY TO MOVE WELL AND FREELY ABILITY TO LEAD PERSISTENCE MAKE MONEY ARTISTIC ENDEAVORS MAKE FRIENDS COORDINATION ABILITY TO RELAX ABILITY TO RELATE

A AFFECT:	**M** MEANING:
External Resources FRIENDS AND FAMILY PEER GROUPS PETS PLAYGROUND MENTORS OBJECTS YOU LOVE	**External Resources** BOOKS STORIES SIMPLE INFORMA-TION AND REAS-SURANCE WORTHY CAUSES SPIRITUAL PRAC-TICE RELIGION
Internal Resources ABILITY TO GET EXCITED ABILITY TO FEEL CALMNESS, JOY, OR ANGER CONTAINMENT OF EMOTIONS CAPACITY FOR WARMTH, CARING, AND COMPASSION ABILITY TO LOVE ABILITY TO CONNECT ABILITY TO TRUST.	**Internal Resources** ABILITY TO MAKE CONNECTIONS ABILITY TO UNDERSTAND, LEARN AND REMEMBER IMAGINATION INTELLIGENCE CURIOSITY HUMOR GRATITUDE DREAM LIFE ART APPRECIATION LANGUAGE

- Allow time for your mind to elaborate on the scenes with the best outcome, then focus on the positive sensations that these outcomes elicit in your body; allow the positive sensations to "wash out," or "digest" the negative ones.

- Notice and enjoy the amazing creativity of the images your body/mind brings forth to evoke your innate healing vortex!

Exercise 13: To Facilitate Importing Resources

Imagine again a situation that left you feeling overwhelmed and helpless.

Ask yourself:

- What would the situation look like if the resource I have today were available then?

- What would I have done differently? What might have happened differently?

- Knowing that I will have this resource in the future, how can this help me in my present difficulties?

- Notice the soothing effect on your body when you bring these resources to mind while thinking of a difficult situation. Give yourself time to discharge.

Exercise 14: Inviting Protective Allies

Think of a situation that you feel is still unresolved for you and which left you feeling helpless and unsupported.

Ask yourself, "If anything and everything were possible right now, who or what would my body call upon to help me and to protect me in that situation?

Think of people you know, as well as imaginary entities, whether mythical, spiritual, or religious figures; angels, dragons, ferocious animals, or a squadron of one's companion soldiers. As you think of any of them helping to protect you, notice the sensations of release.

Exercise 15: Antidote Resource—Inviting the Opposite

Ask yourself:

- What image do I have of this constriction? What is the opposite image?

- What do I feel in my body, when I think of the opposite image?"

- What is the negative thought that occupies my mind and what are the sensations this thought elicits in my body? What would the opposite thought be? As I think of that thought, what sensations come up in me? Pendulate between the sensations the negative thought elicits and those the new positive thought elicits, and feel the release.

- What is the negative emotion that grips my chest, and which sensations does it elicit? What would the opposite emotion be? As I think of this opposite emotion, what sensations come up in me? Pendulate between the sensations elicited by the negative emotion and those elicited by the new positive emotion, and track the release.

5. DEALING WITH ANGER, FEAR, SHAME AND GUILT

Exercise 16: Losing the Fear of Anger

You can start this process by bringing to consciousness the subconscious fears you may have about anger. For example, imagine, in your mind's eye, the kind of angry person that might become a real problem for society. What is this person feeling, saying, and doing?

Now, see yourself as that person and ask yourself the following question: "What is the worst possible thing that might happen if I lost control?" As you see the image of yourself losing control, notice the sensations that emerge in your body; then focus on one sensation at a time and discharge the excess energy contained in the sensation corresponding to this image.

This exercise can help you face and discharge the irrational fears about anger you may have accumulated over the years. It may also bring to your awareness the unfulfilled needs that arouse your anger.

WORKING THROUGH ANGER

You can think of a situation or a person that makes you very angry. Notice the different sensations of tightness or constriction that come up with it. Focus again on one sensation at a time. If the sensation feels very explosive, like a volcano or a fire, imagine what would be the way that this sensation can be released in the most "titrated" way, the least energy at a time. As you imagine your anger getting released as a thin stream of lava going down the mountain to the cool sea, or as the vapor coming out of a pressure cooker, notice the sensations of release you feel in your body.

Exercise 17: Working through Fear

Think of a situation that makes you fearful, and notice the sensations this fear elicits in your body. Focus on one sensation of constriction at a time, be attentive to the discharge response that comes up when the constriction gets released, and give it time to complete.

Notice now if there any thoughts or images that arise in your body. If there are, notice what sensations they elicit and keep following the process of tracking the constricted sensations in your body, choosing one at a time and waiting for the release response.

If there are no thoughts or images that come up, go back in your mind's eye to the situation you fear, and track your body for sensations of tightness and discharge them. Keep going back to the situation you fear until you feel clear and in control and your thoughts make you feel stronger or calmer.

Exercise 18: Working through Shame and Guilt

Think of a situation that made you feel guilty or ashamed, and notice the sensations the guilt or shame elicits in your body. Focus on one sensation of constriction at a time, and be attentive to the discharge response that comes up when the constriction gets released; give it time to complete.

Keep going back to the situation that arouses your guilt and shame, tracking the constriction until it releases, or following the thoughts and images that emerge and tracking the sensations they elicit in your body. Choose one at a time and wait for the release response.

If there are no thoughts or images that come up, go back in your mind's eye to the situation that provoked your guilt or shame, and track your body for sensations of tightness and discharge them. Keep going back to the situation that makes you feel guilty or ashamed, track and discharge until you feel in control of your emotions, have clarity on the action to take, and have thoughts help you feel stronger or calmer.

7/22

International Trauma-Healing Institute
269 South Lorraine Boulevard
Los Angeles, CA 90004 USA

Tel: (323) 954-1400
www.traumainstitute.org
info@traumainstitute.org